THE CROWS

THE CROWS

A Study of the Corvids of Europe

FRANKLIN COOMBS

to Barbara

B.T. Batsford Ltd
London

First published 1978
© Franklin Coombs 1978

ISBN 0 7134 1327 1

Filmset in 'Monophoto' Baskerville by
Servis Filmsetting Ltd, Manchester

Printed in Great Britain by
Redwood Burn Limited Trowbridge & Esher
for the publishers
B.T. Batsford Ltd, 4 Fitzhardinge Street, London W1H 0AH

Contents

The Illustrations

LINE ILLUSTRATIONS

Preface

When I started collecting material for this book my intention was to try to provide as much information as possible, within the limits of the size of the book, on each of the eleven species of European corvids. Most of this material is contained in the species chapters which are subdivided into similar sections: Description, Distribution, Posture and Voice etc. It will be apparent that the literature on some species, the azure-winged magpie for example, is very scanty in contrast to the great number of papers on such species as the carrion/ hooded crow and the rook. The chapters on each species vary in length accordingly; some subsections are omitted from certain chapters where I have been unable to find any reliable information.

I find phonetic renderings of bird sounds very unsatisfactory. Gwinner has included sound spectrograms of raven calls in his papers, but I have not found comparable records for the whole range of European corvids and I have therefore given the phonetic interpretations used by various workers, for all the species.

The line drawings of 'postures' are drawn mostly from my own note-books but in the cases of the raven, carrion crow and jay I have based many of them on published photographs and diagrams and I am grateful to Dr Charles, Mr Goodwin and Dr Gwinner for giving their blessing to this. The captions accompanying the drawings are not intended to indicate all the possible comparisons that can be made but to suggest comparisons where the postures used by different species might be homologous or might have certain elements in common. Bird 'postures' are not as a rule static, they are usually continuing movements or gestures; perhaps the title to the section 'Posture and Voice' would imply communication more clearly if I called it 'Gesture and Voice' but posture is the word in common usage.

The very high cost of translation of foreign papers has presented a problem and will I am afraid have led to some omissions. I have had invaluable help with translations from Mr N.G. Osborne, Mr and Mrs C.V. Smale and my son-in-law and daughter, Dr and Mrs Colin Peacock, and I thank them for it.

My own interest has been especially in rooks, starting in 1935 when I was helped by Mr H. Neal and the late Mr H.H. Davis, but chiefly from 1945 to 1960 in collaboration with the late Professor A.J. Marshall and I am still grateful for his help and stimulating discussion. In addition to rooks I have been able to keep several corvid species in captivity and have been lucky in having carrion crows, rooks, jackdaws, magpies and jays nesting in our garden in most years, with ravens only a few miles away and until the 1960s choughs were still present on the north coast of Cornwall.

Any book of this kind must be very dependent on the published work of others and I am grateful to many whose names appear repeatedly among the references, and especially to Dr J.K. Charles, Dr Eric Grace and Dr David Houston for allowing me to quote their unpublished work. I also wish to thank Miss Foy Quiller-Couch who lent me the only copy of Lewis Harding's diary and has allowed me to publish extracts from it.

I am indebted to many people for help of various kinds, particularly to Professor G.M. Dunnet and Dr Iain Patterson and Mr Derek Goodwin; the latter has also read the whole of this book in draft and Drs Bruce Campbell and C.J. Feare have read various chapters and given me the benefit of their knowledge and experience.

Finally I must thank my daughter Mrs Anthea Paice who was able to read all of my longhand manuscripts and who has done all of the typewriting for me; and my wife for her help with revision and correction of the text at every stage, for reading the proofs and for her continuing encouragement.

I
The Crows and man

One is a sign of mischief,
Two is a sign of mirth.

These are the first two lines of one version of the once popular doggerel verses about magpies. They seem to emphasize man's long held ambivalent feelings towards the crows. Here I shall try to outline the various ways in which man has regarded the crows and the ways in which his activities have affected them.

They may be used as food, appear in folklore, they can be pests and pets, and a source of aesthetic pleasure or scientific interest. It appears that the earliest remains of crows found in Great Britain were in Norfolk and Suffolk, dating from as long ago as the warm Cromerian interglacial 500,000–600,000 years ago, a time of mastodons, extinct kinds of horse, cave lions and forest rhinoceros. But bird bones are small and fragile and evidence from as long ago as that is inevitably scanty. In the Middle to Upper Pleistocene about 100,000 years ago there is evidence that choughs lived in Devon and the Gower Peninsula in South Wales, and that magpies then lived in County Clare, although they later became extinct in Ireland, only much more recently recolonizing again (Fisher, 1966). During a long period of ice cover most of Great Britain must have been outside the range of corvids; the evidence from more recent times is often obtained from areas of human habitation, especially the middens. It seems probable that jays were taken as food by Middle Stone

Age hunters in Yorkshire. England was forested then, much of it with oak, a tree species with which jays of this genus are closely associated. Carrion crow remains were found at the sites of the Glastonbury lake village of about 250 BC. From Roman digs bones of jay and carrion crow were found at Silchester; of jackdaws at St Albans; of rooks at Richborough in Kent; and of ravens from six different settlements. Some of these corvids may have been kept as pets, for it is known that some wealthy Romans owned large collections of wild animals and birds and it is probable that 'ordinary' people also kept their pets. During the period AD 500–600 the dwellers in the Irish lake villages of County Meath kept or ate ravens and crows; and at Jarlshof in Shetland, which cannot have been as bare of trees as it is now, magpie remains were found (Fisher, 1966).

In much more recent times rooks, especially nestling rooks, have been a country food. Lewis Harding (18 May 1848) says: 'Persons are now appointed to watch in the night for the future.' This was to stop the stealing of rooks from the rookery at Trelawne in Cornwall which had taken place on the two or three preceding nights. Richard Jefferies (1848–87), in *Wild Life in a Southern County*, says that the practice of stealing young rooks was less common than it used to be. An old Somerset recipe for rook pie, published by the *Farmers' Weekly* in 1940, says that the rooks should be skinned and only the breast and legs used for the pie as the rest is bitter.

No doubt the earliest sowers of grain were troubled by the presence of the rook flocks, probably less numerous than they are now, for in the Iron Age there were forty million acres of forest, and the rook is not a forest species. Forest was reduced to ten million acres by the Norman Conquest, and only a relic of two million acres remained by the middle of the eighteenth century (Fisher, 1966). This change has almost certainly been favourable for rooks and jackdaws and perhaps carrion crows, and less favourable for jays. As more land was cleared and animal husbandry increased, shepherds felt that carrion crows and ravens were their enemies.

With battlefields, the presence of the gallows, and death as a fact of life being so much closer to ordinary people then, it is not difficult to see how any carrion-eating species came to acquire a sinister reputation. Among the European crows, this applies especially to the carrion/hooded crow and raven and, to some extent, to magpies.

There were widespread beliefs in the raven's supernatural powers of intelligence, memory and long life. In the north, to the Scandinavians the ravens were Odin's birds; he had two of them, Hugin and Munin (Thought and Memory), who perched on his shoulders and flew far and wide bringing him information. Some of the Viking standards bore raven emblems which were a source of prophecy, foretelling victory if they floated out in the breeze, and defeat when they hung limp. In southern Europe, in ancient Greece a raven was supposed to have told Apollo that his lover Coronis had been unfaithful; Apollo slew her and then in remorse

He blacked the raven o'er
and bid him prate in his white plumes no more.
(Addison's translation of Ovid)

The idea that the raven was originally white occurs again in a Tyrolean legend that the child Jesus went down to a stream where some ravens were bathing. He asked them to allow him to drink but they ignored him and went on with their splashing. 'Ungrateful birds,' he said, 'proud you may be of your beauty, but your feathers now so snowy white shall become black and remain so until Judgement Day' (Hare, C.E., 1952).

Ravens appear in biblical stories in two traditional roles, as messenger, and in connection with food. Noah sent the raven forth from the Ark, as a messenger (Genesis 8: 7). Elijah was fed by the ravens (1 Kings 17: 4–6). There is the interesting story of St Benedict, who was sent a poisoned loaf by a wicked priest called Florentius. Benedict commanded a tame raven to carry it away beyond the reach of any living creature and so his life was saved. Perhaps with a similar basis but on more prosaic lines, I remember, when visiting the old Delabole slate quarry in north Cornwall some years ago, being told that a man was sitting eating his pasty when a raven swooped down and stole it. He got up to chase the bird and so escaped being crushed by a rock fall which came down where he had been sitting a moment before. The raven's association with death is reflected in such verse as:

Like the sad-presaging raven, that tolls
The sick man's pass-port in her hollow beak;
And, in the shadow of the silent night
Doth shake contagion from her sable wing.
(Marlowe, *The Jew of Malta*)

Even in recent years I have known country people in Cornwall who are disturbed by the sound of a raven's croak.

There is also another widespread superstition, the origin of which is obscure, that ravens do not look after their own young. Shakespeare, in *Titus Andronicus* says

Some say the ravens foster forlorn children,
The whilst their own birds famish in the nest.

In the book of Job there is this question 'Who provideth the Raven his food? When his young ones cry to God, they wander for lack of meat.' While in Denmark a 'raven-mudder' was a local term for a bad mother.

There are traditions woven round the belief in 'crow' stones. Raven stones and jay stones were supposed to make their possessor invisible and this was said to be why jays' nests were hard to find. The possession of a crow stone could confer such benefits as wealth and fame and the gift of prophecy.

Crows seem nearly always to have been regarded as sinister and even the

BBC has a carrion crow record which is used at 'appropriate' times. Like the raven they were believed to enjoy longevity; there was a Roman saying to 'live the life of two crows' meaning to live to a great age, and a Highland verse:

Thrice the life of a dog, the life of a horse,
Thrice the life of a horse, the life of a man,
Thrice the life of a man, the life of a stag,
Thrice the life of a stag, the life of a raven.

Ravens and crows are also linked in the French tradition that bad priests became ravens and bad nuns became crows.

Based on more accurate observation was the belief that these birds add to their nests fresh pieces of various trees to ward off 'inchantment'.

Rooks seem to have been looked on in a more favourable light and here too the BBC follows suit where the recording seems to indicate rural surroundings rather than something sinister. Several times in Cornwall I have heard the legend that the abandonment of a traditional rookery bodes ill for the estate where it is situated; and this seems to have been a widespread tradition. Rooks have also been credited with the ability to foretell weather changes; usually by special characteristics of flight at the time – high or low, circling or in tumbling dives (see Chapter 16).

There is an immense bird-lore surrounding the magpie. Some of the vernacular names given to it may have been affectionate – Mag or Madge for Margaret – or descriptive – chatter-pie, used also half affectionately for children. In Italy the name *gazza* may also have been semi-affectionate and from this is derived the word gazette for a news-sheet made up of gossip and tit-bits. Many of the local doggerel verses about the magpie have this two-sided view of the species:

One for sorrow
Two for joy (or mirth)
Three for a wedding (or a girl)
Four for a boy (or a birth).

or the Somerset version:

One, zign of anger; two, zign o' mirth;
Dree, zign o' wedding-day; vower, zign o' death;
Vive, zign o' zorrow; zix zign o' joy;
Zevn, zign o' maid; an eight, zign o' boy.

There is an element of the evil eye about magpie traditions. The association of numbers one and three, two and four, sorrow and girl, joy and boy may, according to Thomas (1951), be part of an ancient taboo. Precautions had to be taken to ward off disaster. In Yorkshire they cross the thumb and repeat:

I cross the magpie
The magpie crosses me;
Bad luck to the magpie
And good luck to me.

In Devonshire the tradition was to spit over the right shoulder three times and chant:

Clean birds by sevens
Unclean by twos;
The dove in the heavens
Is the one I choose.

Magpies were also often held to be birds of ill omen on the continent of Europe. The people of Oldenberg cut a cross in the bark of a tree in which a magpie nested, believing that it would then desert and go elsewhere. In the Tyrol they believed that if you drank a broth in which a magpie had been boiled you would go mad. In Dresden on the other hand the same broth was used as a cure for epilepsy.

Choughs were often confused with jackdaws and some of the folklore about the raven is similar to that of the chough. There was a Cornish belief that after his death King Arthur became a chough (or raven) and that for that reason the chough must not be killed; there seem to have been many people, however, who showed little evidence of belief in this.

This brief account of the superstitions about crows may give some idea of how widespread they were. The practice of hanging up dead birds in fields or gardens, perhaps anthropomorphic in motivation, may be a relic of old rural beliefs, for it is certainly no deterrent to other crows, rooks or jackdaws. The possible agricultural damage done by crows, especially rooks, has provided some of the stimulus for research into their biology, although some of the earliest individual species studies were carried out simply because of the personal interest of the observer. The first of such studies, carried out in Cornwall in 1848, is described in Chapter 16.

Murton (1971) surveyed the history of the relationship between man and rooks. He showed that concern about the possible damage caused by rooks was expressed in an Act for their destruction in 1424 in the reign of James I of Scotland. There was a further Act to destroy choughs (probably meaning jackdaws), rooks and crows in 1533, and nets had to be set by villagers for this purpose, and failure to do so was to be punishable by fining. But in 1787 William Marshall, in *A Rural Economy of Norfolk*, expressed the opposite view that 'the notion prevails' that they are more beneficial than harmful, because of the grubs they eat, especially those of the cockchafer.

At the beginning of the 1939–45 war the Agricultural Research Council commissioned the British Trust for Ornithology to investigate the effects of rooks on agriculture. James Fisher was its organizer. This enquiry provided data on the size of the rook population and of their feeding habits and of the types of food taken. There has been a tendency to search for a simple balance statement as to whether rooks do more harm than good – a search destined to failure if the valuation of rooks is to be taken in wide general terms, since their flocking, feeding, population density and other factors vary so much from season to season and from one part of the country to another. This was well illustrated by Feare (1976) who has compared the ecology of rooks in Aberdeen-shire and in Hampshire. The availability of the foods needed by rooks at different times of year, protein when rearing young and perhaps when moult-ing for example, can be affected by such factors as the earlier growth of long grass in the south; for rooks obtain much of their protein food as earthworms where the grass is short. Earlier ploughing in the south and differences in timing of crops also affects the damage that rooks may do, and their value in pest control. Therefore a single comprehensive answer to the question whether rooks are harmful or beneficial is not possible.

In eastern Europe and Russia some attention has been paid to the value of nutcrackers in forestry. Their specialized food-storing methods have probably evolved with the evolution of unwinged seeds by their food trees. This behaviour may now be the most important natural means for the seeding and spread of these pine species (Turcek and Kelso, 1968). Jays too must have been of great, though unrecognized, value to mankind in helping the spread of oaks.

A modern economic problem is that of bird strikes by aircraft, though cor-vids are less frequently involved than some other species. But birds of any kind that frequent arable land are liable to cause accidents by their presence on or near airfields. Common, herring and blackheaded gulls, lapwings, and golden plover, feral and wood pigeons, rooks and jackdaws are all a source of risk. The extent of the economic values, and the dangers to life involved, can be gathered from figures quoted by Murton: the RAF spent £1 million per annum between 1958 and 1963 in repairs as a result of bird strikes, while BOAC had to change 81 engines.

The adaptability of the crows has enabled them to use a number of man-made environmental features. Carrion crows use electricity pylons for nesting in the absence of trees; carrion crows and jays, and to a lesser extent magpies, make use of city parks and suburban gardens as a habitat, while jackdaws nest in chimneys, church towers and ruins. So many plantations and windbreaks are near to farms and houses that it has come to be accepted that rookeries are commonly close to human habitation.

2
Relationships

The crows may be the group which among birds have reached the furthest stage of evolution, for they are highly adaptable to differences in their environment. The red-billed chough, for example, is usually thought of in this country as a bird of the sea cliffs, but in the Himalayas it breeds at levels as high as 17,000ft above sea level, and the closely related Alpine chough followed an Everest expedition up to their camp at over 26,000ft. The climatic range of the raven is unusually wide – from Ethiopia to Greenland, from North Africa to the Arctic cold of Siberia. Choice of nest site can be very variable. The hooded/carrion crow may build according to circumstances on the ground or on cliffs, in low shrubs, tall trees or on buildings, and even on electricity pylons. Many species of crow are practically omnivorous. The group has evolved more than one hundred species throughout the world – except in New Zealand where the only species is the rook, introduced by man. In South America the only members of the family are jays.

There are different systems of nomenclature, and the name *Corvidae* is sometimes used and applied to those species which we normally think of as crows and their relations the choughs, nutcrackers, magpies and jays. Amadon

(1944) uses *Corvidae* to cover the full range of families, and this in his view should include some like the Australian piping crows, the bower birds, and the birds of paradise that we in Europe do not usually think of as crows. The term *Corvinae* is used by him for the more limited group with which we are familiar, and all the European crows belong to this group.

Others (Goodwin, 1976) do not feel that all of these groups should be included, but in Europe we do not have any corvid species outside those genera which are accepted by all as crows. These are *Corvus*, which includes raven, carrion/hooded crow, rook and jackdaw; *Pyrrhocorax*, the red-billed chough and the Alpine chough; *Nucifraga*, with only one European full species, the nutcracker, subdivided into the thick-billed and slender-billed races; *Pica*, the true magpies to which all the black and white magpie races belong, and *Cyano-pica*, the azure-winged magpie; *Garrulus*, the typical jays; and finally *Perisoreus* in which are the species of the northern grey jays. Here we have only to consider the relationships between these seven genera. The much more complex relationships of all the corvine genera are clearly set out by Goodwin (1976).

The earliest fossil 'crow' was found in France and is dated in the Middle Miocene period (Fisher and Peterson, 1964). From the distribution of existing species it is thought that their origins may have been in Asia. The jays are considered to be the most primitive group, and the others may have evolved from the jay-like ancestor. The jays spread to the New World and there branched out into a wide range of species. They remain the only representatives of the *Corvidae* in South America. The Siberian jay, *Perisoreus infaustus*, with its Asiatic and North American relatives, is thought to be the most primitive of the existing European genera. The European jay is one of the genus *Garrulus* and is also of a comparatively primitive type. There are Asiatic magpies, perhaps more closely related to the jays than to either of the two European magpie species; of these two the azure-winged magpie is confined to Spain and Portugal in Europe; but its range is discontinuous and it is also found in the temperate parts of eastern Asia, including Japan. It is not known how it came to have these two widely separated populations; it may at one time have inhabited the whole of the intervening regions and the present distribution may be the result of a division produced by the last Ice Age. It is almost certainly of Asiatic origin and appears to be intermediate between the jays and the true magpies of the genus *Pica*, but placing is difficult as it has no close relatives.

The magpie, *Pica pica*, has not branched off like the jays into a variety of species; in fact all the existing members of the genus may be only geographical races of the one species. We in Europe have only the one species to consider. The nutcracker, *Nucifraga*, also is not too far from the jays and many writers place it nearer to the jays than are the magpies. There are geographical races of the nutcracker in the Old World and in North America a separate species, Clark's nutcracker, belongs to the same genus. The origin was probably

Asiatic spreading to North America, for the Bering Straight has now a width of only about sixty miles and the separation is biologically recent, mammals in North America and Asia having obviously common origins. The name chough is used for a completely different group of corvines in Australia; in Europe it is used only for the two species, red-billed and Alpine. Both the choughs have the black plumage of *Corvus* and, like *Corvus*, they have much longer wings than any of the groups so far mentioned. It has been suggested that they may form a link between the nutcrackers and the *Corvus* group. This final genus *Corvus* has a worldwide spread except for South America and, apart from introductions, New Zealand. They all show some degree of the black glossy 'crow' plumage although a number of species have white or grey areas, and in some the black or the grey may show a degree of brown. This is the most advanced, adaptable and successful genus and in Europe it includes raven, carrion/hooded crow, rook and jackdaw. At one time carrion and hooded crows were classed as separate species under the names *C. corone* and *C. cornix*, but they interbreed freely where the two types overlap in their range, and the offspring are fertile.

The American Ornithologists' Union has recommended that carrion and hooded crows be given the English name of Eurasian crow (*C. corone Linn*), the names carrion and hooded being used for the two separate racial groups – the hooded crow being *C. corone cornix* (*AUK* 93: 378).

Classification can take a great number of features into account and was at one time perhaps thought of in such simple divisions as land birds and water birds. Or animals on the land and fish in the sea. Indeed as recently as the last war the Pope declared that whales were fish, in order to permit eating the then available whale meat on Fridays! Anatomical characteristics, especially bone structure, were important in early scientific attempts to determine animal relationships. More and more aspects are taken into consideration now – ecology, behaviour, biochemistry, parasitology among them – and Kulczycki (1973) has suggested the consideration of nest site and structure as another aspect of related species where a valid and useful comparison can be made. He has analyzed the nest sites used – their altitude, positioning within the tree or other site, and the adaptability of each species – the nest structure, and its materials, and how these may vary, and the methods of construction. He concludes that *Garrulus* falls into the group building the most primitive nest form. *Perisoreus* and *Nucifraga* come into a group building a slightly more developed nest, with the addition of clay or wood pulp and sometimes an additional layer of the structure. *Cyano-pica* comes between the jays and the magpie group *Pica*. The genus *Corvus* form a fairly distinct group, all using some common elements in materials and building nests with clay reinforcement, and constructed in four layers. His conclusions, therefore, agree in the main with the grouping suggested by Amadon and others for the corvine genera found in Europe.

3
Raven
(*Corvus corax*)

European names

Dutch – RAAF
French – GRAND CORBEAU
German – KOLKRABE

Russian – VORON
Spanish – CUERVO
Swedish – KORP

Vernacular names

Cornwall – MARBURAN
Ireland – FIACH

Scotland and Shetland,
   heraldry – CORBIE
Somerset – PARSON

FIELD CHARACTERISTICS

The raven is much the largest of the European crows; it has a wing span comparable with that of a herring gull or buzzard. In flight, except when soaring with widespread primaries, its wings look long and more pointed than those of other crows, the tail too is long and rounded. Its outline is nearer to that of a rook than a crow. Its various resonant calls have a characteristic timbre; and in flight its habit of making a half roll on to its back and levelling out again is typical of this species alone. On the ground the thick bill and large head are very noticeable but its size is usually sufficient to distinguish it from any of the other crows.

DESCRIPTION

The sexes are alike except in size; the male is usually larger often noticeably so, but there is an overlap in size between the sexes. The plumage is all black, with blue, purple and greenish gloss, and is the same throughout the year. The head, neck and throat feathers are elongated and pointed. This plumage is moulted once a year and tail and primaries in particular become faded and browner. The down and feather bases of this species and the rook are brownish grey and of the crow much lighter and a dirty white.

The bill, legs and feet are black, the inside of the bill dark grey or black and the iris is dark brown.

Nestlings develop a covering of grey-brown down, the inside of the mouth is pink or mauve pink, and the edges of the gape are more yellow. The plumage which develops is much duller than in the adult, body and head feathers are brownish-black rather than black, and have only a little gloss, the wing feathers are blacker and glossier but less so than in the adult.

As in other crows the body feathers and most of the wing coverts are moulted towards the end of the bird's first summer, after which these feathers appear identical with those of an adult, while primaries, secondaries and tail feathers get progressively more brown, worn and faded. The entire plumage is moulted during the following summer in the birds second calendar year, and after this the young raven is not distinguishable by age from any other adult. This is the age at which these birds reach sexual maturity and they would normally start to breed in the following spring, the spring of their third calendar year.

DISTRIBUTION

The raven is a species with an unusually wide range which covers the whole of continental North America except for the southern and eastern states of the USA. In the north it extends up the coast of Greenland and the north Canadian islands to nearly 80°. In the Old World it ranges the whole European and Asiatic land mass from west to east and northwards above the 70° line in both Scandinavia and Siberia. India and South-East Asia are excluded, but in Africa it covers the whole of the northern part above about 15°. This enormous range extends over the bulk of the Northern Hemisphere from tropical deserts to high arctic cliffs and from sea level to 4480m in eastern Tibet (Voous, 1960). In the British Isles it is now almost confined to the following areas: Scotland, with the exception of the southern two-thirds of its eastern coast, the Shetlands, Orkneys and Scottish islands; the Lake District and part of the northern Pennines, Wales, Devon and Cornwall with a few other scattered areas. But at one time it accompanied kites as a city scavenger and was widespread as an inland-breeding species over most of the rest of England. In Ireland it is perhaps more evenly spread, with an emphasis on coastal areas, but nowhere is there as concentrated a population as in Wales and South-West England.

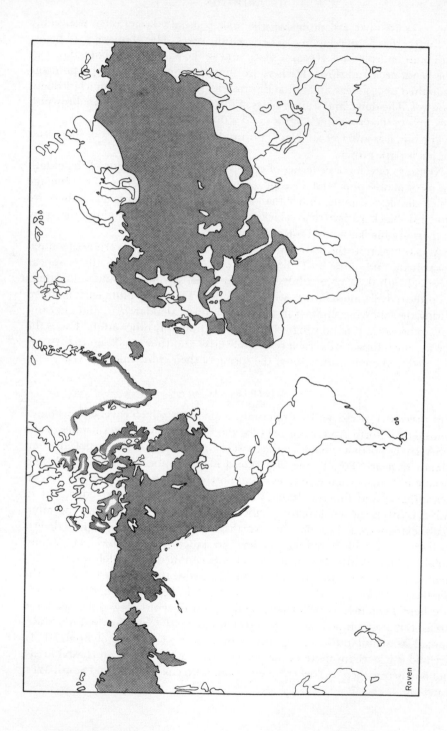

Its numbers probably reached their lowest level before the 1918 war when persecution by man was at its maximum; since then it has shown a gradual increase. Unintentional disturbance is sometimes a problem, and although there are stretches of the Cornish coast with perhaps one pair to every three miles there are some places where the presence of a coastal footpath has not been helpful.

The ravens' fortunes fluctuate with man's attitude towards the species and man's attitude changes; Belon in about 1555 referred to the protection given to kites and ravens in the City of London and Sir Thomas Browne in 1662 said of Norwich that there were a 'good plentie [of ravens] about the Citty which makes so few Kites to be seen hereabout', but times changed and Robert Smith, who described himself as 'late Rat-Catcher' to the Princess Amelia (rodent operatives and pest control please note), published a *Universal Directory for destroying Rats and other kinds of four footed and winged Vermin* (third edition, London, 1786). He gives an account of London ravens and of his methods of trapping them, but says that 'in some places it is very serviceable, in eating up the stinking flesh of Carrion of dead beasts and other Carrion, but in many other places very mischievous, and does a great deal of harm, I having been allowed as much per head for killing them as I had for Kites and Hawks' (Fielden, 1909).

Bounties were paid for heads of many species of bird and mammal in many if not most rural areas, and the local records show how common such species must have been in areas where they are now practically unknown. Thus the church warden's accounts of Tenterden in Kent examined by N.F. Ticehurst (1920) showed that kites were first mentioned in 1654-5, and the number in the records increased from then on, perhaps reflecting a change in attitudes to natural scavengers. Before 1676 fourteen ravens are recorded, but between 1676 and 1690, 198 were accounted for, and the records show that most kites, buzzards and ravens were destroyed during the nesting season. But there are many records of gradual reoccupation of areas by ravens after many years of absence.

In Europe the story of the raven is similar for it has been eliminated from much of France, Germany and the Low Countries. Like other carrion eaters – foxes, wolves and vultures – it suffers from poison put out perhaps for crows and in some places for wolves.

POSTURE AND VOICE AND SOCIAL BEHAVIOUR

Gwinner's (1964) extensive studies of 18 captive ravens drew attention to their ability to vary their behaviour patterns, to make unusual uses of possibly innate activities, and to imitate and use learned sounds. This makes the description and phonetic rendering of the great range of raven sounds particularly difficult. I shall use Gwinner's terms for the various postures and actions described.

The head-forward threat

This is much like that of other passerines and of gulls. It is used by dominant ravens to drive others from food; the action need be no more than the turning of the bill towards the threatened bird. Once a peck order has been established the position is recognized and very little threat is required. If pointing the bill in the right direction is not sufficient then opening and snapping the bill follows. This can be further reinforced with threatening calls, by partly opening the wings, perhaps dropping the wing on the side towards the

1   Raven: head forward. Compare figs 16, 24, 37, 47, 50. Often postures with a tilting or lateral clement

threatened bird (Fig. 1) and then if necessary with bill and wings almost on the ground and a-rhythmic head movements approaching its opponent step by step.

The frontal threat

This is used in its most intense form in nest protection, the bird stands upright with the tarsal joints bent inwards, ruffles its feathers and points the bill vertically down. The wings may be drooped and the tail fanned (fig. 2), and threatening noises may be made. At low intensity, the head feathers only are ruffled. Gwinner describes the plumage in this posture as a smooth fluffing, contrasting with the shaggy texture which it shows in the defensive threat.

The defensive threat

In captive birds this was accentuated because the subordinates could not escape from proximity with dominants by flight, and the impulse to flee is

2   *Raven: frontal threat. Compare fig 45*

important in this action. In its least intense form this amounts to a very variable degree of bill opening and bill snapping, usually with some raising of the crown feathers. Depending on its relationship with the bird confronting it, it may stand up with drooped wings as an intention to fly or it may pull back its head into a more hunched position as a step towards the 'small and thin' posture.

The defence posture

In the defence posture the whole head plumage is raised and some of the back feathers too (fig. 3) so that the ends of the feathers separate. The bill is wide open and either pointing up or at the opponent; and there are special sounds accompanying this. In the most extreme form all the plumage is fluffed up and the bill raised or lowered and accompanied by still louder calls.

The small and thin posture

Appeasement gestures reduce the risk of intraspecific fighting and are, as in many other species, based on reduction in size and in averting the bill. With sleeked feathers and head hunched between its shoulders the bird becomes 'small and thin', and the intertarsal joints are bent inwards in a 'knock-kneed'

3   Raven: defence posture. Compare figs 29, 30, 37
4   Raven: small and thin posture. Compare figs 6, 19

position (fig. 4). Young captive ravens may confront their keeper in this way and components of this position are present in the female's precopulatory actions.

The bill-up posture

The bill-up is an appeasement action common to many species. The bill may be raised only a little above horizontal or straight up (fig. 5). Old ravens

5   *Raven: bill-up posture*

sometimes exaggerate this, by lying flat on the ground or perch with the bill raised or even pointing backwards. Gwinner says that the use of this movement by ravens is much less rigid than with most species.

Head flagging or looking away

'Head flagging' or looking away used as an appeasement gesture by black-headed gulls (*Larus ridibundus*) is also used by ravens; they turn the bill away (fig. 6) slowly, then perhaps look round again and repeat it or preen their wings or peck at the ground. It seems ill-defined with ravens and perhaps only part of a downward stare (see below) or of the displacement preening and pecking.

The bill-down posture

The downward stare or bill-down posture is also less stereotyped with ravens. They lower the head, often in jerks, eventually to a vertically down position and hold it only for a few seconds, but often instead of holding it the bird pecks at the ground or preens its breast feathers. In fact, Gwinner felt that magpies,

6   Raven: head-flagging posture. Compare figs 4, 19

crows and ravens sometimes stare down, without necessarily pecking the ground, in the type of conflict situations that might produce displacement pecking or preening.

The female pre-copulatory posture

The extreme submissiveness in the female pre-copulatory position is adopted only towards those who can be fully trusted (fig. 7), a mate or a keeper who is known.

Begging

During all submissive positions ravens often utter adolescent noises, which are variations originating in the young birds' food begging. This begging is shown as a reaction to the demands of the male and as action with intent to appease. Both male and female can show begging behaviour, whether the partner has food to offer or not; the bird crouches low, flutters the wings and makes the juvenile sounds. Begging with wing fluttering may be shown as social behaviour, sometimes with the female precopulation posture, quite apart from occasions when there is mutual feeding.

Social preening

Mutual allopreening is common among birds shut up together in captivity in more or less established companion groups. It is a means of overcoming the reduced individual distance problems which confinement imposes on them. This behaviour begins while birds are very young and sexual impulses have little or nothing to do with it under these conditions. Young paired birds preen each other most frequently, even here the frequency of mutual preening does not bear a relationship to other parts of courtship.

Intimidatory actions can be used to overawe rivals of the same sex or in the process of attracting and arousing a partner of the other sex, so there are patterns of posture movements and sound used in various combinations in both rivalry and courtship. The range of types of intimidation behaviour are used in succession, one merging with another, stereotyped and in a fixed order at the beginning of contact with the other bird, and later changing.

Ear-tuft intimidation

There is always the ear-tuft intimidation posture at the start of such a contact

7   Raven: female in pre-copulation posture

8   *Raven: ear-tuft display. Compare fig 15*

(fig. 8). In this only the ear tufts (feathers above and behind the eye) are raised, not those of the rest of the head. The wing butts are held away from the body, the flank feathers fluffed out and forward to form impressive 'trousers'.

9   *Raven: thick-head posture. Compare figs 14, 35*

The feathers of neck, breast, and stomach stretch to form an even extension of the flanks and the feathers of the mantle are raised so that the back forms a straight line. The ravens stride around or after each other in a formal manner, and because extra saliva is secreted the continuous swallowing keeps the glossy pointed throat feathers on the move. If the bird takes off to fly while performing these intimidatory actions, the flight is 'slow and heavy like a heron'. In the rhythm of their walk females doing this make 'ko' or 'cho' sounds. The actions may peter out when the birds know each other.

Thick-head intimidation (cf bristle head of *C. corone/cornix*)

This comes in between the ear-tuft actions and the bowing ceremony which may follow it (fig. 9). The whole of the head plumage is erect, especially the pointed throat feathers (fig. 10).

10   Raven: bowing ceremony. Compare fig 23

Sounds

The raven (fig. 11) has such a wide repertoire of sounds that description is exceptionally difficult, particularly so as there are many strongly individual calls and imitations which the younger ravens learn and are also included.

Gwinner provides sound spectrograms of some of these; phonetic renderings of bird sounds are never very satisfactory, and spectrograms need interpreting correctly for comparison to be made. Gwinner says, for example, that male and female intimidation sounds are not only subject to variation, but also capable of being replaced completely by sounds learned from others. The

11 *Raven: sequence of self-assertive displays*
A.   *ear-tuft display, fig 8. Male makes 'ko' sound, female silent*
B.   *thick-head display, fig 9. Male 'kro' or 'krua' or individual sound, female silent*
C.   *bowing ceremony, fig 10. Male vocal and shows nictitating membrane over eye, female*
     makes squeaking and clicking sounds, nictitating membrane used
D.   *male pre-copulatory posture, nictitating membrane used. If female responds with E female*
     pre-copulatory posture, copulation may follow; if not male goes into E female pre-copulatory
     posture, which is submissive (compare this sequence with the rook, fig 26). In posture E
     both sexes show the nictitating membrane, fig 7

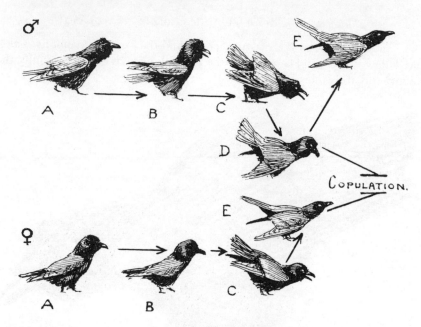

sound variations are learned within the first two or possibly three years, and after that they remain fixed. At the bowing ceremony the two sexes use rather different sounds, and both can introduce special learned sound patterns.

The use of special individual modifications of sounds or borrowed sounds by ravens makes it possible for one bird to recognize its mate by that bird's special sounds. By using its partner's special sounds it can call its mate from a distance and induce it to come immediately.

It is only possible here to summarize the main categories of sound that Gwinner has described without attempting to deal with the variations and intergraded sounds that he recorded.

A   'kra-rufe'. 'Kra', usually written in English as 'pruk' or 'krok', a commonly heard call when there may possibly be some threat, and used in flight chases. One often hears a repetitive version 'pruk-pruk-pruk' when watching ravens, and the threat of the observer's own presence may be the cause of the raven's protestations.

B   'gro-laute'. 'Gro', a deep throaty sound, a contact call between paired
birds, or parent and young.
C   'winsel-laute'. A whining call, given by a young bird preened by its
parents or by a tame hand-reared raven with its keeper. The song given by
young birds may be a variation of this. The whining call has been written as
'gru', 'gri' or 'gwee'.
D   'rüh-rufe'. A soft call given in situations when the bird is submissive,
dependent or perhaps ill at ease or by one bird to its partner in nest building,
as a location call by a young bird, or a subordinate in the presence of a
dominant.
E   'gaux-laute'. This is a soft rattle intergrading with 'gro' (B), sometimes
made by a bird when mutual preening appears to be roughly done.
F   'krä-laute'. Translated by Goodwin as 'kray', a defensive threat call,
when defending nest or food, and never included in the juvenile song.

During the bowing display, which is a self-advertising action, there is a choking
call with clicking, knocking and clapping sounds, which Gwinner thinks may
be in part derived from imitation of the clappering of white storks, although
some clicking sounds can be heard from ravens in the British Isles.

Young ravens and females begging for food use a sound that is recognizably
homologous with that used by crows, rooks and jackdaws, but it has a different
and obviously raven-like quality.

The variability and individual adaptability of ravens in making sounds and
in their behavioural actions was also illustrated by Gwinner's ravens in their
use for other purposes of instinctive actions and of actions derived from 'play'.

Upside-down hanging

A curious habit seen also in wild carrion crows and in my own captive carrion
and hooded crows and recorded over 300 times by Gwinner (1966) in his
ravens is that of hanging head down from a thin branch or from the netting
roof of the aviary (fig. 12); it is difficult to imagine how this arose or what
biological value it can have. Young birds of up to two years probably indulge
in this most frequently. Upside-down hanging is started by a bird perched on
a branch, but tipping forwards or backwards, usually the former, to hang by
its feet, looking around for up to a minute; perhaps changing to one foot or
from one to the other, or swinging to and fro with wings partly open. In this
position they may preen or peck at their perch. This appears to be part of
various play activities indulged in by young ravens, and presumably crows. I
shall refer to play by ravens again shortly; here I want to record Gwinner's
observations that this play was adapted by the ravens as a method of hiding
food in an upper part of the aviary where there was a suitable hiding place but
no perch, so they hung upside down from the roof and pushed the food into
the cavity while in that position. In another aviary surrounded by high shrubs,
but with no perches high enough, the ravens used this upside-down hanging
play to watch and see over the bushes if anyone was approaching.

12   Raven: upside-down hanging

As many ravens, carrion crows, and Alpine choughs will engage in this upside-down hanging there is presumably an innate basis for their behaviour. The special interest lies in the raven's ability to adapt this to different purposes, not obviously connected with the original purpose of the activity.

Young ravens in captivity like to use thin branches for 'play', working their way along them until they hang down, trying to balance with wing flapping or swing over to hang upside down and others will wait to take their turn.

Gwinner had left a piece of hard-board, 2 × 3m, shiny side up, on the ground. After perching at the edges some of the ravens found that they could slide down it, and would do so repeatedly; some young ones not yet flying properly would jump on to the board and slide, and about three weeks later when they could fly, they made half landings on the board, sliding along and taking off again, and then coming round to repeat the process.

In play, when holding an object in one foot, a subordinate bird, instead of giving way to a dominant, would hold the object hidden under its body and threaten. This appears to be a different reaction from the response when a dominant threatens a subordinate over food.

Gwinner gives a very complete account of this type of behaviour by his captive ravens. I have quoted enough to show the reasons for Gwinner's emphasis on the raven's ability to modify its behaviour.

TERRITORY

So many ravens now nest on sea cliffs that they have the sea on one side and no inland neighbour. In Cornwall there are several stretches of cliff with a pair of ravens about every three miles. Allin (1968) examined 70 territories in North Wales, 24 were coastal and below 30m (100ft), and 25 inland at from 300 to 600m (1000 to 2000ft) altitude. The ravens often had several alternative nest sites within their territory. The area required was found by Ratcliffe (1962) to be 16·9, 17·6, 19·2 and 44·5sq. km (6·6, 6·8, 7·4 and 17·6sq. miles) in four different regions, with minimum distance between nests in the same regions of 2·73, 2·73, 2·73 and 4·6km (1·7, 1·7, 1·7 and 2·9 miles).

Some territories were not occupied in some years, and non-breeding pairs might visit those but not remain. There are also small flocks of non-breeding ravens, sometimes visiting special food sources in a region and sometimes using communal roosts.

Actual territorial defence by ravens is rarely seen, and invasion of territories by groups does not seem to have been recorded. However both Ryves (1948) and Ratcliffe (1962) recorded the presence of a third raven or an extra pair in the nesting area during nesting time. This suggests comparison with the carrion crow, Siberian jay and perhaps the red-billed chough. But there have been no studies of individually marked birds.

Where peregrine falcons are sufficiently numerous there is often competition between them and ravens; they may compete for nest sites, or they may nest very close to each other, as close as only 10yd apart. Ratcliffe says that in the ensuing bickering the ravens were more often losers and might desert their nests and move to an alternative site.

Ratcliffe saw no sign of the actual process of the establishment of territory, and no aggression between neighbouring territory holders. He found evidence of flexibility in the minimum distance that ravens will tolerate from one nest to the next, and quotes Nethersole-Thomson's finding of three ravens' nests within a linear distance of 1000yd. Ravens are often gregarious but apparently never colonial nesters. Clearly much remains to be discovered about their territorial requirements.

PAIR FORMATION

Young ravens remain under parental protection for about 150 days. Many then join groups with their brothers and sisters merging with other such groups to form increasingly large flocks (Gwinner, 1965[1]). During the stage of independence from their parents many wander, returning some months later or settling elsewhere. At the beginning of their third calendar year pairs are formed and territories are established.

Mutual allopreening may well be an important element in the actual process of pair formation. It would help in the problem of overcoming the inhibiting effect of individual distance. Gwinner found that allopreening was common between young birds, especially those shut up together, and this started before they were old enough to have any impulse towards courtship. Sick birds, whose aggressiveness is diminished, also like to be preened. In captivity enforced proximity may have increased the importance of this action as compared with free wild birds, but even in wild birds mutual allopreening may be an important element in establishing the pair bond.

NEST SITE AND NESTING

Many nest sites are used again and again and in many raven territories there are several alternative sites. Ravens displaced from the site of their choice by the harassment of neighbouring peregrines may use one of these. Of 30 sites observed by Allin (1968) for five or more years:

2 pairs had 1 site	5 pairs had 5 sites
4 pairs had 2 sites	4 pairs had 6 sites
9 pairs had 3 sites	1 pair had 7 sites
5 pairs had 4 sites	

These sites of choice may in some cases be the same as one chosen by peregrines, as was the case in some years in the Avon Gorge at Bristol, and in different years both species reared families in the one site. I also know of one in Cornwall which was in some years used by buzzards. In the last 12 years or so the site has been abandoned, perhaps because of disturbance. Dr H.J. Moon knew of a site in the Lake District occupied in three successive years by peregrine, buzzard and raven (Moon, 1923).

Ravens seem to have no preference for any particular aspect, but many nests are protected by an overhang from rock, snow, or ice falls. Some sites, after the nest has gone, look remarkably insecure on downward-sloping slabs, and there are accidents to a few nests. In Wales, where there are many inland ravens' nests, trees are still often used, as no doubt they were in much of Britain in the past. Allin's figures show that out of 70 nests, 49 were on cliffs, of 30m high or less, and 25 were inland most at about 370m, with the highest at 610m and four at 91–210m above sea level. Of the inland nests 15 were in trees – 13 in conifers, 2 in oaks – and 5 in quarries. Twenty were in unbroken occupation for 2 or more years. Seven of these were occupied for 4 or 5 years, 1 for 6 years and 1 for 9 years.

This is long enough for names such as Ravenscar, or Raventree to become attached to the site. There were two inland ravens' nests not far from my home, one in the side on an old disused mine tramway cutting only about 16ft up, and one inside an old mine engine house, about 25ft up, where the wall had broken away on the inside.

It is difficult to define the nest-site characteristics that attract a given species of bird, but to the bird they must be clear cut; for example a ledge in a disused quarry in Shropshire was not in use for many years with no ravens in the area, but when they returned in 1918 the same ledge was used again (Forrest, 1918).

Holyoak and Ratcliffe (1968) pointed out that, although ravens do nest on quite low cliffs and trees, where possible they choose cliffs of over 100ft and tall trees; but they mention low-level sites like derelict cottages in Shetland and Northumberland, disused pit-head gear in Wales, and juniper bushes on Exmoor. There are also records of ravens nesting in rookeries (Cowin and Rogers, 1944–5; Harthan, 1944–5; Campbell, 1946) and in heronries (Cox, 1925–6; Onslow, 1946; Hunt, 1946) and on buildings (Hume, R.A., 1975; Kulczycki, 1973; Dementiev and Gladkov, 1951–4).

In Poland the commonest sites are in trees in thinned stands of 60 or more years' growth with large open areas nearby. Scots pine (*Pinus sylvestris*) was the most frequently chosen species of tree, 86 per cent of those examined, the remainder being various deciduous trees. Heights varied from 13 to 31m (43 to 102ft), the average being 21·68m (71ft). The nests were in the top and middle portion of the crowns of trees of an average age of 90 years, and they were usually close to the trunk (Kulczycki, 1973).

Ravens show preference for different tree species in different geographical areas. The trees most used in Germany are beeches; in Sweden beeches when ravens were common and now pines; in England conifers; in southern Poland, Byelo-Russia and in Finland pines. In parkland areas of southern central Russia ravens nest in deciduous trees – oaks, limes and aspens – and in central Siberia in both deciduous and coniferous trees (numerous authors quoted by Kulczycki, 1973).

The nest is built in four layers. The outer layer is of available branches or stems, of pine, deciduous twigs or perhaps heather 30–150cm long and 0·4–2·5cm thick. Sometimes these are brought from a considerable distance. They are tightly interwoven to form a basket, the first twigs being woven in at the base to form a rough triangle, becoming circular higher up the walls. The outer layer is 20cm thick and Kulczycki says that these nests differ from those of other larger birds of prey in not having free ends of sticks projecting beyond the walls. The second layer is circular, made of thin twigs averaging 35cm long and 0·4cm thick, usually fresh deciduous such as birch and hazel and often with forked ends. At the top this ring spreads out to cover part of the upper surface of the outer layer, as it does in carrion crows' nests, and is sometimes made of different materials from the rest of the second layer, perhaps coniferous twigs. The third layer is a cup of clay or earth and rootlets, sometimes with dung added. It is not always a completely formed layer, and varies from 1 to 3cm in thickness. The clay is not used in districts where the ground is frozen at the time of building. Inside this is the lining, first of a mixed structure-

less layer of moss, rootlets, grass, dead leaves, paper, cloth, string and tufts of
animal hair. Lastly comes a more compacted layer of wool, hair and fine grass;
occasionally paper, feathers or some other unusual material like cotton wool
may be used too. All the dimensions of ravens' nests are highly variable and
the size and shape of the nests depends on the site. The most constant measure-
ment is the diameter of the cup which averages 27·60cm between extremes of
19·5 and 36·5cm. The mean depth is 11·06, between extremes of 8·0 and
16·0cm (Kulczycki, 1973).

Ravens are early nesters and nest material may be collected from the
beginning of February. One in Somerset was started on 4 February and in that
case the material was freshly collected, an old nest nearby not being used as a
source of supply; building took 18 days and the first egg was laid on 1 March
(Lewis, 1920–1).

When neither cliffs nor trees are available as in Holstein, ravens may nest
on·the ground, the outer layer of the nest then consists of a mound of twigs and
branches.

Observing his captive ravens, Gwinner (1965[1]) found that the base foundation and sides of the nest are built by the male, with some help from the female.
During the forming of the next layer the female does the major part, the male
still helping. This layer, a sort of outer lining, is compacted into a felt-like mass
of fine twigs, moss, wool, grass, roots, dung and clods of earth and these are
trodden and pressed into place, the female working mainly from within the
nest cup. This felted outer lining may be brought to the top of the sides of the
nest and then turned outwards to form a rim. The final inner lining is also
mainly made by the female with some help from the male.

Ravens when young begin to pick up and carry objects such as twigs and
branches, both dead ones from the ground and live ones twisted off the tree
with the bill. They probably learn the knack of transferring such objects from
bill to feet and back again, even in flight. Thus they already have some skills
with nest materials when they first start nest building, but much more is
learned. A nest built by a young bird takes longer than one built by an
experienced older bird. They fiddle more with the material and drop more of
it than experienced birds.

There are similarities in structure and methods of building between song
birds such as thrushes and ravens; but the pliable material used by the former
do not present the difficulties of transport and insertion into the nest structure
presented by branches up to an inch thick and 5ft long, and ravens acquire
considerable skill in dealing with such uncompromising material.

They learn to find an approximate balance point for picking up long sticks.
They find that holding a long stick too near one end upsets their own equi-
librium especially in flight. Having brought such a branch to the nest they
learn to put it down, hold it with their feet and then take hold of it by its end
with the bill and pull it into place. One of Gwinner's birds was faced with the
problem of getting a long branch through an 80cm opening to reach the nest.

It flew to the opening holding the branch by the middle, landed and, holding the branch in its feet, transferred its bill grip to the end to pull it through the opening; then took it again by the middle to get the balance right for the final distance. Another, having difficulty with branches catching the side of the cage, learned to fly carrying the branch with its head turned through 90° so that the branch was parallel with the cage side and did not catch. Each bird learns its own method and they do not copy each other.

Some twigs are shortened if necessary, for example some of the small ones for the felted outer lining, and small side branches are removed by a twist with the bill, work starting from the end of the main branch.

Although male ravens normally play the larger part in building the base of the nest the female can also do this but they use smaller twigs and the resulting nest is less stable (Gwinner, 1965).

EGGS, INCUBATION AND NESTLINGS

In Britain, the raven lays a clutch of from 3 to 7 eggs, average 5·2 (Holyoak, 1967), with an insignificant variation in the number of eggs in different areas. The mean date of the first egg does vary in different areas:

Ireland	6 March	6 nests
Wales	5 March	73 nests
S. England	8 March	22 nests
N. England	14 March	21 nests
N. Scotland	22 March	15 nests
	(Holyoak, 1967)	

The eggs tend to be laid later at higher altitudes. Allin (1968) gives the following dates for ravens in Wales (dates are for completion of clutch):

	Below 1000ft	Above 1000ft
by 28 February	42%	10·4%
1–10 March	34·5%	27·1%
11–21 March	23·5%	54·2%
22–31 March	—	8·3%

There is a tendency for clutches laid later in the season to be smaller.

Eggs are laid at daily or occasionally two-day intervals and incubation does not start until the last or the next to last egg is laid. Incubation takes 18 to 19 days. Before she starts incubation the female more or less buries the eggs in the deep innermost lining. Only the female incubates and she is fed on the nest by the male with food that he brings in his throat pouch. After being fed the female may leave the nest to stretch, preen or defecate, and Lewis (1920–1) saw a raven perform the two latter functions in flight as it left the nest. While she is briefly away the male may cover the nest. When the eggs are hatching the female keeps them turned so that the young bird's bill is uppermost, and the female helps the young in the process of hatching (Gwinner, 1965[1]).

Hatching is asynchronous at one- or two-day intervals. For the first two days after hatching the young are fed mainly with insects, later with vertebrate prey and carrion. The food may be moistened by the adults, especially when the young are from 3 to 10 days old. If the weather is hot, water is also brought for them and, if they are exposed to the sun, the female may wet her abdominal feathers in a pool and then cover the young. She may also bore a hole through the bottom of the nest so that the young are ventilated from below. On the other hand, if the temperature is low the young are partly buried in the deep nest lining (Gwinner, 1965[1]).

The ravens' great geographical range has been referred to and the nest lining and the specialized nest behaviour are important adaptations to enable the species to cope with these extremes. The lining is carefully maintained by the adults. Droppings which are generally passed immediately after feeding are usually swallowed by the parents.

The female broods the young up to about 18 days old, and they may be covered by the male if she is absent from the nest after being fed (Gwinner, 1965[2]).

The fledging of the whole brood may take five weeks. The process was described by Warren (1955) at a cliff nest on Skokholm. On 9 May five young were on the nest ledge, the oldest looking not unlike an adult apart from its bright pink gape, and the youngest still showed down through its feathers. Wing-flapping exercises were usually done facing the cliff and to the observer carried an obvious risk of overbalancing when performed facing outwards. On 10 May the first young 'flew', a tumbling flight of 3 or 4ft horizontally and 2ft down. On 11 May the parents with three young were on a headland near the nest. By 15 May none of the young were near the nest, two were ½km away; by 16 May the nest area seemed to have no further attraction for them and they were in various parts of the island. Large dead young birds are said not to be removed from the nest.

The rate of success in fledging is probably lower as the season advances and the number of total failures is lower with large clutches. Holyoak (1967) gives the following figures: clutch of 4 – 33 per cent, clutch of 5 – 16 per cent, clutch of 6 – 13 per cent.

FLOCKING AND ROOSTING

Young ravens, after becoming independent of their parents, may wander away from the natal area, some returning later. Some probably remain with their brothers and sisters, later forming larger groups and small flocks. The flocks so formed may contain many young birds, and certainly contain birds which appear to be paired. Such flocks continue throughout the year except perhaps from July to September and must be made up largely of non-breeding birds although courtship and mating take place in the autumn; such flocks may contain some 30 to 50 birds (Coombes, R.A.H., 1948; Bryson, D.K., 1947; Gilbert, H.A., 1946). Flocks may sometimes congregate at especially liberal food supplies like the often quoted example of 800 assembled to feed on whales in Shetland (Saxby, 1860, in Venables; Venables, 1955). On a more modest scale I have seen 64 on a dung heap where offal from a slaughter house was thrown out, but they do not seem to be dependent on such sources – after the very severe winter of 1947 when sheep carcasses were a common sight in most hill areas, there were ravens gathered in flocks in the Lake District although carrion was available everywhere (Coombes, 1948).

Social gatherings may be different from flocks; they seem to be temporary, like the gatherings of other corvids and have already been referred to.

Raven flocks often use communal roosts. A roost about five miles from my house contained a maximum of at least 150 ravens. The plantation was used by jackdaws, rooks, carrion crows and ravens. This flock first came to my notice in August 1945 when I saw about 20 birds. Except at the roost I do not think that all the ravens were together in the same place at the same time, but there was an unusually large number of ravens in an area of about six miles diameter within the roost plantation. The ravens were singletons, in pairs or in small groups of 10 to 20. A larger number might gather at the special food source and by February 1946 there were often as many as 50 feeding near the slaughter house. During March this number decreased to a maximum of about 16; I saw only small numbers after that until August. There was a similar but rather smaller flock and roost lasting until March 1947; this pattern was repeated each autumn and winter, although with smaller numbers, until the spring of 1949 (Coombs, 1946).

Hurrell (1956) described a roost on Dartmoor with up to 50 to 60 ravens in the flock in January decreasing in numbers during March, but continuing on a smaller scale in May and June. An interesting example of many species roosting in the same area was given by Hutson describing a raven roost in Iraq, where ravens and kites (species not specified) shared a roost, and these two species shared the pre-roost assembly area with starlings and goldfinches. A raven roost in Wales is known to have continued throughout the year, including the nesting season from February until May, reaching maximum numbers in September and minimum in June (Cadman, 1947).

FOOD

Carrion is a more important part of the raven's diet in Great Britain than it is of other corvids, but they are omnivorous and also take much vegetable matter.

From an analysis of 433 castings collected in Merionethshire at a communal roost Bolam (1913) gave the following figures:

	Food material		Number of castings in which each material was found

Food material		Number of castings in which each material was found
Animal	Sheep	170
	Moles	54
	Voles } Mice }	49
	Rats	48
	Shells and sea-shore objects	47
	Rabbit	37
	Beetles	31
	Cattle	28
	Birds	25
Vegetable	Vegetable remnants, seeds, fruit, buds, grass and moss	189
Mineral	Pieces of stone	17

An assessment of recorded foods given by Holyoak (1968) placed carrion meat as the most important item. Among vegetable material were grain and wild-plant seeds, and animal material included sick lambs and sheep, live rabbits, live small mammals, birds' eggs, nestling birds, fish carrion, littoral inverte-brates and grassland insects. The young are fed largely on insects for the first two days and 'later mainly with pieces of vertebrate prey' (Gwinner, 1965).

The raven's abilities as a predator are shown in an account given by Tin-bergen (1953). During winter in the Angmagssalic district in east Greenland they were said regularly to catch ptarmigan (*Lagopus mutus reinhardi*) in flight. One was observed by Elkins (1964) chasing a rock dove across an estuary at Stornaway in Lewis. The dove, which had taken refuge behind a lump of peat, was flushed by the raven, which was joined by two others. It was finally caught by the raven's feet and the two birds fell to the ground together. The rock dove, which was dead, appeared to be in good condition. Ravens will also stand over puffin burrows waiting for the unfortunate owners to emerge (Aspden, 1928-9). At the other end of the scale ravens will sometimes join gulls in hawk-ing ants on the wing.

Like most corvines ravens hide food by pushing it into holes or crevices and often cover it up with scraps of available material – leaves, grass, stones or paper, for example (Simmons, 1970).

Gwinner (1965[2]) found that his captive ravens hid more food when they were hungry than at other times; they also hoarded more food during the nesting season than at other times, and hid the kind of food that they were giving to their young. Fat and fatty meat keeps well and was hidden in preference to other foods, and as very young ravens showed this preference it is probably an innate selection (Gwinner, 1965[2]).

PREDATORS, PARASITES, MORBIDITY AND MORTALITY

There are probably no predators on adult ravens other than man, at any rate in the British Isles, but many ravens are still shot (Holyoak, 1971). Carrion crows, jackdaws, and herring gulls rob unattended ravens' nests. There is very little published information about parasites to which the raven is host.

Like other corvids this species is liable to congenital skull malformation, one such was described by Witherby in 1918. A raven in poor condition moulting from juvenile to adult plumage in July 1917 was found to have the right lower mandible twisted from right to left, the right orbit was contracted to half the normal size and there was no trace of an eye on that side; the absence of the developing eye may have contributed to this deformity, by allowing the contraction of the orbit to take place.

Sage (1962) recorded that partial albinism among ravens evolved in the isolation of the Faeroe Islands, and that the white speckled mutant form was named *Corvus varies* by Brunich in 1764. This mutant had been known since the Middle Ages and formed a considerable part of the population at one time. The mutant decreased in numbers after 1850 and was last seen in 1902. Some Faeroe ravens are still recognized as *C. corax varies* because of the pale tip to some of the feathers of the hind neck.

The effects on birds of the very severe winter of 1962–3 were assessed by Dobinson and Richards (1964), who found that ravens were little if at all affected.

Although sheep carrion is a major component in the ravens' food, and there were in 1965 high levels of organo-chlorine residues in wool, skin and flesh of sheep, ravens were less affected than carrion-eating raptors like the buzzard, although some clutches did fail and some young and adults did die.

Ravens mob some raptors like eagles, buzzards and peregrines, but it was suggested by Ratcliffe in 1962 that some of the bickering between ravens and peregrines might be redirected aggression due to the disturbance caused by the presence of the observer. I have the impression, which is hard to measure, that ravens, which are probably not potential prey, mob such raptors less than do carrion crows and rooks, which are.

On the ground at communal feeding areas where several species are gathered together ravens in all cases dominate the smaller corvine species. They usually dominate herring gulls and sometimes great blackbacked gulls also. On all the occasions that I have seen ravens and buzzards feeding at the same carcass the buzzards have taken precedence, and in Wales Walters, Davies, and Davis found that with red kites and ravens sometimes one and sometimes the other would be dominant. Ratcliffe (1962) found that both peregrines and ravens avoid competition with golden eagles for nest sites and usually move elsewhere.

4
Eurasian crow
Carrion (*Corvus corone linn.*) and hooded (*Corvus corone cornix*) crows

C.J.F.C.

FIELD CHARACTERISTICS

The carrion crow is most likely to be confused with the rook, from which it is distinguished by its calls, squarer tail and broader wings and by its slower wing beats. Its bill is heavier and with the nasal bristles which the adult rook lacks appears very much thicker than that of the rook. The adult rook's bare grey face is distinctive. Juveniles are rather more likely to be confused with a crow but the comparative thinness of the bill is still very marked. The carrion crow has more compact flank and abdominal feathers, giving it a less shaggy look, and making it appear to have longer legs. A single carrion crow or a pair at a distance can be mistaken for ravens. The raven's voice is distinctive and in flight its heavier head and bill, its longer more pointed wings and longer rounded tail are very clear diagnostic features. Carrion and hooded crows frequently flick up the closed wings when perched, ravens and rooks rarely do.

The hooded crow is unlikely to be mistaken for any other bird if its colour can be seen. Silhouetted it may be mistaken for a carrion crow. In areas where the grey and black crows are both present hybrids occur.

DESCRIPTION

Carrion and hooded crows are now considered to be different races of one species, the distribution of the races overlapping in some areas.

Adult male and female

The sexes are alike in colour and there is no change between summer and winter. There is a slight overlapping in measurements between the sexes, but males are on average larger. In the carrion crow the entire plumage is black with a blue-purple or blue gloss, except on the primaries, primary coverts and alula where the gloss is greener. The downy bases of the feathers are very pale grey, almost white. The basal half of the upper mandible is covered with black bristles. The feathers of the head, nape and throat are pointed.

The bill, legs and claws are black and the irides are dark brown.

In the hooded crow the back of the neck, mantle, scapulars, back, rump, lower breast, abdomen, flanks, axillaries and under tail coverts are pale ash grey, with narrow dark shaft lines on each feather. Where the black upper breast joins the grey, the black extends in points formed by wide black centres to some feathers, and black on one web of others. The upper tail coverts are black with coloured gloss, but they have grey fringes which are wider on the smaller and more proximal feathers. The tarsal feathers are black.

Nestlings

The newly hatched nestlings of both carrion and hooded crows are naked and pink, the skin becoming grey later; they develop a plentiful dark-grey down which is the same colour in both forms. The mouth lining is bright pink to red, the bill black with pale pink gape flanges. Nestlings are blind at first, but the irides can be seen to be grey when the eye opens.

Juvenile

The juvenile plumage in both types is patterned like the adult, but the body and head feathers are brown black and almost without gloss. The grey on the young hooded crow is darker than the adult and browner in the grey feathers. The greater coverts, secondaries, primaries, primary coverts and tail have some gloss, but much less bright than in the adult. The bill, legs, feet and claws are black.

Moult

This plumage is partly changed during a moult in the later part of the bird's first calendar year. The tail feathers, primaries, and secondaries and some of the larger coverts are retained for a further year and become faded and browner; this faded plumage can sometimes be noticed in the field in a bird that otherwise appears to be adult. This first moult often starts in April and may continue until September.

In the second calendar year the entire plumage is moulted; the moult starts with the innermost primaries and the outermost secondaries and the innermost or central tail feathers; this moult may begin as early as April and continues until September. After this moult the bird is indistinguishable from an adult and is probably adult in its ability to reach physiological breeding condition.

In subsequent years there is a total moult starting in June and continuing until October or November. The process of moult and replacement of feathers is described in great detail by Seel (1976).

In districts where the hooded and carrion crow distribution overlaps, interbreeding is frequent and various mixed plumage types occur. In these the grey areas of the hoodie's plumage is invaded with black. There are often more of the black feathers in the lower mantle and scapulars adjacent to the black of the wing than close to the neck; this gives a collared effect of variable width. The centres of grey feathers in these areas are often black, giving a mottled effect.

The grey of the hoodie varies in different parts of the range. *C. cornix capellanus*, of Iraq and the Persian Gulf, is larger and distinctly paler than the nominate cornix. But *C. cornix khozanicus* from parts of Russia and *Corvus cornix minox* and *pallescens* from Crete and Cyprus are hard to separate from *C. cornix cornix*. For measurements see Appendix 1. The Far-Eastern carrion crow, *C. corone orientalis*, is larger.

DISTRIBUTION

This species is found throughout the whole of Europe, with the exception of a small area of northern Russia, and including *C. corone orientalis*, over the whole

of Asia including Japan, with the exception of the arctic tundra areas of northern Siberia. It reaches into Africa in the lower Nile area, and in southern Asia as far south as the northern end of the Persian Gulf. It does not extend to the south of the central Asian mountains.

The western and eastern black crows are separated by the large central area occupied by the grey hooded crows. The two races are presumed to have evolved in isolation from each other during a separation caused by the last ice age. Later the centrally placed hooded crows must have extended westwards from Scandinavia to Scotland and Ireland (Voous, 1960). Where the black and grey crows meet there is a zone of hybridization varying from 24 to 170km in width. It extends for about 1300km across Europe. In the west the hooded crow occupies Ireland and the north and west of Scotland, and the dividing line runs north east across Scotland approximately from the Firth of Clyde to the Beauly Firth. In Europe the two groups are divided by a line running from the Gulf of Genoa round the northern side of the Alps (there are carrion crows in Switzerland) and north across Germany to the Baltic Sea east of Denmark. In eastern Asia the overlap zone is about 3200km long, curving eastwards from the Aral Sea towards Mongolia before turning north again.

In the British Isles it is found in every area including Orkney, Shetland and St Kilda.

Related species of comparable size take its place in India, Africa, and North America. In Britain the numbers of both grey and black crows have increased during the past 50 years, perhaps because of decreased persecution, and there has been a tendency for the carrion crow to extend north and west into northern Scotland and into Ireland, and for the hooded crow to recede some-what in the same direction (Parslow, 1967; Cook, 1975). It has been suggested that this shift may be due to climatic change; but any assessment should take the entire overlap zone into consideration. Here in the British Isles it is easy to think of the carrion crow as a lowland bird and the hooded crow as belonging to highland areas, but this obviously does not apply throughout the range of the species.

Carrion/hooded crows are usually found in country where trees abound and the species will nest in denser woods than the rook. It does not favour high bare mountain areas, nor tree-less desert as the raven does, but it is adaptable and will nest on the ground as the hooded crow sometimes does – for example in Sutherland and Shetland. In the British Isles it is a non-migratory species; there is some dispersion of juveniles after the nesting season, but the records of recovery of British hatched young are within a maximum distance of 130km from where they were hatched, and only 5 have come from more than 32km (Holyoak, 1971).

Both black and grey crows are migratory in north and eastern Europe and northern Asia where conditions make this necessary. The migratory or resident status and the movements of the species were summarized by Busse in 1969.

C. corone

In the British Isles, resident.

In northern France, Belgium and Holland, nearly resident.

In Switzerland, resident, although some move south west as far as the Pyrenean foothills and I have myself seen them at up to about 4500ft in the Alps in winter.

C. cornix

In Ireland and Scotland, resident.

In Denmark and Sweden, migratory to England.

From Scandinavia and Finland migratory to eastern England, Belgium, Holland, Denmark and the southernmost point in Norway (a Norwegian bird was recovered as far north as Lockerbie in Scotland, Leach, 1956).

From Poland, migratory (not many records but one was found in central France).

There are a number of records from ships at sea as well as from land observers which give some idea of the dates of migratory movements. In the autumn the first arrivals on the east coast are in early October, and continue throughout the month (Cornwallis, 1954–5). Over the North Sea crows were recorded by Wolfe Murray (1927–8) at 54°30'N, 4°10'E on 23 October and in the spring at 54°30'N, 5°30'E on 29 March. This is about 305km east of Flamborough Head on the Yorkshire coast. In 1918 at the end of World War I Medlicott noted that the last hoodie had left the Pas de Calais by mid-April.

Experiments on displacement of migrant hooded crows west-southwestwards of their normal route produced evidence that adults were better able to correct this displacement than were juveniles; of the latter the displacement was lasting and they bred south-west of the correct area (Lack, 1962, quoting Ruppell, 1944).

POSTURE AND VOICE

When I am describing the important and complicated territorial organization of carrion/hooded crows I shall go into more detail, but it will make it easier to understand the postures and sounds made by crows if I give a brief outline here. Breeding birds are territory holders and are dominant. Juveniles of the previous year and some paired adults are in a flock formation and without territories they cannot breed, and as there is pressure to obtain a territory flock birds intrude into the established territories of other pairs when they can. Some male flock birds become partially accepted within territories and may help to defend them. Charles calls these 'third birds'.

I shall first describe the behaviour concerned with obtaining and defending a territory.

During his researches into territorial behaviour of carrion crows in 1972, Charles studied the relevant postures, behaviour and calls, while Wittenberg (1968) in Brunswick in Germany examined the breeding biology of the carrion crow. I have combined these records with some that I made myself on a captive carrion crow and a captive hooded crow and two territory-holding crows within whose area the hooded crow's aviary was. I use Charles's terminology.

The postures associated with attack are:

A   the upright (fig. 13) used by territory-holding birds standing on prom-

13   Carrion crow: upright posture. Compare fig 54

inent perches, possibly song posts. The head and neck are nearly upright in line with the body, the bill is held horizontally while the bird looks around, the tail lowered but not fanned. No calls are particularly associated with this. It is used by territorial birds before and after eviction of intruders, and sometimes close to the territorial boundary when the holders of the nest territory are not far away, and acting in the same manner.

B   the bristle-head posture (compare the raven's thick-headed posture). The bill is pointed down, sometimes so much so that it almost touches the neck feathers. The head and neck feathers are raised, the belly feathers fluffed and the wings drooped; the tail is lowered and partly spread (fig. 14). The bird moves by walking or with short hops with the wings held out. No sound is especially associated with this posture. Territorial neighbours use this at their common boundary and territory holders use it in the presence of a persistent intruder. My captive hooded crow was willy-nilly a persistent intruder in the

14   Carrion crow : bristle head. Compare figs 9, 35

territory of a pair of local carrion crows, both of whom walked about the aviary roof in this posture.

C   the pot-bellied posture (the raven's ear tuft display). In this the head and neck are upright and arched forward, the belly feathers are fluffed out, the wings held close to the body and the tail held down (fig. 15). Locomotion is by hopping and running, often close to and parallel to an intruding bird who

15   Carrion crow : pot-bellied posture. Compare fig 8

may do the same. While running the bird may give a 'mew' call or in this position a 'karr' cawing call.

D   the head-forward posture is used by a territory holder on the ground or in a tree. It stretches the head forward and makes a token or threatening peck, sometimes gaping or actually pecking. The neck is slightly fluffed, the tail below the horizontal and with the wings held at the sides, but at high intensity the wings and tail may be partly spread. Locomotion is by running at the intruder or by hopping towards him through the branches. There are no calls associated with this (fig. 16). These actions are used: when a 'third

16   Carrion crow: head-forward posture. Compare figs 1, 24, 37, 47, 50, 53

bird' (a male tolerated within the territory in certain circumstances, see the next section) is approaching residents within their own territory; when subordinate flock birds approach too close to a dominant flock member (see flock in next section); and sometimes by a territory-holding pair in defending their nest against persistent intruders. (The term 'persistent intruder' will also be fully explained in the description of territory.)

E   the cawing display. This is given by a crow standing on the ground or often on an elevated perch. The head and neck are held forward, the throat hackles and belly feathers are raised. The wings are closed but slightly raised from the sides, the tail is fanned and depressed and the legs are partly flexed. This is really a series of actions and not a static posture. The head and neck are first lowered then, as the bird caws, the head and neck are suddenly bobbed up to normal, and at the same time the nictitating membrane, which is pale in colour, is drawn across the eye. The whole body tends to move with the upward bob with each caw and there is often a series of caws and bobs (fig. 17). This was used repeatedly by the carrion crows on the roof of my aviary, and on other occasions when they were not present by the hooded crow inside it. Several calls are associated with this self-advertising posture. These were rendered phonetically by Charles as:

A   'kraang', given with the bill more open than in other calls; it is a loud and resounding sound audible at 700m, usually repeated three times (2–6) and then a long pause. Variants of these are 'krong' (like 'honk') and 'kraa'. This call is often used at dawn by a territory holder from a prominent point when it arrives from the communal roost during the non-breeding season;

17   Carrion crow : cawing display. Compare figs 22, 42

sometimes during a slow-wing-beat flight, described below, sometimes in a cawing duel with other territory holders, or during an intrusion into a territory by flock birds

B   'aaah', a loud call, three times repeated and followed by an interval, often given at dawn by the female of a territorial pair and distinct from the male's call.

These two calls are clearly advertisement of the fact that the birds giving them occupy a territory.

C   'karr' or mewing call; a short-range aggressive call (fig. 18) described

18   Carrion crow: 'kaar' or mewing call

by Charles as a single low guttural call muffled and with the bill hardly open
and sometimes sounding like a mew. The head is bobbed by rotation in a
vertical plane. This was used by a territory holder: when a persistent intruding
flock landed near; during the hop and run in the pot-bellied posture; at continuous boundaries; and when confronting a dominant flock bird at a common
feeding ground (territory holders are dominant over flock birds, and some
flock birds are dominant within the flock; see section on territory).

D   'krr' usually repeated three times. This is a softer sound used by a flock
bird finding food and possibly a short-range warning to others in the flock not
to approach and fight over it, which they will often do.

E   a rapid 'kraah', loud and harsh and repeated two to four times. This
sound, rendered by Wittenberg as 'ark-ark', may be given by a territorial bird
during an aerial chase and sometimes from a perch when the territory has been
invaded by a single bird or a flock.

Postures associated with avoidance

A   the sleeked posture. In this the feathers of the head, neck and body are
sleeked down so that the bird looks small and thin; it is shown by a subordinate
in the presence of a dominant, or by an intruder if near to the owner of the
territory (who will in any case be dominant). This posture is common to most
passerines and may precede actual fleeing (cf the raven).

B   the hunched posture, used in somewhat similar situations to the above,
such as when a subordinate bird waits and watches a dominant one feeding
(fig. 19). The head is drawn back into the shoulders with feathers flattened,
but the body feathers are raised and fluffed out

C   wing and tail flipping, used in a varying degree by a great many 'crows'
– rooks, jackdaws, choughs, magpies and *Garrulus* jays, for example. This is an
action and posture used by alert birds, generally the action increases as alertness increases, but sometimes it is reduced or inhibited by action, even action
when an element of alarm is present and alertness is essential. Inhibition of
wing and tail flick was shown by my captive hooded crow approaching a rat
which had taken refuge under some rocks but was not fully concealed. Wing
and tail flipping is a simultaneous quick movement of spreading the tail and
lifting the closed wings from the back. The action is very marked with carrion
and hooded crows (fig. 20) (Goodwin, 1966).

Actions of avoidance, chase and combat

These are actions involving locomotion, mainly flight.

Aerial chase is usually a direct, swift, aggressive flight by a territory holder
after a bird or pair at the territory boundary, but used in different contexts it
produces different results. A territory holder may fly after an intruder sometimes with rapid 'kraah' calls but may not attempt to overtake. Alternatively
it may pursue an intruder or subordinate which has food until the latter drops

19   Carrion crow : hunched posture. Compare figs 4, 6

20   Carrion crow : wing and tail flip. Compare figs 21, 41, 46, 51

it; the dominant bird feeds and the dispossessed bird goes into the sleeked posture. If a territory holder does catch up with an intruder combat is inevitable. The intruder is pecked at in flight although fleeing; they may grapple in the air and fall to the ground with the territory holder on top. Males always attack males, and females attack females, and if two females fight the male may watch and caw or attack the subordinate intruding mate.

A carrion crow attacking its reflection in a window pane has 'caught up with a persistent intruder and a fight results'. A very unusual case of territorial invasion in a London square was recorded by England in 1970. The intruder was threatened with intense head-forward display, followed by an aerial chase and actual attack. The intruder was brought down and killed. After 19 minutes the victorious territory holder disengaged himself and 'went into a frenzy of display', probably very intense self-advertising cawing display. The loser was found to have lost most of its head feathers, and to have been blinded, having almost lost one eye. This attack on the eye may be rather unusual, as Lorenz and others have suggested that 'crows' avoid such attacks. The restricted area (a London square) available for avoidance in that case was probably responsible for the ferocity of this fight. An aerial chase may simply end in a soaring flight, when the resident bird rises above the intruder with a slow flapping flight to look down on the enemy from a threatening position of advantage. As well as aerial chases there are often supplanting attacks. The territory holder flies at the perched intruder who leaves, the resident landing on the exact spot where he was. There are no calls with this. The supplanting may be repeated two or three times, against persistent intruders, or flock birds and other subordinates, or the 'third bird'. The persistent intruder, or flock bird who is the victim of an aerial chase, may fly in circles, turn left or right or swoop to the ground in avoidance flight.

Most, if not all, corvine species and many other passerines too have some form of special wing action in flight, which may be part of self-advertising display (Goodwin, 1956; Coombs, 1960). The carrion/hooded crows use a slow wing-beat flight in displays at their territorial boundaries. The wing action is a slow deliberate wing beat with increased dihedral angle (wings raised higher above horizontal than is normal). The wings are fully spread with a slow downstroke, followed by a rapid upstroke which is accompanied by a flick of the wing tips. Sometimes the wings are held horizontal and still for a few moments, while the wing tips make a series of quick upward flicks. Usually this is performed in silence, but can be accompanied by cawing with a partial wing closure and slight dive forward with each caw.

This slow wing beat is used in a type of flight which Charles calls circling: the territorial bird would fly towards a perched neighbour using the slow flap but wheeling round before reaching him. The neighbour either flies back to his own territory or chases the displayer back to his. This only happens at territorial boundaries and helps to determine their position. The boundaries are also defined by border patrolling; the territory holder flies silently along the boundaries, watched by the neighbouring territorial birds perched on prominent boundary positions. This usually happens in the early morning. Charles did not see any mutual aerial patrolling comparable with the parallel walking. In this two pairs of territorial neighbours would walk parallel to each other, often about 2m apart for from 3 to 14 minutes without a break. One or both of the same sex would be in the bristle head position and they would often stop and peck at the ground and sometimes turn and reverse their direction. Sometimes only the two males did this, while the females fed. The whole performance is in silence and only at continuous territory borders, and without haste or fighting and eventually the pairs return to their own territories.

Copulation often takes place on or near the nest, sometimes on the ground, and very often without any easily observed display. The 'typical' male pre-copulatory posture involves fluffing of the head and body feathers, part spreading of the wings and tail, the latter is not raised. C. and D. Nethersole-Thompson also recount that 'prior to the act the male for over a minute violently shook his raised wings and this he also continued to do after coition'. In another display that I have seen and which has been described by other observers (Nethersole-Thompson, 1939–40; Tebbut, 1949) the presumed male, with a wing flap, jumps into the air vertically for 4ft or so and then lands again, on the spot from which he jumped. In Tebbut's record the male was a carrion crow which approached a hoodie feeding on the ground, and when ignored by the latter gave this jumping display.

In the female precopulatory submissive display, the bird crouches with flexed legs, holds the tail slightly above horizontal and the head only a little higher than the back. The bill is level or tilted slightly upwards, and the wings partly open, drooped or almost level, and the tail, which is not spread, is quivered, mainly in a vertical plane. The nictitating membrane is often drawn across the eye and held there for a few seconds. Sometimes the bird pivots on its flexed legs.

Mutual preening is mainly of the feathers of head, nape and mantle, and may well serve to enhance the pair bond, and although crows are often paired for several years, there may be a need to overcome the instinctive defensiveness against close approach and infringement of individual distance.

Both sexes take part in early spring gatherings in which pursuit flights and slow wing flapping occur. During one such flight described by McIntyre in 1951 a pursued bird landed and may have been knocked over, and then hung below the branch looking about it for about two minutes. It may have got into this position voluntarily as this curious habit of hanging upside down has been described by various observers, and in detail in the raven by Gwinner (1966). Sometimes the bill is pointing straight down and the tail slightly spread (Pettit and Butt, 1949).

'Play' with small objects perhaps a stone or small bone is another activity which is hard to explain. One or perhaps two birds fly up with the object, sometimes held in the feet, and sometimes in the bill, drop it and quickly retrieve it and repeat the process several times (Denny, 1950; McKendry, 1972; Hayman, 1953). The behaviour has obvious resemblance to the dropping of shell fish on rocks to break them open. Displacement activities most frequently seen are bill wiping, pecking at the perch on which the bird stands, and displacement preening.

Anting is a feather maintenance activity and both active and passive anting have been observed in the carrion/hooded crow (Coombs, 1947; Simmons, 1957). In passive anting the bird lies and wallows among the ants, allowing them to run over and among its plumage. In active anting ants are also taken up in the bill deliberately applied to the feathers, especially to the tips of long feathers such as the primaries.

TERRITORY

For the carrion/hooded crow territory is an area within which it nests and during the nesting season also obtains its food. Within this area it can breed without excessive interference with nest building, and copulation, and can care for its eggs and young. Tenovuo and Wittenberg in 1963 and Charles in 1972 have thrown light on the complicated social system of the species, and I shall quote especially from Charles's work in the country round the Ythan Estuary in Aberdeenshire.

The crow population is divided into territory-holding pairs and a flock of non-breeders, mostly immature although some are adult and may be paired and up to five years' old. These may be in a physiological condition to breed but without a territory it is impossible for a pair of crows to do so. Those that hold territories are the dominant birds, and males are the more important in territory defence. Males are dominant over females, and a male crow without a female can still maintain his territory, but a female on her own cannot do so. The territory is from 14 to 49ha (35·6 to 110 acres), is defended most vigorously near the nest, and the boundaries are less aggressively defended against neighbours who are recognized, than against intruders from the flock or other areas. This automatically produces some overlap and mutual defence against non-territory holders at the borders.

The birds remain paired and together throughout the year, but the area within which they are active is not constant. Here we have to distinguish between range and territory. All the places that a pair or a single bird may visit in a day add up to form what Charles calls their daily activity space; all the different daily activity spaces add up to form the bird's or pair's range – its range is not defended, but the territory is a defended part of its range.

The nesting period from intensive nest building until the fledging of the young, is a time when the range becomes much reduced to an average size of about 28ha (16–41) (73 acres). Outside the nesting season the average is 53·17ha (36–75) (131 acres) or nearly twice the size. The importance for a breeding crow of staying within easy range of its nest is shown by the fact that while the pre-breeding range is 53·17ha (131 acres) during nest building it is reduced to 34·25ha (84·6 acres) and during incubation to 8·26ha (24.4 acres) or only a little more than one-seventh of the pre-nesting size. While nestlings are in the nest it extends again to 20·36ha (50·2 acres). When the range is at its smallest, there are large gaps between the ranges of adjacent territory holders. But the ranges of adjacent pairs may overlap outside the nesting season and this overlap involves the recognition of neighbours and a degree of tolerance of their presence. In the Ythan Valley the area occupied by the flock birds was mainly along the estuary, and the ranges of territory holders nearest to the estuary overlapped the area occupied by the flock. Territories close to the estuary were much smaller, probably because of the greater pressure of intrusion by flock birds. However, there were large food supplies at some piggeries and a rubbish dump nearby which might have made it unnecessary to have a large territory. Territory size does not increase at times of food scarcity, nor does it decrease when extra food is supplied experimentally, so the food available in this area is unlikely to have produced these small territories.

The territory and with it the nest site must be defended throughout the year: 52·6 per cent of nests were re-used and the males spent much time there using the self-advertising cawing, and some aggressive postures. During the nesting season territory holders remain near the nest at night, and they do not always go to the communal roost during the whole of the period between one nesting season and the next. If the territory holders do go to the communal roost (p. 66) some will go to the pre-roost assembly about one hour before sunset, but some go direct to the roost after sunset. In the morning the territory holders go back to the territories about 15 minutes before the flock returns. It is essential for them to leave late at night and arrive early in the morning to maintain their territories and to avoid the need for repeated eviction of intruders.

The threat to the territory comes from the members of the non-breeding flock. They may intrude as single birds, casually, and usually leave at once when they are threatened, but some single male intruders are very persistent and become temporarily tolerated: these are the 'third birds'. Only males are sufficiently persistent and aggressive to become third birds. Some flock intrusions are made by paired birds and some by groups. In Charles's experience some pairs were casual and some were persistent but all were eventually evicted by the owner. Members of pairs were never accepted as third birds but a few succeeded in establishing small temporary territories of 3–6ha (7·5–15 acres) during the months between December and May. When nesting begins, any nest that the intruders have succeeded in building is liable to be destroyed by the combined efforts of adjacent territory holders. Such intruders will be continually pursued and will eventually return to the flock.

Experimental removal of the territory holders showed that the holders of a temporary territory would take over. A female left on her own by loss of her mate would be evicted, a male on his own could maintain his territory, but might relinquish it and the tenant of a temporary territory would at once move in.

The third bird, a male, is tolerated in the territory; he may be a juvenile of the pair that bred there the previous year. He will help the owner with defence and eviction of the flock intruders, and he will roost within the territory but not close to the resident pair. Third birds and temporary territory holders are dominant birds in the flock.

Although no flock pair ever succeeded in establishing a territory by reduction of an existing one (contrast with the rook), their intrusions into the territories exert great pressure on the resident birds. Firstly because intrusions continue throughout the year except from June to August (the testis refractory period when aggressiveness is minimal), and any relaxation of their defence might deprive a territorial pair of their territory and with it the chance of breeding in the following nesting season. And secondly because of the direct threat to the nest contents. For a flock pair invading a territory goes straight to the nest site and in the absence of the owner lands on the nest tree or nest, but flees at once if the owner returns. Many are persistent and retreat only as far as the territory border where defence is less intense, returning for a second try at the first opportunity. Groups of 5 to 24 birds from the flock may invade the territory and assemble in the nest tree or near it, and fly to the nest and try to land on it. If the resident pair are present they can prevent a landing on the nest and on trees up to about 20m away. But it can easily take as much as an hour before the whole of such a group has been evicted from the territory. Groups of birds are able to remain longer within the territories than are individuals or pairs. There are more group intrusions close to the estuary where the flock birds live and, due to disturbance and more frequent predation of the eggs and young nesting, success is lower in these territories than in those further away. Most intrusions take place from January to May with a peak in April, but not in the months from June to August. They occur again from September to December with a peak between September and November, but not as many as in the spring.

When a pair of intruders approach a nest, the resident male chases away one of them, probably the male (as males attack males and females attack females). The other goes to the nest and the incubating female leaves to chase it. One of the two intruders tries to wheel round to the nest and an egg or young bird may be taken.

The flock of non-breeders varies in size. There is a winter peak in numbers, probably due to immigrants doubling the summer number, which remains more or less constant. Fifty-eight per cent of flock birds are males, most juveniles leave their parental territories and join the flock at between 2 and 10 months; they are not chased out of their natal territories by the parents, but they are chased out of neighbouring territories and from one to another until they end up in the flock.

In Charles's study, the average age at which a young bird would first make an intrusion into a territory was 21 months. Prior to reproductive sexual maturity it would probably not be sufficiently aggressive, and in any case adults are dominant over young birds; no one year old, recognizable as such by wing tags, was ever seen to rob a nest. The flock is not so much a cohesive group, as a collection of birds who, through being subordinate to the territory holders in confrontation, have failed to establish a territory and so cannot breed.

I have given an account of some of the actions and postures used by crows in these confrontations between territory owners and the flock members, and here I can only briefly indicate how this behaviour is used.

The mere presence of the owner is not sufficient to protect his territory and he must use displays such as the bristle head, head forward, and chasing to keep away intruders, who remain at a distance, usually in the sleeked position. Intruders are threatened or attacked at the border, but are often successful in getting as near as 20m from the nest (124 times out of 134) but resistance then becomes much more intense and only 17 attempts to reach the nest were successful out of a series of 104. The residents' aggressiveness increases with intense nest building (cf rook) at which time all third birds are evicted from their territories.

If a group of flock members lands in an area of continuous territorial borders, the neighbouring territory holders land at the edge of such a group, and any flock members near one of the residents is 'supplanted' or attacked. Most such intruders sit silent and in the sleeked posture, while the residents use the cawing display, the bristle head, the pot-bellied posture, aerial chases, and supplanting to remove them. Those few flock birds not sleeked and subdued may also use the cawing display, the pot-bellied posture and bristle head; but in spite of this no resident was evicted from a territory by these group intrusions during the years of Charles's study.

The size of the territory is constant, and no additional territories were ever found in the spaces left by the reduction of ranges of the breeding birds while nesting. The experimental introduction of additional new nest sites (trees or whole branches in which crows had previously nested were set up) never enabled an additional pair to establish a territory; adding extra food supplies also failed to alter the size and number of the territories.

NEST SITE AND NEST BUILDING

These birds have a preference for trees as nest sites but are very adaptable. In the more northerly parts of the range, and on islands where trees are few, nests may be built on the ground among the heather, or on cliff ledges, and sometimes in small stunted birch, fir or hawthorn trees. Recently, electricity pylons have been used for nest sites. Trees are, however, the normal site for the nest, the species of tree varying in different parts of the range. Wittenberg (1968) in Brunswick found oak (*Quercus*) to be the favourite, while in Poland black poplar (*Populus nigra*) was most commonly used (Kulczycki, 1973), and in north-east Scotland most nests were in Scots firs (*Pinus sylvestris*) (Picozzi, 1975). The mean height of the tree was very similar in two instances, 14m in Kulczycki's study and 14·8m in Wittenberg's, but the range was from 0 to 30m.

The top and middle of the crown of the tree is often chosen and sometimes a many-pronged fork of the trunk or a bough. In Cornwall many nests are in the introduced *Pinus radiata* where the dense foliage gives wind protection and many branches spread out horizontally, and the nests are often among the spiny leaves on the flat spread of the branch up to 4 or 5m from the trunk.

New sites are often chosen. Of 98 nests examined by Picozzi in 1975 only three were re-used, although Charles had found 53 per cent of old nests used again.

Nest building both in Brunswick and in north-east Scotland begins in mid-March and takes about 20 days. The nest is built 'normally by the female accompanied by the male' (Picozzi, 1975). The nest is very strongly built and may last for many years, especially those built in pines. It is formed in four layers. First an external foundation and wall structure is made of twigs of local trees or heather stems, with sheep and rabbit bones sometimes added; and Walford (1930) described one made mainly of wire and rabbit bones and placed halfway up the iron-work supporting structure of a wind pump. The outer walls are filled with bark strips and other fibrous material arranged circularly; fine birch twigs are often used in this way. The bottom is lined with earth and mud pushed in between the twigs and fibres to make a firm base, and this extends up the sides to a varying extent. The structure so formed is lined with a variety of available soft material, including feathers and down, wool and red-deer hair, string, cloth and pieces of paper. The average diameter of the cup is from 19 to 20cm and the depth from 10 to 13cm (Kulczyki, 1973; Abshagan, 1963). The outer dimensions of the nest are more variable, because of the difference in site and type of twigs available.

EGGS TO FLEDGING OF YOUNG

The average size of the eggs is 43·3 × 30·4mm; they are pale greenish blue, but some are bluer or greener than the average. They are marked with spots, blotches and streaks of grey-brown, shades of grey and olive. The markings vary from almost complete absence to almost total covering, and erythristic eggs occasionally occur; these have a pink ground colour and red and purple markings.

Holyoak's (1967) analysis of carrion crow breeding records shows that in the British Isles there is a range of mean dates for the laying of the first egg from 13 April in Wales to 27 April in the north of Scotland. The earliest eggs can be found at the end of the first third of March and the latest are at the end of May. Laying is later at higher altitudes in the north of England and Scotland: 0–150m, 20 April; 150–300m, 24 April; 300–600m, 2 May. Various other factors have an influence on these dates, such as weather and food supply. But an all-important factor in carrion crow breeding is the cannibalism by the flock birds, and Yom Tov (1975) has shown that there is a tendency for birds nesting close together to be better synchronized in their nesting times than those which were more widely scattered, and those that were synchronized were significantly more successful than the others. This may be because when there is synchronization there is less cannibalism and less interference in such matters as nest building and copulation.

The mean clutch size varies a little from about 4 in the south to about 4·5 in the north and there is a slight reduction in clutch size at higher altitude from 4·1 in nests below 150m to 3·9 in those between 150 and 300m in comparable areas of the British Isles. Usually one egg is laid each day but occasionally there are two-day intervals. The incubation period is from 17 to 22 days (mean 19·5). Charles found 59·5 per cent of nests to be successful and the greatest cause of failure is nest robbing by other crows, with human interference next. Eggs that fail to hatch are generally removed by the parents, possibly by eating them, but any that are still in the nest after 12 days are usually left. Dead young of any age are removed by carrion and hooded crows.

Although Picozzi (1975) found that on average successful pairs rear 2·94 young per nest, the overall result of all pairs is much lower, varying from about 1·1 to 1·7 in different areas and years.

There are three causes of total loss of nest contents: human predation; chilling when parents are kept from the nest for too long; gradual loss of nest contents by repeated robbing (nest robbing by other crows was by far the most frequent of these). Where the non-breeders lived by the Ythan Estuary there were more total losses than in territories further away.

The nesting season lasts for about 75 days from mid-April until the end of June and this is the period when predation by other crows takes its effect: 91 per cent of egg losses, 68 per cent of desertions and 82·5 per cent of nestling disappearance were attributed to crow predation by Yom Tov.

Total failure increases as the season advances, and the majority (59 per cent) fledge in the first week of June, and almost all (94 per cent) within that month in the Aberdeen area (Charles, 1972). There would be appropriately later or earlier variations in other parts of the continent of Europe.

If a nest or the clutch are destroyed a new nest is often made. This does not appear to happen after hatching, the regression of the bird's breeding condition having by then gone too far. The time taken to replace a nest and clutch varies from 12 to 17 days (Pring, 1924–5; Symes, 1925–6). All incubation is normally done by the female.

The female is fed on or near the nest by the male, for about the first 9 or 10 days after the eggs have hatched. During that time the female broods the young fully for the first week, and leaves the nest only to receive food from the male and roosts there. After that, she may leave the young by day to help collect food for them and will continue to brood them at night for another three or four days. The young remain in the nest for 30 to 34 days and then follow the adults in the field and are dependent on them for several weeks. Picozzi (1975) found that hatching success varied from 65 to 83 per cent and of fledging from 50 to 70 per cent, hatching and fledging both being high in good years.

Yom Tov (1974) provided additional food both during the winter before nesting and during the nesting season, and distributed it in various ways: concentrated close to the nest, more scattered or in more distant parts of the territory, for example. He found that the provision of extra food did not alter the number of eggs laid nor the weight of the fledglings. Extra food given during the winter enabled the crows to start nesting about five days earlier than those that received no extra food – an advantage because there is more predation by flock crows later in the season. Extra food concentrated in an area close to the nest reduced the number of desertions, reduced the number of eggs lost and increased the proportion of eggs that hatched and the survival chances of the young birds.

	Desertions	Eggs lost	Proportion hatching	Survival of young
Control	21·6%	27·3%	9·0%	1·2
Extra food near the nest	2·1%	4·3%	15·2%	2·6

The effect is less if extra food is provided in parts of the territory. Remote from the nest, for example, the proportion of eggs producing young is 28 per cent where no extra food is provided; 37 per cent where food is provided in far parts of the territory; but if the same amount of food is provided near to the nest the proportion of eggs that hatch, 67 per cent, is nearly twice as high.

The breeding, territory-holding birds can always defend the nest if they are present, but obviously if they have to go far in their foraging and are therefore away for longer periods they cannot make so successful a defence as when adequate food is available near the nest, so predation is greater. It has been suggested that carrion crows maintain their numbers at below the level of food shortage. While this clearly applies to territory holders who do not lack food and remain in good condition throughout the year, the flock birds who are the subordinate members of the whole population do not get adequate food, are not in good condition and some starve. Food distribution has a great effect on the territorial birds, but food quantity and quality clearly affects the population as a whole.

The balance between the flock and the territory holders provides a mechanism for self-regulation of the population: in a good year for crows more young will fledge and there will be more recruitment to the flock, so competition and confrontations will increase, so lowering breeding success and reducing the rate of recruitment again the following year.

It was found that after the end of the nesting season the behaviour of the young bird varies and some were independent of their parents by September.

Some – and it was usual for all of a brood to act in the same way – joined the flock, some stayed with their parents until the next nesting season. In one territory young of three successive years fed in the same field as their parents on 13 September – and no other crows were present. None of the tagged birds in this study moved very far, 23km being the greatest distance, but because many had been tagged as juveniles the ages of 28 'dispersed' crows, recovered or sighted, were known, and are shown in this table. Ages are for tagged, 'dispersed' crows when recovered or sighted.

1 year	29%	4 years	4%
2 years	46%	5 years	4%
3 years	14%	6 years	4%

One bird tagged in March was seen 17km away in April but had returned by May and later held a territory in the original area in which it was tagged.

They probably reach physiological maturity (ability to breed) at the end of summer of the second calendar year, 15 to 17 months after hatching.

ROOSTING

Communal winter roosting of carrion/hooded crows is probably their normal habit. They gather at pre-roost assemblies and if such an assembly happens to be within a territory its members are not evicted – outside the nesting season, of course. Sometimes this species roosts alone and sometimes with other 'crows'. At a roost in Cornwall there were up to 150 ravens, about 200 carrion crows, 2500 rooks and 7–8000 jackdaws; these numbers changed from year to year. Rooks and jackdaws assembled in a particular area and flew in to roost in more or less the same part of the plantation; ravens and carrion crows each had their own assembly area and roosted in separate parts of the plantation. There was some overlap between species, caused by the very numerous jackdaws, which could not all be accommodated in one area and tended to overflow into the raven and crow parts of the roost. At this roost, ravens tended to go to their trees about 20 minutes before the rooks and jackdaws; the carrion crows went last of all. In the morning the ravens and carrion crows had all left before the rooks and jackdaws began to move.

Within the catchment area of these two 'crow' roosts there were several smaller carrion crow roosts of from 3 or 4 to about 30 birds and one large one of about 200 birds. It is possible that carrion crows usually do not fly so far to their roosts as rooks and jackdaws.

Numbers in the roost tend to vary and Picozzi (1975) suggested that there might be interchange of birds with another roost about 4km from the one he studied. In eastern and northern Britain numbers may be augmented by immigrant birds and the roosting numbers may then be more than would be accounted for by the local population – there was, for example, a count of 400 roosting birds in an area where it was estimated that only 60 pairs were resident (Brock, 1913–14).

Charles found that during the nesting season all territory-holding breeding pairs roosted within their territories on or near their nest trees and when the female is incubating the male roosts on or near the nest tree.

Outside the nesting season there was some variation. Some territory-holding pairs did not go regularly to the communal roost, and the number roosting within their own territory changed with the season as follows:

Aug–Dec	0
January	5%
by 3rd week in February	31%
by 1st week in March	80%
by 2nd week in March	100%

(These changes could be delayed for up to three weeks by exceptionally cold weather.)

Communal roosting, as opposed to remaining in the territory, must have some special value for crows. Perhaps it originally served as a protection against predators, although in Britain there are now almost no enemies of adult crows other than man. For many species, including crows, communal roost may serve as information centres for locating good feeding grounds as suggested by Ward and Zahavi (1973). The advantages of flock feeding do not seem to apply as forcibly to crows as to rooks, but communal roosting persists for many birds, even in treeless areas where they may have to roost on the ground.

FOOD

One of the most striking things about the crow is the adaptability of its behaviour, and this is also apparent in its choice of food. Basic foods can vary from one area to another, and there is a long list of, sometimes, surprising opportunistic feeding by crows.

Holyoak (1968) showed that the basic foods as determined by gizzard analysis of 234 carrion crows from an agricultural area in southern England were as follows:

Vegetable

Grain**	Cherries
Wild-plant seeds*	Plums
Potatoes	Acorns
Apples	Beechnuts
Pears	Walnuts

Animal

Live small mammals** (especially March–August inclusive)
Carrion*
Earthworms (January–April inclusive)
Grassland and woodland insects
Full-grown live birds
Nestling birds
Birds' eggs
Fish carrion
Territorial and fresh-water molluscs
Littoral invertebrates
Spiders
Woodlice
Centipedes
Ticks
Bread
Animal feed stuffs

** especially important   * important foods

In a very different environment in Argyllshire Dr David Houston undertook an investigation of the effects of hooded crows on sheep farming. He found that between November and February stomach contents contained by volume 62 per cent carrion, 27 per cent grain, 6 per cent small mammals, and 5 per cent beetles. During the summer, spiders, click beetles, ground beetles, crane flies, and dung beetles were the chief food sources and berries were important at the end of the summer and during the autumn. Examples are rowan (*Sorbus aucuparia*), elder (*Sambucus edulus*) and blaeberry (*Vaccinium myrtillus*). Compared with the diet of lowland birds, carrion was much more important and wild fruit and berries also figured more largely. Grain was taken mainly as oats, for which the hoodies made long flights from hill ground to farms. Young birds were given protein food and the parent hoodies collected the spiders, flies and beetles from which this diet was made from the hill pastures, probably fed themselves on insects as they did so, but also exploited any special source such as bread from bird tables, but did not give this to the young. Birds in Argyll feeding in lowland areas were found to have a wider choice of insect species than those living on higher ground. Animal food, both invertebrate and vertebrate, is also a source of fluid for young crows.

The non-breeding flock tended in Houston's study area to feed on such places as Oban town rubbish dump, where they were in direct food competition with the much larger herring gulls and ravens. There, most of the crows were just sitting about without getting any food, and those whose stomach contents were examined had been feeding on grain and not on material from the rubbish dump. The flock birds also fed on the foreshore where they were still in competition with herring gulls and where the nutritional value of the food that they could obtain was low. Thus in this area shore and dump were mainly congregating areas for non-breeders, the underfed subordinate part of the crow population:

> They must chiefly rely on other sources of food. Both shore and rubbish dump are probably chiefly used as congregating areas where birds can join feeding parties that are leaving to visit cattle-feed sites and other feeding areas. During the winter these feeding sites are widely distributed, very localized and transient. An individual is more likely to find a source of food if it joins a flock and follows other groups of birds that are leaving to feed.

The size of the individual bird is important in determining its position in the social hierarchy, and in the relationship between the sexes. Holyoak (1969) showed that there are statistically significant differences in the methods used by the two sexes in obtaining food. Females picked the food from the surface of the ground more than males and used clod-turning far more often. The males used surface probing and deep probing more. There was also a statistically significant difference in the size of invertebrates and larvae brought to the young by the two sexes, the males on average brought the larger items. Holyoak (1969) pointed out the possibility that these differences might be of behavioural importance, because the bill is conspicuous in the threat and aggressive behaviour of the species. He also suggested that bill size and probably body size might, because of the difference in food selection, be important in reducing competition for food between the sexes.

In the social order, male carrion crows are dominant over females; and Charles found that in 'flock males' dominance correlated with the weight of the birds and among captives dominance correlated with weight and also with the size of the gape. He pointed out that a dominant bird might be able to feed better and so become heavier, but among his captive birds a linear dominance was established from seven months and did not change. Males are larger than females, have larger bills, are dominant and have priority over them in food competition. Yom Tov and Ollason (1976) presented a hypothesis, based on mathematical calculations, that 'in some cases intersexual competition over food and sexual dimorphism are responsible for uneven sex ratio'. It seems possible that such competition does exist, as the number of males in the flock is greater than the number of females, and the males are dominant, and therefore presumably get an advantage when food is scarce.

Dr Houston's main brief was to find out what effect crows were having on the hill sheep farming and to try to make an objective assessment. Ewes that roll over when they have a heavy fleece cannot regain their feet. Couped ewes, as they are called, are at risk from suffocation, unless they are found within twelve hours, and also from attack by predators. Such ewes are found most often between February and April, the time when their mortality is highest. The annual mortality in hill conditions was 6–7 per cent and post mortems showed that almost all couped ewes attacked by crows were dead as a result of their position before the shepherd found them.

Overall lamb mortality was about 17 per cent from birth to six weeks, with a higher percentage in bad weather. But the percentage of lambs killed by crows was exceedingly low – about 0·7 per cent of lambs that die, or about 0·06 per cent of lambs born, that is about 1 in 1700.

Carrion and hooded crows often drop shellfish on rocks to break them, sometimes letting the shell go during a dive. Is this to increase the impact? To aim? Or just because the bird 'forgets' to let go at the top of its flight? Crows are said to make a choice of hard ground as compared with gulls which sometimes make their drop on to soft ground (Tinbergen, 1953). They will take live fish out of running water, and dead fish off the surface; and a few weeks before writing this I watched one repeatedly landing in fresh water that must have been about 25cm deep – for when it landed only its upraised wings were visible as it put its head right under each time to capture a frog. It made several such captures within 20 minutes. A bird that becomes responsive to a particular pattern of its prey and the environment of that prey develops a 'search image'. In exploiting new food sources and in the efficient use of known ones crows (and other species) gain an advantage from hunting by search image. Croze (1970) showed that the crow's ability to find prey, once recognized, was enhanced by success. Crows learned features of the habitat as well as features of the prey. Prey species of a polymorphic population (more than one search image for the crows) had a better chance of survival than those with a single form. Camouflage by prey is an antipredator adaptation and the search image is a means of overcoming this.

Crows sometimes catch adult birds and the following have been recorded: house sparrows often; swallows attacked but not caught (Hanford, 1969; Radford, 1970); young house martins (Yapp, 1975); a starling caught in full flight and carried off by the crow in its claws (Warren, 1969); nestling magpies from their nest (Cawkell, 1948); wood pigeons as nestlings in the nest and as fully grown (Geoghegan and Fileman, 1950; Bromley, 1947; Husband, 1966). Perhaps the most surprising was an apparently normal adult lapwing attacked repeatedly in flight and eventually brought to the ground by one of three crows (Tinbergen, 1953). Small mammals are a staple part of their diet, but a bat caught in·flight must be a rarity, especially as it was caught at a second attempt, the first having failed (Arnold, 1955).

PREDATORS, PARASITES, MORBIDITY AND MORTALITY

Charles has shown that the two most important predators on the carrion crow are carrion crows at nesting time and man. Apart from those destroyed by man there must be very few fully grown carrion crows killed by predators. There are records of a fully grown carrion crow as identified among the prey of the red kite (Walters-Davies and Davis) and more surprisingly an adult carrion crow as the prey of a sparrow hawk (Newton, 1973).

That the predatory habits of crows are not free of risk was shown by Blackett's

(1970) account of a crow being drowned by a coot. Two other coots joined in. The usual reaction of 'black crows' when one of their number is held by a predator is mobbing and this was shown by six other crows. There is also a record of a carrion crow probably killed by a heron and this may have been the result of attempted nest robbing by the crow (Aspden, 1928–9). Hooded crows are among the species of which individuals have been found to have died after being soaked in fulmar oil (Broad, 1974). Carrion crows are among the species parasitized by the hippoboscid fly *Ornithonyia avicularia*. A captive hooded crow that I kept clearly recognized these as different from other flies of similar size, even when they were in flight, trying to catch them before they landed, but ignoring them once they were among the feathers. Larvae of the small fly *Neottiophilum praestum*, a nest fly, inhabits the nests of several passerine bird species, including the carrion crow, and the larvae are parasitic on the nestlings (Rothschild and Clay, 1952). The gape worm, the nematode *Syngamus trachea*, has been found in nestling carrion crows. It is found far more frequently in the rook, but Picozzi (1975) did comment on the number of nestling crows that were wheezing. Another nematode which has been found in the carrion crow is *Oxyspirura mansoni*, a species comparable with *O. sygamodea*, parasitic on poultry and with the cockroach as an intermediate host. When the insect is eaten the larvae are released and quickly migrate to the host's eye where they remain. Many parasites have evolved with their host species and in the British Isles the tapeworm *Anomotaenia constricta* has been found in carrion crows and rooks; it is also found in American crows and may be confined to corvids.

Carrion crows are also honoured by having their own specific flea, *Ceratophyllus rossittensis*, and the poultry flea *C. gallinae* is also found in crows' nests. I have already described anting by hooded and carrion crows and this may be an anti-ectoparasitic measure: Rothschild and Clay quote the story that 'Russian soldiers were said to clear their lousy garments by putting them on ants' nests', and the function of anting by birds was discussed by Simmons (1957).

As with other corvid species, cases of abnormal pigmentation are not uncommon. Fully albino carrion and hooded crows have been recorded; a pigment deficiency especially affecting the primaries seems to be comparatively common and to be an inherited defect (Harrison, 1963; Sage, 1962).

Abnormal bill formations occur in this species as with other corvines. Pomeroy (1962) recorded a hooded crow with crossed mandibles.

Crows have been sufficiently adaptable in their feeding not to be as much affected by cold as are many species. In the abnormally cold winter of 1962–3 they may possibly even have benefited from the presence of dead birds or other animals (Dobinson and Richards, 1964).

Ratcliffe (1965) found that organo-chlorine pollution had had little effect on carrion or hooded crows, either in their numbers or in their breeding success, although there were slightly higher concentrations of organo-chlorine residues in the eggs of crows in hilly sheep-rearing areas than in those from lowland nests.

MOBBING AND DEFENCE

Most ornithologists must have seen 'crows' mobbing raptors: carrion crows mobbing buzzards, kestrels or sparrowhawks; hooded crows mobbing golden eagles and occasionally actually striking them (I have seen feathers knocked from a buzzard's back). On the ground, the approach to any potentially dangerous object is very cautious, and if that object is living the approach is always from behind. The crow with most of its feathers sleeked and in a semi-crouched position is obviously ready for instant flight. Probably there is some degree of readiness to flee in a crow making aerial attacks too but many birds show a confidence in the air which they would probably never exhibit on the ground. A house sparrow may pursue a feral pigeon. On the ground, at any shared food source, my experience has been that buzzards always take precedence over ravens, herring gulls, carrion/hooded crows, rooks and jackdaws and magpies. The interspecific dominance is in that order, except sometimes in the case of the last two. At refuse dumps crows may be present but because of the dominant herring gulls they obtain almost no food (Houston, 1974), but in a gull colony the position can be very different and Axell (1956) described the depredations of carrion crows in a herring gull colony, and the application of a commonly used crow tactic to rob the gulls. One Crow would walk round the nest at 3–5yd distance, occasionally making short provocative flights at the sitter; the second crow waited about 45m away to rob the nest as soon as the gull made an attack. He also described one or two crows on each side of a nest making short vertical flights of up to 3 or 5m, possibly to try to induce the gull to leave its nest and attack them.

Just as the crow and other species may alter their behaviour on the ground or in the air according to the degree of risk involved, so the crow may act differently in mobbing different raptor species. With some, one can see the aggressive fluffed-up feathers of the crow's head and neck, the bristle-head position in flight; a kestrel has been killed by mobbing crows (Sage, 1962) and a barn own clutched and brought to the ground by an attacking crow gripping the owl with its feet (Dickson, 1972). The attacks are accompanied by a harsh grating call, which may be threatening or aggressive and it is said by Lohrl (1950) that this call is not used when crows mob a goshawk, probably their main avian predator, and Lohrl suggested that the crow has then much more fear than when attacking a kestrel or buzzard. With some species it is difficult to be certain whether they are attacked as potential predators, as a potential meal, or because they have interfered with the crow obtaining a meal (in that case a food competitor from the viewpoint of the crow). Thus a jay (Cross, 1947) attacked in April and severely injured might have been trying to defend its own nest (to prevent the crow eating the food it had found), but the crow was apparently trying to carry off the jay in its claws, as they sometimes do with food that is too heavy to carry in the bill.

Was a grey squirrel prey or predator? It was running and leaping through the grass and followed by a carrion crow which struck it repeatedly with bill and feet. This was in May when the crows would perhaps have had young (Rowberry, 1931–2) and in June of the same year a somewhat similar attack, but this time in a tree top, was also put on record (Ferrier, 1931–2).

Perhaps the distinction between mobbing and attacking is the degree of the crow's fear of the victim of its attack. Carrion crows, like jackdaws and rooks, join the combined mobbing by corvids when one of their number is held by a predator.

5
Rook
(Corvus frugilegus)

European names

Dutch – ROEK
French – CORBEAUX-FREUX
German – SAATKRAHE

Russian – GRACH
Spanish – CORVACHONES DE PICO
    BLANCO
Swedish – RÅKA

Vernacular names

BARE-FACED CROW
Cheshire – LORD BARRYMORE'S
    PIGEON

Cornwall – BRAN
Somerset – CHURCH PARSON

FIELD CHARACTERISTICS

Few bird colonies can have aroused as much interest as rookeries. The activities of rooks need to be watched from nest level as Lewis Harding (1848) did from his window, or better still from a hide among the nests. I was particularly lucky that 'my' rookery at Roundwood, Cornwall, was in the trees on a wooded peninsula with two creeks of the Fal Estuary on either side of it. From the hide I could watch the activities of a small fishing community as well as all the excitement of the twenty or so rooks' nests within easy view in a colony of more than 200 birds (Coombs, 1960).

Under reasonable viewing conditions, confusion is likely only between this species and the carrion crow. The rook has a more slender bill, and this is even more noticeable in the bare-faced adults when the light-grey colour of the face makes diagnosis certain. On the ground, the flank feathers of the rook are more shaggy and hang looser and lower than those of the crow; this is less noticeable in juveniles but is more marked even in them than in the carrion crow. In flight, the wing beat is rather quicker.

DESCRIPTION

Adult male and female

The sexes are alike and there is no difference between winter and summer plumage. All the feathers are black, but show iridescence in various shades of blue and purple. The gloss on the primaries, primary coverts, alula and tail is greenish. The face and chin are bare, usually pale ash-grey but the colour varies. The bill, legs and feet are black and the irides are dark brown.

Newly hatched nestling

This is dark-skinned and develops a scanty grey down. The inside of the mouth is bright crimson, the spurs at the base of the tongue are pale orange. The bill is dark grey to black with yellow edges at the gape. As the bird gets older the mouth colour becomes pinker and less red. The irides are bluish grey and the feet black.

The nestling/juvenile

The face is feathered and there are black nasal bristles, comparable in length and density with those of other crows. All the feathers are black but with little gloss, the head and neck often appearing brownish.

The bill remains black externally, although at first some birds have a yellowish base to the sides of the bill, especially around the gape. This is sometimes associated with a small area of white feathers on the anterior part of the chin between the rami of the lower mandible. There are sometimes a few white feathers on the face. Some young birds have grey areas beginning to appear inside the mouth before they leave the nest, but many do not become fully dark until the moult into adult plumage in their second calendar year. The young bird may begin to loose the nasal bristles and face feathers of the juvenile plumage at the beginning of the second calendar year, perhaps in January. The loss of these feathers is slow and only about 50 per cent of first-year birds retain feathered faces after May of their second calendar year, when the following year's crop of young birds is fledging (Dunnet, Fordham and Patterson, 1969).

Summarizing the age classes and stages of moult will make for clarity.

A   nestling. From hatching in March/April until leaving the nest in May/June.

B   first-year bird. From leaving the nest until 31 December. A moult takes place, starting in late April or early May, and ending towards the end of the summer. The body and head feathers are changed from the juvenile type to adult type and colour. The lesser and median coverts and some outer greater coverts are also moulted. The remaining greater coverts, the primary coverts, primaries, secondaries and tail feathers are retained and gradually become brown and worn.

C   second-year bird (second calendar year). There is no change from 1 January until the end of March, when the brown faded primaries, secondaries, alula, remaining coverts and the tail feathers are moulted gradually between April and September. As I have already mentioned, the nasal bristles and face feathers are usually lost by May. The birds are then indistinguishable from adults in the field and are said to have changed from juvenile to adult plumage, although a number of juvenile flight and tail feathers may be present.

D   fully grown bird. October until 31 December. By this stage all the juvenile feathers have gone and the bird is indistinguishable from an adult even in the hand.

E   post-second-year bird. There is an annual moult starting in early May with the shedding of the innermost primaries and continuing until the late autumn with the final replacements in some of the body-feather tracts.

In this summary I have used the terminology and some of the data provided by Seel (1976). A few second-year birds retaining feathered faces are present in the rookeries when nesting starts in February or March and a few breed. A few males in this plumage are involved in the attacks on incubating females to be described later. Although some of these immature birds have obviously reached a sexually active stage the testis development of the males is incomplete (Marshall and Coombs, 1957).

DISTRIBUTION

The rook is distributed throughout much of Europe and Asia in areas clear of dense woodland but with plenty of trees; agricultural land with access to both grain and pasture is preferred. They are found in the north to about 65°, east to about 90° and south to about 30°. This is a more restricted distribution than that of the Eurasian crow and in the Far East its place is taken by a subspecies *C.f. dastinator*, which has a partly feathered face and feathered chin. In Europe the rook is absent from all but the extreme north of the Iberian Peninsula; it is also absent from Italy and much of the mountainous area of central Europe. In the north there are a few colonies in the Hebrides, Orkneys and Shetlands; and although rooks may feed from the shore to rough upland pastures at 360m there are large areas in north-west Scotland devoid of them. The species is commoner in eastern Denmark than in the west and found only in small areas of Southern Norway and Sweden and western Finland.

In some parts of its range the climate makes winter feeding impossible for

Rook

the rook, which obtains much of its food by probing the ground; in these areas it is a migrant. During the 1939–45 war observations on rook migration were made by some British ornithologists while in German prisoner-of-war camps (Waterhouse, 1949). Much of the spring movement was protracted and spread over five or six weeks, but at all the places where observations were made there were peak days in which a very high proportion of the total number of birds passed. For example at Sagan a total of 18,000 birds were recorded and of these 11,700 were on 18–19 March. These peak days were all between 10 March and 22 March, by which time rooks in Cornwall and in Aberdeenshire would in many cases be incubating eggs. The autumn migration also showed peak periods between 25 October and 1 November, but the total time of these migrations was between 52 and 58 days. As well as the rook movements across Germany and further east, there are movements down the north-west European coast, south westerly, until the point where the coastline turns south at Cap Gris-Nez; at that point rooks turn north west towards a wintering area in the British Isles (Nijhoft, 1958). However some cross wider stretches of sea and were observed at sea by Captain Wolf Murray, who made three observations in March and April 1927 in a North Sea area approximately 320km east of the north Yorkshire coast and about 100 miles from the Dutch coast. Overland rooks have been seen to travel in flocks at 180m and sometimes up to a probable height of 900m. Above this height they would probably not be visible from the ground. Some travel in small straggling parties and at heights of only 100ft or so (Waterhouse, 1949).

Rooks from inhospitable areas winter as far afield as Algeria, northern Egypt, Sinai, Palestine, Asia Minor, Trans-Caucasia, central Asia, Afghanistan and Kashmir. They return early to their summer quarters and by 13 March 'the rook is the first harbinger of spring' in Moscow (Dementiev and Gladov, 1951–4).

The pattern of roosting in the area where flocks of immigrant rooks spend the winter in the United Kingdom is confused, because they often use the same roosts as the resident birds, but do not always collect before roosting at the local rookeries. Some do go direct to the second assembly points close to the roost (Burns, 1957).

POSTURE AND VOICE

Some of the seasonal changes in behaviour of any bird are at least in part under the control of the hormones produced by the endocrine glands. The various display postures involved in the reproductive cycle of the rook have been studied in relation to the cycle of gonad changes and these can be briefly summarized. There is a primary autumnal sexual season, which is normally inhibited – probably by the decreasing day length – until the following spring when the increasing day length allows continuation to the full secondary phase in which reproduction is completed. The spring production of reproductive cells begins in both sexes early in February and reproductive behaviour becomes ever more active, reaching its highest level in March. By the end of April the testes are becoming inactive in terms both of the production of reproductive cells and of the production of male sex hormone. This refractory period lasts until the end of July or early August, and during that time displays of apparent sexual significance are rarely seen. After the refractory period the interstitial cells, which are the source of male hormone, begin to show renewed activity and there is then an increase in sexual behaviour, including certain displays, which reaches a level in September and October comparable with that of February, when display is intense and nest building beginning. Although in November really successful reproduction (viable young) must be extremely rare, there are several records of young birds in the nest, some of these records were given by Yarrell as long ago as 1845.

Although the spring increase in day length seems to be the factor that ensures that the rooks breed at the right time of year, the actual date of egg laying varies from year to year as was shown by D.F. Owen in 1959. During his six-year study the mean date of first egg laying varied from 9 to 23 March and these variations in egg-laying date appear to be related to the mean air temperature in the area (Owen, 1959).

Display postures

About a dozen of these are described here, but some merge with one another without any sharp demarcation, and there are several common components. Some have obvious counterparts in other species, especially of course, in other crows.

Wing-and tail-flipping

21   Rook : wing and tail flip.
Compare figs 20, 41, 46, 51

This occurs in many passerine species. The folded wings are quickly lifted from the back and if the action is at all marked the wing tips separate and at the same time the tail is slightly spread, the head and body not being involved. There seems to be a close connection between the wing and the tail movements. Rooks often perch with the wings held rather loosely over the back, so that one or other wing tip may slip down to lie below the tail, and is usually quickly replaced; the action is very similar to the wing-and-tail-flipping action, and as the wing is replaced the tail is often slightly ópened. Both adult and juvenile rooks use the wing-and-tail-flipping action but less frequently and with less emphasized movement than do carrion/hooded crows.

This movement resembles the bowing and tail-fanning display described below but the action is much quicker. During quarrelling wing-and-tail-flipping may continue between the bouts of bowing and fanning. The action might signify readiness to fly but it does not occur as an intention movement for flight.

Bowing and tail-fanning

22   Rook: bowing and tail fanning. Compare figs 17, 42

This is a self-advertising posture in which the bird bows its whole body forward and caws. As it does so, the tail is raised above the horizontal and spread. The angle varies with the intensity of the action, and the raised position is maintained for some moments and continues when the bird's body is stationary after the forward part of the bowing movement. At the same time as the bowing and tail-fanning, the wings which are kept closed, are raised from the sides. Then with greater intensity they are lifted above horizontal, the legs being flexed at the same time. Bowing and tail-fanning is rarely seen during May, June and July. It occurs during all other months, especially in late February and March, and during this time the sound most often heard in the rookery is the cawing that accompanies it. It occurs most often before and after quarrelling over territory, before and after pursuit flights (cf the posture of the great tit between flights, Hinde, 1952), and on the arrival of another rook nearby. In these circumstances the cawing accompanying the posture has a deeper tone than when there is an element of alarm. Then the birds stand in the branches with head feathers sleeked but crests raised, cawing shrilly until the alarm has passed or fear becomes sufficient to make them fly. The significance of this shrill caw is not really clear because one sometimes hears an isolated bird using this perhaps as part of its song. It might be effective as a long-range sound.

The male and female precopulatory postures described below can both develop from bowing and tail-fanning. All have an element of slow wing raising, and one posture can merge into another without a perceptible break in the bird's movements. Bowing and tail-fanning can also merge with the threat postures described later.

The male pre-copulatory display

23   Rook: male pre-copulatory display, frontal. Compare fig 10

In some respects the male posture looks like an exaggeration of the bowing and tail-fanning. The movements are slower and the tail is raised higher, and more fully spread, and then held in that position. The wings are raised from the sides more slowly, are partially spread and may remain so for several seconds.

24   Rook: male pre-copulatory display, lateral. Compare figs 1, 16, 37, 47, 50

The head is raised with the bill pointing down and the head and nape feathers raised, with the flank feathers markedly fluffed out. Usually the male faces the female but, if he happens to be sideways on towards her, the tail is twisted and the body tilted so that the upper surfaces of wings and tail are towards her (fig. 24). I have never seen this posture used in the autumn, and it has been seen less often in February and April than in March. It is nearly always followed by copulation or attempted copulation and usually occurs near the nests, where copulation usually takes place. This posture is sometimes shown by a rook on the ground or away from the rookery. Most copulation takes place without any noticeable display, so this posture is not often seen. In fact 94 per cent of observed copulations were the result of attacks by a male on an incubating and therefore previously fertilized female, and in over 60 per cent of cases the male was known not to be paired to the female. It appears that the incubating female is in a position very similar to the female pre-copulatory or soliciting posture and that this may account for the frequency of attacks on incubating birds. The male pre-copulatory posture is more often seen early in the season when presumably the female does not appear as co-operative as she seems to be when incubating.

Usually a sexual intent is recognized by a female rook as the male approaches without any full precopulatory display, and while he is still some distance away. He usually approaches slowly and hesitantly, sidling along the branches or jumping from one branch to the next. The crest and head feathers are raised, and the flank feathers markedly so. The bill is pointed down. I have seen this posture used by birds in the rookery, and only very occasionally outside it, but it was described by Lockie (1956) as 'elaborate bill-down', used exclusively in sexual situations, and Lockie's observations were mainly of winter feeding flocks.

The female precopulatory display

25   Rook : incubating (below) female pre-copulatory posture (above).
Compare figs 7, 38, 43, 56

This posture can be used by birds of both sexes, and appears to have a strong 'releasing' effect, as on every occasion that I have seen it it has been followed by mounting or attempted mounting by either the male or female. The bird crouches with back level, head lowered and level, and tail slightly above the horizontal. The wings are partly spread and raised, rather similar to the wing action in the equivalent male posture. When in this position the bird remains still, apart from a rapid vibrating of the tail – though this does not always happen. The vibration appears to be in both vertical and horizontal planes. The nictitating membrane may be drawn across the eye slowly and repeatedly. At low intensity the posture bears a marked resemblance to the position of the incubating female for the tail may be still and the wings only just freed from the body (fig. 26).

Copulation
In most rookeries copulation is nearly always on the nest (Yeates, 1934). In

26   Rook: transition of male postures
A.   bowing and tail fanning, self-assertive
B.   male pre-copulatory display
C.   drooping the tail in transition to D
D.   female pre-copulatory display, submissive

1789, in his observations on birds, Gilbert White says: 'These birds do not pair on trees, nor in their nests, but on the ground in the open fields.' However, I believe that when observed from the ground many acts of copulation in the trees are not recognized by the observer because of the interference of other birds and this results in fighting with which the action can be confused. In any case it only occurs during a limited period, starting when the first males are found to reach maximum development of the testes. This is in early March in Cornwall and the earliest copulation that I observed was on 8 March. Every mature male examined during March had reached the height of spermato-genesis and copulation continued to be frequent until the end of the month, after which the frequency decreased rapidly. More and more males become occupied with collecting food, and display and posturing quickly decrease after the eggs are laid. As these events take place, the contents of the testis tubule change, so that reproduction ceases to be possible, and the male hormone disappears from the interstitial cells. The refractory period is be-ginning. It is very striking that incubation does not of itself bring about a decrease in the frequency of copulation, although every incubating female has, of course, been fertilized. In many of these incidents more than one male was observed and this is because of the frequency with which other birds interfere with copulation – only 17 per cent of copulation attempts were not interfered with.

There seems to be a very strong urge to interfere with any action which bears any resemblance to mounting, or perhaps any unusual action. For example, a rook made what appeared to me to be an accidental landing on the back of another in a field and two others promptly flew some distance to threaten them. This happened on 9 July when gonad activity is minimal and sexual responses unusual.

When interference occurs, a male rook approaches an incubating female, perhaps crossing the territories of other females, and the female who is his objective may be on a nest in an area defended by a neighbour (see under Territory). Sometimes as the male approaches he may be attacked by those whose territory he has infringed and the female, seeing him approach, may leave her nest to chase him away, but if he flies direct there may be no opportunity for her to do so. When copulation takes place in this way the female usually resists. At the same time other male rooks, each trying to take his place, may attack him. Some of these males may well have infringed nearby territories and the incubating females from these nests may then join in the fray.

Dihedral wing flapping
This is a slow wing-flapping action in which the wings are raised to a greater angle above horizontal than normal, and brought down more stiffly with less flexion at the wrist and elbow than normal. Analysis of slow-motion film shows that the upstroke is the part that is slowed. This manner of flying may appear for a few flaps only, during ordinary flight, or it may be used continuously for a considerable distance, especially during pursuit flights. The slow stiff upstroke somewhat resembles the wing-raising component of the display postures already described, and like those postures is very rarely seen during the testis refractory period. The display is more common in September than in August and October. It may indeed be seen through the winter, especially on sunny days, but is most frequent in February, decreasing rapidly in March and April.

Pursuit flights

27   *Rook : pursuit flight*

These flights, in which rooks pursue one another around their nesting trees, were described by Lewis Harding in 1848 under the term 'sporting' and more correctly as 'mating flights' by Burkitt in 1935. The number of birds and the time involved vary – two birds may chase for only a few metres but I have seen as many as 12 in a rookery with a spring population of 220 and the displays can continue for as long as 20 minutes. Some may leave and others join as the flight proceeds, and the group may break up into two or more smaller flights, each then taking its own separate course. During the flight the positions of the birds involved change: the leader of one group may join the rear of another, or one of the pursuers may overshoot the front bird and itself become pursued. Both sexes take part and either may be the leading – and thus the pursued – bird. During the flight, all the birds of both sexes use the dihedral type of wing flap for a large part of the time. Sometimes one bird may seem to be trying to peck downwards at one below, which may appear to be resisting, but it could equally well be that as in mutual feeding they are in reality trying to engage bills. These flights often start after quarrelling in the nest trees, usually over territory, but also perhaps in pair formation, and they are usually preceded and followed by bouts of bowing and tail-fanning display with much cawing. I have seen them most frequently in September, January and February, less often in October, August and November, and not normally at all in May, June and July. In August, when the flights first appear, they seem rather half-hearted affairs, but within a week or two the characteristics of the pursuit flight become clearly defined.

Song

28   Rook: song

'Rooks in the breeding season, attempt sometimes, in the gaiety of their hearts, to sing, but with no great success.' So wrote Gilbert White in a letter to his friend the Hon. Daines Barrington in 1778. Rooks sing mainly in early spring and in the autumn. Song posts, usually a prominent perch such as a telegraph pole, are often fairly near to the rookery but have no connection with the territorial boundaries. There is no evidence as to whether or not particular birds use particular song posts. Richards (1976) produced evidence of the importance of song in pair formation (p. 93). The singing rook uses a modified version of the bowing-tail fanning posture. It remains in a more-or-less bowed position, with legs flexed and tail raised and slightly spread, and wings closed but raised a little from the sides. A series of rather staccato notes is produced, some shrill and some guttural. During the production of these the bird's head moves forward and back and at the same time the bird may pivot to and fro in the manner of some finches (Newton, 1972), and make movements rather similar to the bowing and tail-fanning display.

Fluffing as a response to aggression

*29–30   Rook (above) fluffing as a
response to aggression (below)
Higher intensity
Compare figs 3, 29, 30, 37, 53*

Rooks adopt a variety of positions when they are threatened. Some of these positions are most noticeable when the threatened bird is for some reason unwilling to leave – for example, a female at the nest threatened by a male or sometimes a rook in its own territory. The general posture of the bird depends partly on how the antagonists are placed in relation to each other, above and below, on the same level, or perhaps on a moving branch. The most constant feature is the raising and fluffing of the back feathers – flank feathers are also raised, but as these are always held rather loosely it is much harder to tell whether there is a significant difference here. She may also jab with her bill towards the aggressor, and she may leave her eggs and fly towards him or her or go from branch to branch. Females brooding young are less reluctant to leave the nest in this way than are those still brooding eggs. A more intense version of this posture is similar but with the bill down, and the head and neck feathers more obviously fluffed out (fig. 30). If the danger passes and the bird relaxes, the head slowly comes up to a less 'bill-down' posture. This position is very often used in territorial quarrelling, and the rook may actually take off in this position with feathers still fluffed out. I saw this posture used only in the rookery and it does not appear among those described by Lockie (1956) in the winter flocks.

Another posture of aggression often seen in food fighting was labelled by Lockie (1956) as 'full-forward' or 'forward threat'. This to some extent over-laps the attitude just described since positions indicating that a bird is threatening another or being threatened by another are clearly interchangeable. The bill points towards the opponent and at maximum intensity is markedly raised; the tail is held level and a little spread. Wing- and tail-flipping may continue but sometimes become inhibited when this posture is adopted. When several birds are at sheep troughs or feeding in rickyards, actual fighting is more frequent than at any other time (Lockie, 1956; Marler, 1955). When two birds face each other and neither is prepared to give way the threatening attitude becomes extreme and much resembles that of the robin described by Lack (1943) and perhaps the head-up of the great tit described by Hinde (1952). Lockie gave the name 'take-off' to this posture. The head is stretched up with the feathers sleeked, except for the crest which is erect. The tail is raised in relation to the back but often the stretching up is so marked that in spite of this the tail may slope downwards towards the tip. Sometimes the wings are held outwards, extended at both elbow and wrist but drooping slightly (fig. 31). This seems to be an intention movement for flying or jumping up and forwards to get above and attack the opponent, because from time to time this actually happens.

Food begging
Nestling and juvenile rooks beg for food with a wing-fluttering accompaniment to their calls. Adult female rooks use the same action and similar calls when they are fed at the nest by the males, and each bird greets its mate in this way.

31   Rook : take-off. Compare fig 36

32   Rook : food begging. Compare fig 48

Even before the start of incubation and when they are well able to get food for themselves they use the same actions and calls and are fed by their mates. This may have a submissive, or as Goodwin (1956) put it, a dependent significance. A winged captive male rook that I had was able to reach the ground to feed only by working his way down a long sloping branch; he used the wing fluttering and begging call towards a female and this appeared to be important in stimulating this female into pair formation and subsequently into a partially male role in territory and nest building. Royama (1966), however, produced evidence that the feeding of female great and blue tits (*Parus major* and *Parus coeruleus*) by the males played an essential part in the nourishment of the female, and argued that this was probably more important than any courtship function that such feeding might have. When young rooks grow too big for the male to bring enough food for them and the female, the latter may become hungry and she will then call for food and use the wing fluttering as a demand for food, and if sufficiently hungry she will do this when males other than her mate appear. Hunger may finally drive her to go in search of food for herself. When this happens she may take off while fluttering her wings so that the wing action merges with that of flight, as it often does when young birds are following their parents in the fields.

Mutual allopreening

This is usually confined to the head, neck and mantle, and it may be performed by either sex. The active partner puts the tip of the bill between the feathers, most often those at the back of the head, and separates them by opening the mandibles. I have never been able to see that ectoparasites are actually removed but it seems very likely that this is done. Allopreening may serve to remove parasites from an area inaccessible to the bird itself and it also probably helps to strengthen the pair bond. It is most often seen during the weeks in early spring and in August and September when the birds spend much time together in pairs but are not actually nest building or otherwise occupied in the rookery.

Displacement activities

The displacement activities that I have been able to see are similar to those already mentioned for the carrion/hooded crow and appear to arise in the same situations. They are: bill wiping – usually in situations arising from sexual relationships, pecking – usually at the branch on which the bird is perched, and seeming to be connected with quarrelling or aggression, and least often with displacement preening.

'Outflights' or 'dreads'

Many gregarious and colonial nesting species perform what have been termed 'outflights' or 'dreads'. In 1937 Kirkman described the outflights of the blackheaded gull (*Larus ridibundus*); in 1934 Marples and Marples described a similar movement of terns as 'dreads'; and in 1958 Mountfort drew attention to the same phenomenon among bee-eaters (*Merops apiaster*). In none of these cases was it possible to assign a cause. There are sudden flights of rooks from their nest trees, which may also be comparable. From a hide one gets a detailed but limited view and the possible causes of these outflights often seem to occur outside that narrow fie d of vision. However, out of 140 records it was possible to determine the cause in 34. The cause of alarm came from within the nesting area 14 times, 7 were caused by rooks quarrelling, 4 by an alarm from the local jackdaw population, 2 by close approach and calling by a carrion crow, and once by a sound from the hide. Various causes, mostly sounds from outside the nesting area, caused the remaining 20. Among these were gunshots, aircraft, a buzzard, the rustling of leaves on the ground below, caused sometimes by poultry and sometimes by people.

These outflights take place when there are many birds in the rookery but not much activity. There will be a sudden bout of cawing and almost at once the rooks take off, sometimes only those from one tree, or from part of the rookery, but sometimes the entire colony is involved. These actions were not recorded during May, June and July (when the rooks only spend a short time each day at the rookery) and only once in August. They are most frequent in March and then decrease rapidly as rooks become more occupied with their nests. In the autumn they are most often seen in September. Tinbergen (1956) suggested that in a colony there might be a 'build up of a fleeing urge with very little movement to de-activate it'.

Rooks sometimes make tumbling dives. These may happen when a flock of rooks, perhaps with jackdaws, is flying fairly high over the place where they wish to land, whether rookery, roost or feeding ground, and most commonly in windy weather. Similar manoeuvres can take place over a sloping hillside facing the wind so that an updraught is created. This seems to be 'play' as several species may take part, mixed flocks of rooks and jackdaws, sometimes with ravens and carrion crows, and even herring gulls fly to and fro along the hillside, rising with the updraught and diving and turning down again. There are records of various species taking part in forms of 'play' involving sensations of being carried along or of movement: eiders (*Somateria mollissima*) travelling down a tide race and returning to repeat the ride (Roberts, 1934); a pied wagtail (*Motacilla alba*) perched on the arm of a rotating spray and returning again and again to be carried round (Parsons, personal communication).

Maintenance activities

Rooks usually scratch with the leg over the wing like most passerines but that this is not an absolutely rigid behaviour pattern is shown by Simmons's (1966) observation of a rook in flight scratching by the direct method, that is with the leg brought up and directly under the wing – the indirect would admittedly be difficult in flight!

Both active and passive anting are used by rooks (Simmons, 1966). One rook that I saw anting in a field was chased away by another which did not take its place. It looked like an attack on a bird indulging in an unusual activity. Rooks frequently bathe in water, but do not use dust baths. Water bathing often follows anting. Preening and oiling, and water bathing and anting are all part of feather maintenance, and the active application of ants and their formic acid to rather inaccessible areas like the ends of the primaries may help in limiting the presence and activities of ectoparasites.

TERRITORY

Rooks, being colonial nesters, cannot have large nesting territories. The area defended by each pair is a small part of the tree round each nest. It is easily variable and in every year of my own study I observed instances where, in the early part of the nesting season established territory holders would defend the area around their nest against all comers, but a persistent intruder or pair would eventually be able to establish a territory, build a nest and become accepted by those neighbours who had previously tried to drive them away. The aggressiveness of each male is at its maximum during the most intensive stage of nest building, probably the time of maximum output of male hormone. The resulting changes in aggressiveness appear to alter the order of dominance among the birds. Perhaps such changes are a factor in enabling an intruding pair to establish themselves. Once established, they are recognized and return to their nest without being attacked by their neighbours, who continue to attack strangers, and who are apparently defending the area which was originally their territory. The overlap of such territories would provide a system of localized mutual territorial defence which would have obvious survival value in a colony, in preventing excessive nest robbing and interference, and a comparable form of group defence was described by Lorenz among jackdaws. In many instances the same pair of rooks re-use the old nest each spring, and during most of the intervening months the birds are present to maintain the territory. In some rookeries the territory may be the roosting place of the pair during the autumn.

Many of the nests used each year are reoccupied by the pair that built them, but it is a fact that nests have an attraction for birds that have no claim to them: a pair of rooks may land on a nest, remain for a few minutes until they are driven off, and not return. This type of action is most common at the end of February and in early March when gonad activity is increasing, when there is a rising interest in nesting territories, and before most birds have reached the peak of nest-building activity and territorial defence. In February there may be some fighting in parts of a rookery not used for breeding but used by arriving birds. Both sexes are involved and this fighting appears to start when another rook approaches too closely, in other words an infringement of 'individual distance' (Conder, 1949). Song does not appear to be used in the establishment of a territory.

The bowing and tail-fanning posture is much used before and after territorial quarrelling, and such quarrelling often ends with the whole group of birds departing in pursuit flight.

Some rooks pair for several consecutive years, perhaps for life, and use the same nest for several seasons. Of a group of nests that I had under observation in 1946, 71 per cent had been occupied for more than two years but the birds were not individually marked. One bird, recognizable by an abnormal voice, occupied the same nest in 1944, 1945 and 1946. Outside the nesting months rooks feed in pairs, visit the rookery in pairs, roost in pairs and fly to and fro between these various places in pairs.

But changes in the number of birds seen in pairs can be counted. Of course, during nesting, when the females are at their nests, the birds are separated and are not seen in pairs away from the nest. Counts that I made in July, August and September, taken together, showed that 52 per cent were in pairs, by October and November the figure was 66 per cent and by January and February 81 per cent.

Adult birds are in potential breeding condition in autumn and display and posturing are intense in September and October. In addition to the self-advertising and stimulating displays taking place, there is also food begging in autumn, and Goodwin (1956) suggested that this might be important in over-coming aggressiveness due to 'individual distance' – the innate resistance shown by one bird to close approach by another. Among captive rooks that I had, food begging certainly seemed to be important in establishing pairs. If rooks pair for several seasons, the formation of a new pair must often involve young birds. After becoming independent of their parents, juveniles may wander long distances from their natal rookery. The return of juveniles to their own or another rookery may be linked to pair formation. Dr Eric Grace, in a study of recruitment to rookeries in Aberdeenshire, was able to show that some were more attractive than others to new birds. There were differences between rookeries in the frequency of use of the different types of display and posturing. Self-advertising bowing and tail-fanning and the action of bill wiping (perhaps a displacement activity) were less common in attractive rookeries than in unattractive ones, possibly indicating a difficulty in obtaining a mate. Pursuit flights and aggression, mutual feeding and nest building were more often seen in attractive rookeries, indicating pair formation, territorial defence and success in finding a mate. The actual process of the formation of a pair may not have been observed in marked individuals but we can judge some of the conditions in which it takes place and some of the behaviour involved, and in a study of captive rooks Richards (1976) described the use of song in attracting the hen birds. The males may spend several hours 'on warm autumn and winter days' in singing. The other males ignore this but unpaired females show interest. The singing male may collect food, carry it in his throat pouch and continue to sing. The food is presented by the male to the female. If the singing male is already paired his mate will drive away the unpaired hens, beg for food and be fed: 'When an unpaired hen is attracted by a singing male, the pair is formed as soon as she accepts food.' Among Richards's captive rooks, pairs were usually formed in 'the first few weeks of October'.

NEST-SITE SELECTION

Many old nests are re-occupied, often by their original owners, and they defend the territory continuously apart from a short gap from May or June until the end of July or early August. Territories without nests may be abandoned – for example, when a nest is blown out by gales. Unclaimed nests may be dismantled, the materials being used to construct new nests. Nest sites are chosen in both spring and autumn and by both males and females, but there is insufficient information to indicate which sex most commonly does so. When the autumn resurgence of sexual activity occurs, many rooks show an interest in nest material, and in September and October sticks are often carried, but nest-lining material only occasionally. Although there are a number of records of the completion of nests and of the presence of eggs and even of young, usually in November (Yarrell, 1845), there does not appear to be any account of successful breeding. With such frequent autumn nest-building activity it is not surprising that some of the sites chosen for autumn building should be maintained as territories through the winter and used for breeding in the spring. The material put in position in the autumn is usually too scanty and the whole procedure too incomplete for anything more than a very temporary structure to result. I have seen nest material brought to a defended area of tree top as early as 16 August; I have observed from nest level a territory established on 20 September; the first nest material of a very sketchy autumn nest brought on 19 October; and then continuous territory defence through the winter with successful breeding the following spring. The nest proper was begun at the end of February. Nest-site selection in the autumn must presumably require some degree of physiological sexual activity, and it may be that some of the nests built rather late in the spring are made by young birds which only reached maturity during the preceding autumn.

Some sites are chosen in spring, but whether by old or young birds is uncertain. A male rook new to a particular tree top was first seen on 23 March and although not yet accepted without threat by the owners of three other nests, seemed to have established a mutual territory. It soon became apparent that his mate also had a territory a few branches away, and both started building and the female sometimes visited the male's territory, wing fluttering and begging for food. Both continued to build and both spent most of their time in their own territories but the male's nest became more complete and eventually the nest built by the female and her territory were abandoned.

But female rooks may choose the territory: an unpaired female built a complete nest close to one occupied by a pair already with eggs and repeatedly begged for food from the male who was, of course, much further advanced in the reproductive cycle. She often had to leave the nest to obtain her own food and the undefended nest was frequently pilfered for nest material and was eventually abandoned. I also had a captive pair of rooks of which the male, having a wing injury, could only climb into the branches instead of flying; he was very dependent on the female, begging for food from her in the manner normally used by the female, and the female of this pair collected the nest material and built the nest at a site which she had chosen the previous autumn and defended during the winter.

Most colonies are in trees growing on low ground from just above sea level to about 150m above. Continuous woodland is not often used, the colonies being more often in groups of trees, lines of hedgerow trees, wind-break belts or small copses.

The species of trees used by rooks for nesting must vary with their availability. Thus in France, poplar, oak, plane, chestnut, beech, ash and birch are mentioned in that order by Deramond (1952), who also records that in Vendée the Corsican pine (*P. maritima*) was much used.

In Poland Kulczycki (1973) showed that rooks nest in old and high trees in habitats similar to those in the British Isles, the average height above the ground was 19·01m with extremes of 7 and 30m. Poplar and alder are the most commonly used tree species, together accounting for 50 per cent of the sites. Oak (*Q. robur*), sycamore and Scots fir are also used. Rookeries in beech trees (*Fagus sylvatica*) are much less common than in Britain and in birch (*Betula verrucosa*) much more so. In parts of Britain where a study has been made, it has been found that most nests are in deciduous trees. For example, in the Oxford area 90 per cent were in elm (*Ulmus campestris*) (Nicholson and Nicholson, 1930); in the Wirral Peninsula less than 1 per cent were in conifers (Marples, 1932); in the Isle of Wight 90 per cent were in elm (Wynne, 1932). Yapp, 1934, in west Gloucestershire, found 78 per cent in elm, 19 per cent in oak (*Quercus* sp.) and 3 per cent in beech (*Fagus sylvatica*), sycamore (*Acer pseudoplantanus*) and Scots fir (*Pinus sylvestris*) combined. In the Falmouth area of Cornwall, where high wind speeds are frequent (wind speeds of over 70mph in 28 months between 1944 and 1954, highest 103·6mph), a much higher proportion of nests are in evergreen trees: 49 per cent in 1945 and 52 per cent in 1953, the tree species used being pines (*P. sylvestris*, *P. radiata*, and *P. pinaster*). The deciduous trees used were especially beech, oak and sycamore, but hornbeam (*Carfinus bitulus*), Spanish chestnut (*Castanea satira*) and ash (*Fraxinus excelsior*) were also used. Most nests are built near the top of tall trees 70ft or so from the ground but, where nothing higher is available, quite short trees of 9m or even less may have to serve. Electricity pylons are occasionally chosen as nest sites (*West Midland Bird Report*, 1953; *Report on Somerset Birds*, 1953).

In New Zealand, where the rook is an introduced species, most nests were in eucalyptus until about 1926, when an epidemic reduced the number of these trees. There was then a change to pines, although eucalyptus are still used extensively. Bull (1957) and Coleman (1971) say that at West Melton and Banks Peninsula *Pinus radiata* were mainly used. *Pinus maritima* and *P. radiata* are used by rooks in Cornwall, the latter extensively.

There are more small rookeries than large ones. This was shown clearly by the recently completed British Trust for Ornithology enquiry.

	Scottish	Welsh	English
1–25	33·76%	68·31%	70·15%
26–50	20·34%	20·38%	18·32%
51–100	21·74%	9·12%	8·87%
Under 50	54·10%	88·69%	88·47%
Under 100	75·84%	97·81%	97·25%

However there are some very large rookeries in some parts of the country, notably in north-east Scotland, where as many as 3000 pairs may nest in a single colony. Large rookeries well spaced out seem to be the rule in that area (Patterson, Dunnett and Fordham, 1971).

Population density varies from about 5 nests per square mile in North Wales (Walton, 1928) to about 90 per square mile near Bishops Stortford (Burns, 1957).

NEST BUILDING

Nestling rooks peck at the nest and pull at leaves of the trees and lift twigs and then later, when following their parents in the field, they often pick up leaves and twigs and moulted feathers, potential nest material in fact, in which they show an interest from an early age. Nest material is purposefully carried and manipulated during the autumn activities at the rookery and this happens from time to time throughout the winter, possibly more often on fine warm days. Towards the end of February, when display activities and pursuit flights are increasing, the carrying of nest-building material also becomes more frequent and more continuous. In Cornwall, where the climate is mild and the spring early, intense nest building usually begins about 1 March, but very cold weather at the end of February (fig. 33) can cause a delay of as much as two or three weeks (Marshall and Coombs, 1957). Feare (personal communication) reports that the maximum number of nests in both Aberdeenshire and Hampshire is reached soon after the middle of April. Late nests are still being built during April and there is sometimes a sharp rise in the number of nests built at that time. It has been suggested that these may be built by juveniles that have reached maturity with the completion of the preceding autumn moult. Although a female rook can build a nest alone, normally a large part of the work is done by the male. Most often sticks are collected and fitted into place by the male, although they are sometimes brought to the nest by the male and

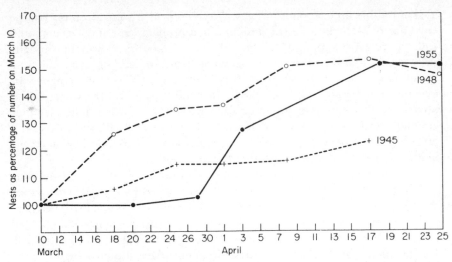

33   Rook: graph of weather factors and nesting in an inclement year (1955) compared with two 'normal' years (1945 and 1948). Nest building was delayed in 1955 when the weather was unusually cold and heavy snow fell in late February and persisted until the beginning of March. The maximum number of nests (in one colony) is indicated on each curve. The number of March 10 is taken as a base line (100) and the counts made on later dates are converted into a percentage increase

given to the female to build into the nest. Excluding the case of the nest built by an unpaired female, on 32 out of 49 occasions when the sex of the bird bringing twigs was definitely known, it was the male. From the start of nest building or soon after, the females appear to become much more reluctant to leave the nest site than the males, and this might also account for the much shorter distances that the females go in search of material (see also Goodwin, 1955).

The actual process of nest building goes by steps of which the first seems rather slow and unco-ordinated. A twig usually fresh or taken from another nest will be brought to the chosen nest site and rested in the branches in a random manner, whether it stays in place seems to be a matter of chance. When a few twigs have remained in position the method used by the birds changes and instead of simply resting the material on the twigs already there they push each new one into place. Two movements are used in doing this, a forward and upward thrust of the whole head with the stick firmly held in the bill, and quick short lateral movements. Sometimes the feet are used to hold the twig on the perch.

Nest-building rooks do not appear to have any insight into the difficulties that may arise in fitting twigs into place by using these movements. But when a twig partly falls and has to be pulled up again the action is similar to that used in pulling up food on a string, examples of which were given by Thorpe (1943) as possibly showing true insight into a problem and may be compared with the raven (see pp. 38–9). This chance method of construction usually takes two or three days before a recognizable platform has appeared, and from the ground it is quite easy to see right through it. The rook bringing the material now usually stands on the platform and works on the various twigs around it. Twigs may be anything from a few cms to 60cm long and they gradually form a dense ring around the bird, contrasting with the frail central platform. Sometimes strips of bark are used and these are placed around the inside of the outer ring, thus starting the nest cup.

Construction of the nest lining begins with an increase in nest-building activity; dead deciduous leaves, green conifer tufts, grass and earth are added and thrust into the spaces between the twigs by the bird standing in the nest cup.

As the cup forms, the female spends more and more time in it, turning round and round, pressing the sides with her breast, treading down the centre with her feet and pulling out bits of material from one place and pushing them into another.

Sometimes specially available material such as paper is added. A particularly striking example was in 1938 and 1939 when rooks used great quantities of feathers collected from an adjacent field, where large folding mobile units housed poultry and were moved daily. In 1939 75 per cent of the nests examined contained feathers, some so many that the eggs were almost buried (Tayler, 1939–40). To a lesser extent the male also carries out these actions. From the manner in which so much of the nest is constructed, it seemed likely that the cup shape was solely the result of the bird standing in the middle and building around itself in the same way as the long-tailed tit (*Aegithales caudatus*) formed the dome of its nest by building upwards and over its head (Tinbergen, 1953). But an accident made it clear that this is not necessarily so. The reason for the bird standing in the middle of the nest platform may be that it is the most convenient position from which to work. A nest was completed by 11 March and the young were hatched by 4 April. On 18 April the nest and young were normal, but on the 20th part of the side of the nest had broken away and one of the three young had fallen to the ground. On 22 April one more young bird had fallen and the remaining one was precariously resting on the fragile and scanty remains of the central nest platform, one side of the nest having completely disappeared. On that day, although the female pecked at twigs from time to time, she made no purposeful effort to repair it. By 25 April, however, it was obvious that the side of the nest had been considerably built up. More had been done by 29 April although there was no nest lining and it was easy to see through the cup from below. Further additions had been made by 2 May, and more again by the 6th, when the young bird left the nest. No earth or nest lining was added, reconstruction was limited to the stick cup. Apart from the fact that only half the nest cup had to be rebuilt, and the normal working position was occupied by a well-grown young bird, this reconstruction was carried out at a stage in the reproductive cycle when gonad regression must have been well advanced. Normally that particular part of the nest building is carried out at a stage of great reproductive activity. It is difficult to explain the motivation of this bird's behaviour, without assuming that it recognized its problem.

EGGS, INCUBATION AND YOUNG

The eggs, which have an average size of 40×28.3mm, have a pale blue/green ground colour, sometimes green or grey-green and are densely marked with shades of ash-grey and brown.

The average date of egg laying gets later in more easterly and colder countries. In south England and Belgium it occurs in mid-March (Marshall and Coombs, 1957; Verhayen, 1946); in Holland in late March (Niethammer, 1937); in Germany from the beginning to 20 April (Friderich, 1923), (Tischler, 1941); in Poland in the second week in April (Prazak, 1897); and in USSR from the middle of April until the beginning of May (Dementiev and Gladov, 1951, 1954). In all of these places the day length and the rate of change in day length are similar but the end of winter conditions comes later the farther one moves eastward. So that although the spring increase in day length appears to be the external factor which ensures spring rather than autumn breeding, temperature and sunshine may also have some retarding or advancing effect on the breeding dates.

In the Truro area of Cornwall intensive nest building begins at the beginning of March, copulation is first observed in the second week, is most frequent towards the end of March and then becomes rapidly less common after the end of the month. The first eggs are laid about the middle of the month. Clutches are from two to seven in number and the eggs are laid daily with occasional two-day intervals (Holyoak, 1967). Lockie found a mean clutch size of 4.3 eggs in the Oxford area; late clutches, laid after 31 March, were smaller and averaged 3.5 eggs.

The female does all the incubating, although Nethersole-Thomson and Musselwhite (1940–1) watched a male rook feed the female and then take her place brooding the eggs. Over 80 per cent of eggs hatch and clutch size makes little difference to the success of hatching. Unhatched eggs are removed by the adults but often not until the others have been hatched for some days.

The young are closely brooded by the female at first and food is brought by the male. Some of this he gives to the female, and she will often give part of what she has received to the young. Young rooks require protein food and especially fluid for the first 21 days and Lockie showed the importance of earthworms in their diet in providing these essentials. Earthworms have to be near to the surface to be accessible to rooks and in cold and dry weather, such as occurred in March and April 1953, they go to too great a depth; in that year Lockie found them making good the deficiency with other food, especially the larvae of the moth *Celaena secalis*. This proved to be an insufficient substitute and there was a very high mortality, especially among large broods.

Food brought to nestling rooks near Oxford in April 1952 and 1953 is shown below, expressed as percentages by volume. Samples were obtained by placing a collar round the neck sufficiently tightly to prevent swallowing without restricting breathing. Samples were removed from nestlings immediately after a feed, in rookeries A and C.

		Earthworms	Leatherjackets	Other animals	Grain
1952	A	73	8	6	13
	C	80	2	17	1
1953	A	32	–	28	40
	C	53	–	29	18

As the young rooks hatch asynchronously, the last to hatch are smaller and weaker than those that hatched earlier. The young bird that stretches up most strongly is fed first and the weakest is clearly the one that is most likely to suffer. In 29 broods, 90 per cent of marked nestling rooks that died in Lockie's study had been the last to hatch. The total number reared will, of course, vary with the available food supply; in a difficult year, broods of four and five will both fledge about the same number of young, while in a year when it is possible to rear 5, 'broods of 5 will on average be more productive per nest than broods of 4'.

The difference in the difficulties the parents have in feeding larger broods was clearly demonstrated to me by the case I have already described when part of a nest broke away and two of the brood of three had been lost. Before this happened, the female had started foraging flights and bringing back food for the young. As the young grew they took more of the food that the male was able to bring, and the female had shown signs of hunger and so had begun her own foraging. The eggs had hatched on 4 April, she was collecting food for the young before 18 April, by 20 April one young had been lost, and by 22 April a second had gone. On that day the female was fed on the nest by the male twice in three hours and, although she did leave the nest from time to time, she spent far more time brooding the one remaining young bird than she did when there were three. She continued to do so until the young bird left the nest on 6 May, 34 days after hatching. Even in normal circumstances some rooks brood their young for a long period, and at three nests the female was first seen to go in search of food when the young were 21, 32, and 33 days respectively.

Nest sanitation is carried out by both parents, not merely the one that has just brought food; droppings are taken either direct from the young, which may be stimulated by prodding the chick's anus or from the side of the nest. The faecal sac is occasionally carried in the tip of the bill, more often hidden in the throat pouch, and usually dropped a few feet from the nest as the bird flies away. As the young grow bigger, they position themselves so that some of the droppings are projected clear of the nest. If the faeces are dropped clear of the nest, no attempt is made by either parent to collect the faecal sac, and droppings that foul the nest are removed by the adults, whether they have brought food or not. So the action of removing droppings is a response to fouling the nest and neither part of the act of feeding the young nor a response simply to the young bird's defaecation.

Small young that die in the nest are, like unhatched eggs, removed by the adults, but after the young reach about 12 days this reaction of the parents ceases to operate and dead large young are left in the nest.

The young leave the nest at about 32 days and follow their parents in the fields, and late juveniles may be dependent on them until mid-August. At first they roost near to the rookery; in my experience they do not often return to their own nest trees. Young birds picked up from the ground and kept in captivity began to pick up some food for themselves at about 8 weeks after hatching. They did so by picking up again food that they had themselves regurgitated. While young birds accompany their parents in the field they often pick at objects they find, twigs, grasses, feathers, or even their own feet, and they often peck at the ground just scratched up by the sideways flicks of the parents' bill.

When they become independent of their parents, juveniles may wander. The British populations are non-migratory but the young may move as far as 160km (100 miles) from their natal rookery (Dunnet and Patterson, 1968). This dispersion of young birds and the irregular presence in some areas of small flocks made up entirely of young birds makes it difficult to assess the proportion of the whole population which the juveniles represent.

ROOSTING AND FLOCKING

Roosting patterns are not identical. There are seasonal changes in roosting habits in all parts of the country, even among resident British rooks, and in addition, in some parts especially of the east of England, there are large flocks of continental wintering birds. There are seasonal changes in roosting habits.

Winter roosts break up within a few days in February or early March, probably when egg laying begins. The roosts often also contain jackdaws, which nest about five weeks later and continue to use the communal roost for that much longer: they also use the rookeries as collecting points before flying with the rooks to the roost (see p. 124). During the few days of the break up of the roost the rooks get more and more reluctant to leave the nest colony with the jackdaws; some fly out a little way and return; some still feel the 'pull' of the communal roost and I have heard them depart in its direction as late as 1.30 am on 6 April. A few, mainly juveniles, from some rookeries continue to use the winter roost.

After nesting has started, females roost on the nest and males use a branch nearby, often the same branch as is used for landing when arriving at the nest. When the young have flown, but are still dependent on their parents for food, some birds begin to go to the winter roost and some still roost at the rookeries. But in south-west Cornwall some roost in small parties or flocks in convenient groups of trees or hedgerows near their last evening feeding place; this is an area of small fields and although by no means heavily wooded there are more accessible clumps of isolated trees than in the north east of Scotland, where this nomadic habit of roosting does not occur.

In both north-east Scotland and in Cornwall communal roosts are well formed by mid-July. Not all of them are permanent; birds from several of the rookeries in an area, and these are not necessarily the closest ones, may go to the site of the winter roost and continue to use it until the following nesting season. Those from a number of other rookeries may roost at some other site, often a rookery (at some rookeries used as roosts, the roosting trees are not the same as the nesting trees, and a separate area among the same trees is used) and continue there perhaps until early November. Then all make an abrupt change and go direct to the main winter roost, not going via this autumn roost site (see map). This pattern in my area of Cornwall was similar to that in the Ythan Valley in Aberdeenshire, but in the latter in one year a small roost was formed at a different site in January and this continued to be used until March when nesting began (Patterson, Dunnet and Fordham, 1971).

In some areas there are small autumn and winter roosts made up of juvenile birds which live during the day in juvenile flocks.

Naturalists and country people have been aware for hundreds of years that rooks from many rookeries in winter form large units for roosting. The area of all the rookeries which go to make up a single roost has been termed a rook parish. This is an imprecise but convenient term to describe the whole area of the rookeries contributing to one roost; 'catchment area' is perhaps better, but the catchment area itself is neither constant nor does it have boundaries. The birds from one of the rookeries that contributed to the roost at which I made most of my own observations (Coombs, 1961) divided and went to two roosts, both about four miles from the rookery and in opposite directions. At the beginning a few only went northwards to Four Burrow, but by the end of the study a gradual change had taken place and the majority were going to this northern roost. In Aberdeenshire, one rookery had a seasonal cycle involving four different roost sites.

Many rook roosts are shared by other corvids, mainly jackdaws but also carrion crows, ravens, and magpies. When gregarious roosting is fully established the rooks collect in the late afternoon at their own rookeries as assembly points. With them are many jackdaws, although when there are sufficient numbers there may be some assembly points for jackdaws only. (One roost in Cornwall contained about 14,000 birds, mostly jackdaws, but in Aberdeenshire a roost was estimated to contain 65,000 rooks.)

From these first collecting points they fly, mainly along regular flight lines, to the fields and trees close to the actual roost. Here rooks from all the different rookeries collect, many on the ground, but many along hedges and trees and

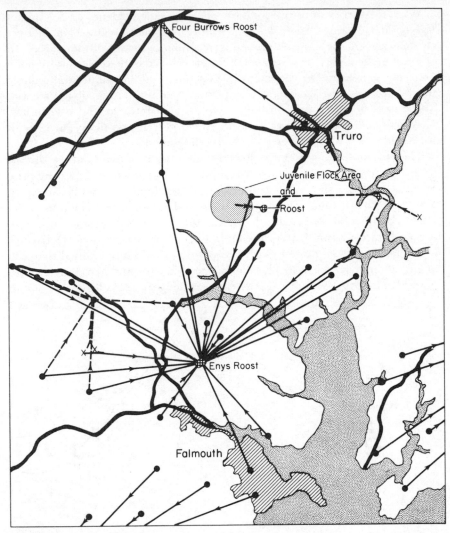

Rook: roosting
Dotted lines – temporary flight lines to autumn roosts
Solid lines – flight lines to winter roosts

parts of wooded areas in which the actual roost trees are situated. The flight from these second assembly points to the roost trees starts quite suddenly.

At the final assembly points near to the roost many birds feed, especially when they first arrive, but there is movement from the fields to the trees and back and birds on the periphery appear uneasy and try to fly in to the centre. Before the final flight in to roost, feeding has usually stopped. The flocks may have been there for 20 to 30 minutes, and all is quiet before the sudden take-off and flight in to the roost.

When they arrive at the roosting trees there is some tendency for the species to separate. At Enys, rooks settled in taller trees and jackdaws in shorter; carrion crows in the same plantation were a hundred yards or more away. In contrast to the silence before the flight to the roost trees there is constant noise and movement to and fro, perhaps while the birds find their mates and suitable perches; by this time the light is very poor and captive 'crows' do not see well in the dark, so the incessant calling may enable birds to find each other. Eventually all becomes quiet and movement ceases, and many birds, both rooks and jackdaws, can be seen to be roosting in pairs.

The time of roosting is closely linked to the time of sunset, and the time of departure from the roost is linked to sunrise, as the diagram shows (fig. 34). Sevingland (1976) showed that there is a relationship between light intensity and the departure time from the primary assembly, that the arrival time at the final assembly is also related to light, and that allowance is made for this by earlier departure from distant assemblies than from nearer ones. Departure from the roost in the morning in Cornwall was often more gradual than the arrival at night, the birds flying away in ones and pairs and straggling groups. Sevingland (1976) also noticed that 'each morning the rooks leave the roost in

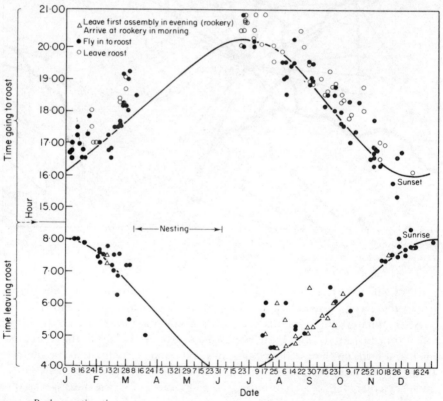

34   *Rook: roosting times*

parties'. But Feare (personal communication) has found an abrupt departure commoner both in Aberdeenshire and in Hampshire. In September and October, and again in February and March, they go straight back to their rookeries without stopping to feed on the way, while in winter, when the rookery activities have declined, these roosting flocks may feed in very large numbers close to the roost before returning gradually to the rookeries and then dispersing to feed. Why do birds congregate at a communal roost? Wynne-Edwards (1962) put forward the hypothesis 'that the primary function of the roost is to bring the members of the population unit together, so that whenever prevailing conditions demand it they can hold an epideictic demonstration'. These are 'specially timed communal displays', 'evolved to provide the necessary feed-back when the balance of population is about to be restored' – means of providing information which could enable the population to adjust its numbers. Ward (1965) concluded that it provided the means whereby an unevenly distributed food supply might be more efficiently exploited. Birds that had fed well would return next day to the same feeding ground and those that had not would follow them. Zahavi (1971) pointed out that it is much easier (for a bird ringer) to approach birds roosting in isolation than members of a flock roosting together, but that although the warning that communal roosting provides might be of value, communal roosts do attract predators. He went on to conclude 'that birds which converge on a communal roost from different feeding areas thereby benefit in their feeding'. Ravens often use communal roosts and it is difficult to imagine that any predator has exerted sufficient pressure on this species to cause it to evolve a communal roosting habit; on the other hand many records of communal roosting by ravens also mention the presence of unusual food supplies within the feeding area of the roost.

One value of the communal roost may be that exceptionally large flocks feeding together intensively enable rooks to make up for the long night in cold weather by highly efficient feeding as soon as they wake (Feare, Dunnet and Patterson, 1974).

Apart from the short time from about the beginning of June until mid-July (in Cornwall), some rooks use the rookery as a point to congregate and from which to disperse to their feeding places, especially at the beginning and the end of the day. The distances to which they go out from the rookery vary with the season; during the autumn and winter rooks feed in an area around their own and perhaps any nearby rookery. There are no feeding territories belonging to the rookery (cf Wynne-Edwards, 1962) and the birds from one colony mix with others in overlapping feeding areas. In the breeding season they tend to go further afield but still fairly close to their own rookeries, within about 2·4km. At this time males have to provide protein food for their young, and for their mates, as well as feeding themselves and making frequent flights from feeding ground to rookery. Rooks average more than 50 flights to the rookery per day.

In the summer, when food is harder to obtain (see next section), and interest in the rookery is at its lowest, the birds spread over a wider area.

FOOD

In many countries and for hundreds of years men have tried to answer the question 'Are rooks harmful or beneficial to agriculture?' No universal answer is possible, but the question has been asked sufficiently often for it to have provided the stimulus and finance for extensive research.

A great range of food substances is taken and there are problems in determining the relative quantities of each. Stomach analysis, for example, cannot be relied upon for evaluation of either volume or numbers of certain food items, because much animal food is digested far more rapidly than is grain.

Rooks obtain the bulk of their animal food from grassland and about 50 per cent of feeding time in all months is spent feeding there. Earthworms are the most important animal food in terms of bulk with leatherjackets next. These are obtained from the top 5cm of the soil by probing, an action used more by rooks than by other crows. Animal food is also obtained by pecking from the surface and by jumping in the air to catch disturbed flying insects, for beetles, flies, ants, spiders and so on are additions to the animal part of the diet (Lockie, 1956; Holyoak, 1968; Feare, Dunnet and Patterson, 1974).

Large quantities of grain are taken if available at all times of the year although the source from which it is obtained varies: in the autumn from lodged grain, in winter from stubbles, in spring from newly sown seed. Late sowings and food troughs are sources also, but sprouted grain is less often taken. The practice of stooking, which used to provide a liberal supply of grain, has nearly disappeared with the universal use of combine harvesters. Root crops, potatoes, acorns and 'weed' seeds are taken as and when they are available. Rooks also eat apples and will occasionally raid apple trees. They take acorns both from the tree and fallen ones from the ground, and break them open, discarding the shell pieces before swallowing the kernel. A feeding flock can adopt the advantageous habit of spreading out so that the flock as a whole covers the ground more completely in its search for food. In such a spread-out flock, if one individual happens to find a concentrated food supply, others quickly fly to that point to take advantage of the find (Pinowski, 1959). Rooks in flocks feed faster and spend less time looking about them, perhaps for predators or for competitors.

In places with intense seasonal cold from which they may not have migrated, or through which they may pass on migration, rooks may feed in large numbers on food which they find on floating ice floes. Rooks, like some other crows and like some gulls, will drop shell-fish on to rocks to break them open, and one was seen to fly up with a pot egg (a china egg used to induce hens to lay in a particular nest) to try to break it.

Nestlings are given a higher proportion of protein food, and the nesting season seems timed to take advantage of the seasonal availability of the earthworm. The proportion of non-protein food increases as they grow older; the non-protein food is mainly grain but includes potato, turnip and a little bread. Lockie (1959) found that weather can have a marked effect on the diet; non-protein food increased from 1 per cent to 22 per cent of the total during the time the nestlings were growing in 1952, and from 16 to 37 per cent in the equivalent period during the dry cold April of 1953.

Rooks are omnivorous, but their requirements are not the same throughout the year, nor are the foods available to them. To some extent they are specialized feeders, more so perhaps than the Eurasian crow and this may account for their more limited world distribution.

The nesting period is difficult for adult rooks. The incubating female expends little energy until the young are perhaps 12 days, when she will join the male in foraging. But the male has to find sufficient food for the young, his mate and himself, in spite of the fact that much time is spent in flying to and fro between rookery and feeding ground, which requires energy. Feare, Dunnet and Patterson (1974) observed that during that time 'adults obtained little food for their own use, the majority being given to the young. The resulting weight loss (and death in some cases) at a time of maximum availability was due to their having to spend so much time caring for their young.' The same authors have shown at Newburgh in Aberdeenshire that summer is a time of food shortage for rooks. Earthworms and leatherjackets in the surface soil decrease in numbers from June onwards. At that time the rook's food requirements are increased by about 20 per cent because they are then in full moult.

The birds spend more time feeding than at any other time of the year and in spite of that obtain less food. In the summer there is a drop in the mean body weight of adults and a severe mortality among juveniles (Feare, Dunnet and Patterson, 1974).

Food is usually abundant in winter; there may be local difficulties as when the ground is snow covered and the birds are forced into confined spaces like rick yards or near animal feeding troughs. There is then an increase in threat and fighting, but this is probably not over food but infringement of individual distance.

The rook's feeding habits are necessarily closely linked with agricultural practice, and although so much of their time is spent on pasture, searching for animal food, this causes no problems to the farmer. It is the rook's vegetable requirements that are the source of the damage they do, especially perhaps to spring-sown grain and turnips, to 'lodged grain' at the end of the summer, to stacked grain in the autumn, and to stocks where these are used. They also take potatoes and stock foods in both summer and winter in appreciable quantity. Other examples of crop damage by rooks were given by Fog (1963), referring to rooks in Denmark, who recorded that 97 per cent of rooks examined contained vegetable matter, frequently grain, especially barley and oats, also potatoes.

As far as grain is concerned the rooks usually lose interest once it has sprouted. The shoots emerge more quickly as the season progresses, so early sowings are vulnerable for a longer period. When it is possible to sow at a low density damage may also be lessened, as it was found that below a density of 27 grains per sq. m rooks had to spend more time searching and their rate of feeding was reduced. Some forms of grain capable of developing side shoots can be sown more thinly and are less subject to damage. Maize is also a vulnerable crop in some areas. As well as the timing of damage by rooks and whether a particular crop continues to be subject to their depredations, the rook's innate feeding habits have an influence on the problem. Rooks feed on open ground, probing for invertebrates and taking seeds (grain) from the surface; they do not feed in long grass and thick foliage can protect a crop from them – for example potato varieties that grow tall foliage are less vulnerable than slow-growing varieties leaving much ground exposed. The losses caused to the farmer can be quite large in financial terms, but the type of crop, the timing of sowing, the development of the crop, harvesting and storing of the produce vary so much in different parts of the country that no generalizations are possible.

In southern England, for example, sowing may be a month earlier than in north-east Scotland, and grain and other crops such as peas may be available in the south, reducing the period of summer food shortage. In addition, in the summer rooks are among the many species that prey on the defoliating caterpillars in oaks and this is a protein source not available in north-east Scotland (Feare, 1976). Methods of scaring rooks were tested by Feare (1974), and shooting has been shown to be an ineffectual method of local population control, although it may have some value for scaring. Scarecrows, polythene bags and dead rooks have no worthwhile effect, and rooks even get used to gas guns after a couple of days, which is too short a time for effectual protection. Grain needs protection for at least two weeks (time for the seed to sprout). Balloons filled with hydrogen and tethered at a height of about 20ft had some lasting effect, and were cost effective in terms of increasing yield. However, further research on control is needed.

PREDATORS, PARASITES, MORBIDITY AND MORTALITY

The only important predator of adult rooks in the British Isles is man. No doubt a few are taken by peregrines (*Falco peregrinus*) and by goshawks (*Accipiter gentilis*) in some countries. In 1955, after the enormous reduction in the rabbit population by myxomatosis, buzzards (*Buteo buteo*) were in many areas starving; well-grown nestling rooks were repeatedly taken from the nest and tree branches at a rookery near King Harry Ferry in Cornwall, and more than once I saw a buzzard attempt, unsuccessfully, to catch rooks from the feeding parties of adults and juveniles in the fields in July. Young rooks are taken by red kites in Wales (*Milvus milvus*) (Walters Davies and Davis, 1973).

I have also found their remains in a tawny owl's nest. Feijen (1976), writing of the decline of the rook population in the Netherlands and other parts of Europe, gives poisoning, shooting and disturbance as possible causes but mentions martens (*Martes* spp.) and several kinds of birds of prey as predators of the rook.

Rooks mob a number of predatory animals – for example fox (*Vulpes vulp*), buzzard, kite, kestrel (*Falco tinnunculus*) peregrine and sparrowhawk (*Accipine nisus*). There is a record of nests in one rookery being robbed by grey squirrels (*Neusciurus carolinensis*) for three years in succession (Harthan, 1940–1) and cannibalism has been recorded (Caldwell, 1949), but unlike the carrion crow this is probably a rare occurrence – I did not see any instance during several seasons of nest-level observation.

Of the ectoparasites to which the rook is host, the most spectacular to the human observer are the hippoboscid or louse flies. Anyone who handles many rooks will soon become familiar with these rather unpleasant, 6mm long, flies, flattened in appearance and running sideways and forwards among the feathers.

I found these flies (*Ornithmyia aricularia*) on rooks between 27 August and 7 November and, of 18 male rooks, 12 were infested. One unfortunate had nine. Of 25 females, four were infested, each with a single fly.

A number of species of mallophaga are carried by rooks including *Philopterus atratus* (Nitsch), *Colpocephalus subaequale* (Burmeister), *Brulia varia* (Burmeister), *Myrsidiaxisostoma* (Nitsch), *Analges corvinus* (Megn), *Megningia corvinus* (Megn), *Gabucinia delibata* (Robin) and *Montsauria corvinicola* (Ouds). Leg mange has been reported in one rook and this is caused by a mite (*Cnemidocopte mutans*) burrowing beneath the skin (Keymer and Blackmore, 1964).

Nearly all nestlings appear to have the nematode *Syngamus trachaea*, the gape worms of poultry, sometimes in large numbers and a possible cause of death. Earthworms are an intermediate host to this parasite. A specialized study of the helminth fauna of the rook was made by Barus and his colleagues (1972), who described 21 helminth species, this diversity being a result of the host's omnivorous feeding habits.

Most nests have a fauna of their own, and in bulky 'earthy' nests this can be quite a community. One nest occupied in spring and examined in June was reported to me as containing two pails full of dry sticks and grass roots; a pail full of damp leaf and root litter, with pieces of egg shell, and many potatoes and seeds. The live animal contents were about 50 earthworms; many brachyletrous beetles; dozens of nematodes of four species; hundreds of wood-lice; one slug (*Limax flavus*); collembola of genera *Entomobra*, *Lepidocyrtus*, *Orchesella*, *Pogonognathellus*; a few diptrous larvae and pupae; several spiders; a millipede (*Blaniulus guttulatus*); acaris of genera *Nanorchestes* (20), Oribatid (1), Parasitid (1), and a flea (*Dasypsyllus gallimulae*). Many other commensal species of animal have been found in other nests (Coombs, 1960[1]; Rothschild and Clay, 1952).

Congenital abnormalities are defects which must usually be a handicap to the sufferer. As a family, corvids seem liable to bill abnormalities, usually exceptional length of one or other mandible and several examples in rooks have been described. Feeding can be very difficult but it is sometimes overcome by using the side of the bill. Preening can only be very inefficiently done and the feathers may get into poor condition (King and Rolls, 1968; McKendry, 1973).

Pigment defects occur and true complete albinism is a genetic defect as are the various shades of grey and brown affecting the whole plumage. On 30 March 1768 Gilbert White wrote to Thomas Pennant Esquire:

A Gentleman in this neighbourhood had two milk-white Rooks in one nest. A booby of a carter, finding them before they were able to fly, threw them down and destroyed them to the regret of the owner, who would have been glad to have preserved such a curiosity in his rookery. I saw the birds myself nailed against the end of a barn, and was surprised to find that their bills, legs, feet and claws were milk-white.

Some rooks have complete feathers or one or other web of an individual feather which look grey; some barbs are often paler than others, giving an overall grey effect. Individual wholly white feathers can result from injury. They can also appear temporarily – possibly due to feeding deficiencies during the moult – the colour becoming normal again at the end of the next moult (White, 1768; Harding, 1848; Sage, 1962, 1963; Harrison, 1963).

Ratcliffe's (1965) analysis of raptor and corvid eggs showed that, apart from the raven, corvid eggs contained much lower concentrations of organo-chlorines than did those of raptors taken in the same area. Ratcliffe pointed out that the crows are partly vegetable eaters and, although they are also scavengers and predators, they might have been taking a less contaminated diet than the wholly predatory raptors. On the other hand the crows might be more efficient at metabolizing and excreting organo-chlorine residues than the raptors.

The exceptionally severe winter of 1962–3 caused great losses among some species but, like most corvids, the adaptable omnivorous rooks seemed to be little affected. Reductions in population occurred in a few areas but such changes take place without winters of that degree of severity and it is uncertain whether the weather conditions were the cause (Ash, 1964; Dobinson and Richards, 1964). Man's most direct effect is by shooting. Although destruction of most of the young birds of the year will greatly reduce the number of juveniles in a local population in the early summer, this is made up by the autumn recruitment, and no lasting reduction takes place. Obviously this can only happen if the young birds over the wide range from which the recruitment may take place are not themselves part of a heavily shot population, but the fact that the population of any one rookery is replenished with young birds from a wide area does mean that rook shooting is an expensive and useless method of trying to control their numbers (Dunnet and Patterson, 1968).

6
Jackdaw
(*Corvus monedula*)

FIELD CHARACTERISTICS

The smallest of the true crows in Europe, the jackdaw is about two-thirds the size of a rook or carrion crow. Its movements, in both walking and flying are quicker; in flight the separation of the primaries is much less obvious than in any of the larger species and the wing action is more pigeon-like. In some of its habitats it is most likely to be confused with the chough. The latter is larger and has much longer wings, reaching to the end of the tail or just beyond when closed, whereas the jackdaw's closed wings are noticeably shorter than the tail tip. Mistaken identification of flying birds is most likely when there is a strong wind, and either species may fly with half-closed wings and no flapping. At other times the larger wings and lighter flight of the chough are distinctive and so is its voice.

DESCRIPTION (Plate III)

In the nominate form of the jackdaw, *Corvus monedula monedula* (the Scandin-avian jackdaw of the *Handbook of British Birds*), the forehead and crown are black, glossed with blue-purple. The back of the head, nape and sides of the neck are grey, contrasting with the black of the crown, but contrasting less at the sides where the ear coverts are a darker grey. The grey feathers have a very soft texture. The grey colour becomes paler at the lower part of the sides of the neck, so that in this race a partial white collar is formed. The nasal bristles and lores are black. The mantle is dark grey, the colour tending to merge with that of the nape. The back and rump are blue-black with inconspicuous grey fringes. The scapulars and upper tail coverts are similar, but blacker and with more gloss. The lesser, median and greater coverts, secondaries and the tertiaries have a purple gloss. The alula, primary coverts and primaries and the tail are black and the gloss is blue-green. The chin and throat are black, the feathers having grey centres. At the front of the neck the grey-black feathers have lighter fringes. The breast, abdomen and tarsal feathers are dark grey with narrow lighter tips. The under-tail coverts are black with a slight bluish gloss and very narrow light edges. The bill and feet are black. The irides are white or pearl-grey.

The variations between the races are mainly in the lightness of the grey 'hood', whether there is a white patch at each side of the neck or not, and the greyness or blackness of the mantle, back and rump and of the underparts. These variations will be discussed in the section on distribution.

Nestlings have short and rather sparse pale-grey down, through which the skin can be seen. The gape flanges are yellow and the mouth lining bright pinkish-red, or purplish-pink (R.M. Lockley, quoted by Witherby, 1938). Juveniles have the crown brownish-black, the grey hood is much browner than in the adult, the mantle, back and rump are brownish-black and the under parts brownish-grey. Lesser and median coverts are brownish-black, only the greater coverts, the remiges and retrices have any gloss and this is very much less than in the adult.

First winter and summer

After the first moult the plumage is like that of the adult, but those feathers that have not been renewed, the primaries, secondaries, tail feathers and greater and some of the median coverts are more faded and browner and with little gloss. The iris in the juvenile is blue-grey becoming a brownish-white and this colour is usually visible during the following spring when the bird is up to a year old. At close range, for example at a nest box, this colour can be used to determine the age of the bird.

Young birds hatched in the spring undergo a partial moult in the late summer and autumn, all the head, neck and body feathers and the lesser, median, and many greater coverts are renewed. The flight and tail feathers are retained until the bird is about one year old. Then the bird undergoes a complete moult, the mean starting date of which in the United Kingdom is 22 May for males and 24 May for females. The mean duration is 149 days. The following year the bird is fully adult by the spring, and the moult starts later, the mean starting date is then 20 June and the duration is shorter, 122 days (Seel, 1976).

DISTRIBUTION

The distribution of the colour phases of the jackdaw is complicated. Voous (1950) gave a clear analysis of the variations of size and colour as geographical characteristics, and traced the post-glacial origins of each group and their subsequent movements. There are variations in size among jackdaws from any area and size can therefore only be regarded as a supplementary factor in distinguishing the origins of the birds. He drew attention to the following characteristics which could have a geographical significance:

1   size.
2   intensity of the grey colour of the under parts.
3   intensity of the grey colour of upper parts.
4   development of a grey neck band.
5   presence and development of white patches on the sides of the neck below the ear coverts.

In eastern Asia the full species *C. dauricus* has a white breast and neck band but does not come into the area that we are considering, except as a vagrant. The members of the group that Voous feels are sufficiently distinguishable are:

1   Iberian Peninsula (*Ibericus*, Kleiner).
2   western Europe and northern Italy (*Spermologus*, Vieillot).
3   Moroccan (*Nigerimus*, Kleiner).
4   Algerian (*Cirtensis*, Rothschild and Hartert).
5   south-eastern Europe (*Collaris*, Drummond).
6   Russian and west and central Siberian (*Soemmeringi*, Fischer).

He distinguishes these by the tendencies in colour and size. Such subdivision of a continuous cline may seem overcomplicated, but they are interesting, taken in conjunction with Voous's views of how the colour and size separation came to take place. Wing measurements were used as a standard size, although they vary widely between the sexes and within the same sex and the same race, mean values are none the less a guide. The main characteristics of the six races described are usually that *Ibericus* is of medium size with very dark upper parts, a slight white neck band and no white patch, and the under parts are rather light. *Nigerimus*, an Atlas-mountain type, is larger and very dark in both upper and under parts, and has no pale neck band. *Cirtensis* is smaller and darker still, the darkest of all the races, a rather scarce and isolated group. Voous

suggests that these three types probably became isolated from the remainder before the last ice age. The remaining European populations may be made up from components from Asia, south-east and south-west Europe, also isolated from each other by the last ice age.

The characteristics of these groups are: *Spermologus* from Western Europe is medium in size, has dark upper parts, no pale neck band and no white patch; *Collaris* from south-east Europe is again medium in size, rather light below and not quite so dark on the upper parts as the west European birds, and with a very marked pale neck band and a very marked white patch; *Soemmeringi* from Russia and Asia is medium in size with very dark underparts, moderately dark upper parts, and no pale neck band, but it does have the white patch, although not quite as conspicuous as in *Collaris*. Specimens are sometimes recorded in the United Kingdom as continental or Scandinavian jackdaws. For example Venables (1947) recorded that two pairs of jackdaws with white neck patches nested at the head of Weisdale Voe in Shetland for a year or two before 1945. In 1945 two pairs reared three or four young there, and in 1946 there were three pairs which showed white neck patches. These were presumably of *Soemmeringi* origin.

The jackdaw breeds throughout most of Europe, with the possible exception of the north of Spain and parts of the south of France, although it breeds in the Camargue (Nicholson, Ferguson-Lees and Hollom, 1957; Hoffmann, 1958). In the north it nests in Orkney and Shetland (Lea and Bourne, 1975) but not in the Faeroes.

It breeds in the southern parts of Norway, Sweden, Finland and eastwards across Russia to about 90° east. It only extends south of the Mediterranean in Morocco and Algeria. It is present in Asiatic Turkey and the northern two-thirds of Iran and northern Pakistan. It is an increasing species in many areas, is opportunistic and adaptable and may well be extending its range.

DISTRIBUTION, MIGRATION AND GEOGRAPHICAL MOVEMENT

In much of their continental range jackdaws are migratory – although fairly sedentary in the United Kingdom – and Busse (1969) has summarized their migrations. The races of the jackdaw have their own migration patterns, although no doubt there are great variations and overlaps in a group in which the divisions between the races have become very blurred with time and inter-breeding. *Corvus monedula spermologus* can be split into three groups. Those in the United Kingdom make mainly local movements of less than 100km, although there are ringing records which suggest some degree of movement between the United Kingdom and the Netherlands, and between the United Kingdom and Ireland (Spencer, 1961; Spencer, 1962; Hudson, 1967; Hudson, 1969). There have been coastal observations of migrating jackdaws (*British Birds* 13: 80; Cornwallis, 1955) and some from ships in the North Sea (Wolfe-Murray, 1931–2) which may refer to these birds or to the Danish birds referred to

below. Birds of this group breeding in northern France tend to go south west
and west-south-west as far as the French Atlantic coast. There is also an
emigration from the mountainous areas of Switzerland to the Rhone Valley
and the foot of the Pyrenees.

Birds of the *Corvus monedula monedula* group from Denmark reach the Low
Countries, northern France and south-east England; those from Scandinavia
move to southern Sweden, Denmark and the Low Countries; those from
Finland make a similar migration with perhaps a slightly more easterly but
overlapping destination. The *Corvus monedula soemmeringi* birds from the Baltic
states and north-east Poland travel to central France, Bulgaria, Germany and
north-west Poland; those from south-east Poland and the Ukraine go west-
south-west to north-west Czechoslovakia and south Germany and south west
to the Hungarian plains. These migrations may be influenced by the rook
flocks with which the jackdaws often travel.

Although jackdaws in the United Kingdom are more sedentary than those
of some continental areas, they are probably more active travellers than the
remaining British crows. Their first fledgling dispersal may be more extensive
than in the other species and several young birds have moved more than a
hundred miles from their birth place, though there may be a partial return in
the second year. Some Danish and Swedish birds, after wintering here, remain
through the summer as adults and may possibly breed (Holyoak, 1971). Just
as migrants like the blackcap may occasionally winter in the United Kingdom
so jackdaws may occasionally remain through the winter in the far north.
Larsson (1944) records such a case at Boden in northern Sweden.

POSTURE AND VOICE

In *King Solomon's Ring* (1970), Lorenz illustrated the jackdaw's self-advertising
posture (fig. 35) with nape and head feathers erect and bill slightly down, and

35   Jackdaw: self-advertising. Compare figs 9, 14

body more or less horizontal. He also described a very similar posture, which he regards as specific intimidation, and this seems to be the same as that which Lockie called bill-down. The threat by the jackdaw at its own nest, which Lorenz also described, is a more sleeked posture with bill up and body inclined upwards and forwards. This is similar to the intention movement posture of the rook as a preparation to fly above its enemy and to attack (fig. 36), and is

36 Jackdaw: take-off. Compare fig 31
37 Jackdaw: final defence posture (above). Compare figs 3, 29, 30: full-forward (Lockie) (below). Compare figs 1, 16, 29, 44, 47, 53

similar to Lockie's bill-up and take-off postures, used both in food fighting and in sexual situations. The jackdaw has a defensive threat posture, used when it is not going to give way, for example in its own nest. With this threat it will usually win any encounter with another jackdaw. The head and bill are down and the feathers of the mantle and flanks and underparts are fluffed; the tail is spread, and if the position is lateral to its enemy the side of the tail towards the enemy is spread – in this position they may stand jabbing their bills at each other. The posture Lockie described as elaborate full forward is a similar type of threat with spread tail and some fluffing of the body feathers, but with more emphasis on the jabbing part of the action, with bill pointing at the enemy. And Lockie's half and full forwards are, I think, simply less intense versions of this.

Lorenz described two submissive postures, both with legs much flexed. In one the front part of the body is raised and the bill down, so as to expose the nape which is made very conspicuous. He considered it to be used in appeasement in reproductive encounters between males. The female's submissive and pre-coital posture is common to many species, crouching with wings slightly drooped and perhaps a little held out from the side, head lowered and bill inclined a little upwards and the tail flat or slightly raised, and often quivered.

38   Jackdaw: female pre-copulatory posture. Compare figs 7, 25, 43, 56

39   Jackdaw: anhedral glide

This posture (fig. 38), but with the wings drooping element increased, is remarkably similar to the anhedral glide position of the jackdaw (fig. 39). The quivering action of the tail is usually part of the submissive or pre-coital postures. The tail quivering in the jackdaw is very marked and can be either lateral or vertical and when the movement is vertical the range of movement is often small. The partly spread and drooped wings also appear at moments of meeting – for example, when one of a pair lands beside the other. The anhedral glide is often used during pursuit flights. These quite often involve three birds (fig. 40) but sometimes several, and I have seen as many as twelve. There is

40   *Jackdaw: posture on meeting*

sometimes a wing-tip flutter during the glide. Goodwin has described this as performed by a perched bird too, and this wing-tip action is very reminiscent of the same action of ravens, perhaps when disturbed near the nest. I have recorded the anhedral glide most frequently in March, but also in April, September, October and once in January. During food begging by either adult females or young birds there is the usual wing fluttering action discussed already (see pp. 88, 90). Coitus usually takes place on the nest, but was recorded by Morley (1943) between two jackdaws among a flock of rooks in a field. The action was followed by loud cawing by the rooks (see pp. 84–5, 92).

The vocalizations that have been described, mainly by Lorenz (1970), are first a song made up of the jackdaw's own colloquial calls and each delivered with its appropriate posture, and added to these various imitated sounds; second, 'kia' which Lorenz describes as a sessile call; third an aerial guide call given by him as 'kioo'. Fourth, in defence, a rattling sound accompanied by bending forwards and flapping the wings. And fifth, in the final defence posture a short call which he renders as 'jup'.

During the glides there is often – perhaps usually – a long call made up of repeated syllables.

In food begging both females and young use the same juvenile-type sound, comparable with that of other crows. The 'jup' call is, Lorenz says, a means of preventing any one bird becoming excessively dominant in a close colony, as it is part of a successful defence by even a subordinate in its own territory. The rattling sound is used against predators and 'jupping' against conspecifics who press home attacks too closely. In food competition, birds finding small particles can swallow them at once. With large pieces of food they tend to take avoiding action as aggressive attacks by others are often successful in robbing the finder. In the interspecific fighting among feeding flocks, rooks and carrion crows always dominate jackdaws, and magpies often do (personal observation), but intraspecific fighting is much commoner than interspecific fighting (Lockie, 1956).

Lorenz also describes an action used to induce a companion, and this may be a young bird or a human companion, to follow: the jackdaw swoops over the companion and wags its tail as it does so.

TERRITORY

The jackdaw is a colonial species often nesting very close together. I had six occupied nest boxes made from tea chests on the outside of a hide in a rookery that I was using in 1948. Three of the tea chests were in contact with each other along each side of the hide. For birds that breed so close together a modification of the territorial habit is essential as it is with rooks. The nest box and the immediate area around it are defended with the 'jup' call, and other jackdaws learn to avoid the area even when the owners are absent. But I have seen this small territory defended in the autumn in another colony that I watched and filmed. Here the nest sites were in chimneys and the males in particular were actively defending the immediate part of the top of the chimney stack, the surroundings of the nest entrance.

PAIR FORMATION

It is very difficult to be certain how, or exactly when, jackdaws form pairs. In many cases it probably happens in the autumn. Lorenz (1970) records that the earliest pairing among his semi-captive flock was at five months. They are certainly to be seen in pairs in the autumn and right through the winter, sit close together almost or actually in contact, fly to and from their roosts and feeding ground in pairs and roost in pairs. The distance separating a pair from another pair or from a single bird is much greater than that between the paired birds themselves (Hinde, 1947; Lockie, 1956). If these distances are infringed they are met by aggressive threats. In the pursuit flights the commonest number of birds taking part seems to be three, and I have recorded more of these in March than in any other month, but they do occur during the autumn and winter too. These flights may be no more than an expression of a mood of self-assertion and sexual excitement, but occurring among groups of birds, some of them unpaired, they could be important in pair formation and in strengthening the pair bond.

Because jackdaws are seen in pairs during all parts of the year it is usually assumed that barring accidents they pair for life, and this may well happen quite often, but changes in partnership do occur as they did among Lorenz's flock. The jackdaws used the nest boxes attached to my hide from 1947 to 1955 and I was able to catch and mark seven adult jackdaws, six of them in pairs in the spring of 1948, and another seven, six in three pairs, during the autumn of that year and the spring of 1949. In addition I marked ten young birds individually. Pressure of work prevented my continuing observation on this group beyond the autumn of 1949 until 1953. Of the seven adults ringed at their nests in the spring of 1948 only one was seen in the autumn of the same year. Of the four adults ringed at the nest boxes in the autumn of 1948 one pair were probably together at the same colony in the spring of 1953; I say probably because part of the colour code of rings that identified the individuals had been lost by the time I was able to make any further observation in March 1953. Of the three adults ringed in the spring of 1949 none was identified in 1953 and none of the ten young birds ringed was seen for more than six months at that colony.

NEST SITE AND NESTING

The male bird builds the stick foundation of the nest and the female arranges the lining and will throw out some of his sticks if he overfills a confined nest hole (Lorenz, 1970). In fact, as Kulczycki (1973) makes clear, the nest structure is usually well adapted to the site. Chimneys are filled to the required level, as are other deep vertical holes, using sticks, mostly dry ones picked up from the ground, and measuring 15–20cm long by 0·3cm in diameter. The filling-up process is random and without order, depending on a few sticks catching in the hole and then supporting others as they are dropped in. But the nest is finished by an arrangement of sticks around the sides and against the walls of the nest hole. The cup thus formed is lined by the bird standing in the middle. The thick lining is made of fibres, bark strips, dead leaves, moss, paper, sometimes with a base of clods of earth, and then with a final cup of fur, hair, sometimes taken from the backs of animals, and sometimes feathers. According to the site, part of the early stick stages of building may be omitted, for example in a horizontal and small hole in a cliff. The cup diameter is from 12 to 16cm.

Nest sites are chosen in the autumn in some cases; when old nests are used again this simply involves continued use of the site with the maintenance of the territory from one breeding season to the next. I filmed part of the selection of a nest site in a chimney. Both of the pair visited the chimney and there was some mutual preening and very brief wing-drooping display; the male examined the chimney carefully, letting himself down into it as far as he could but maintaining a firm hold on the rim of the chimney pot with one foot as he did so.

The jackdaw has an extraordinary adaptability in its choice of nest sites. A few make open nests. Those that I have seen have been in dense ornamental conifers where they are very much enclosed by the tree structure, but they are particularly liable to predation and a high rate of failure (Holyoak, 1967). Nests in holes are usual: these may be in trees, using natural holes, woodpecker holes, and sometimes in suitably sized nest boxes, such as those put up for goldeneye ducks in Scandinavia. Nests in holes in cliffs are common, both by the sea and inland in quarries, and in Cornwall there are many nests in cavities in the broken-down shuttering of disused mine shafts (plate 5). Ruined buildings, church towers, and especially chimneys are very much used. Large holes dug out in old sand martin colonies are sometimes used by jackdaws from year to year (Mead and Pepler, 1975). Kulczycki's 1973 survey of corvine nesting provides additional data from Poland, from which we learn that the mean nest height chosen by jackdaws there was 9·41m in trees and nest boxes; 20·7m in buildings; and 15·3m on rocks.

The time taken over nest-site selection and nest building is obviously variable. I first opened the doors of four of my experimental nest boxes on 15 February. Three had some nest material in them by 18 March; in one nest the cup was formed by 27 March and some lining had been added by 8 April. Additional lining was added gradually and there were two eggs on 18 April. In that case it took about four weeks to build the nest.

EGGS, INCUBATION AND NESTLINGS

The jackdaw eggs are pale greenish blue, blotched and spotted with dark brown and shades of grey. The markings may vary in size or be almost absent. The average size of 100 British eggs was 35·7 × 25 × 49mm (Witherby, 1938). The clutch varied from three to eight eggs, with a mean of 4·3 in Britain (Holyoak, 1967). Holyoak found a slight decrease in mean clutch size as the altitude of the habitat increased and also a decrease in size of clutches laid later in the season.

The mean laying dates are variable, more so than in the three preceding species. Laying can take place from the beginning of April until mid-May but over 60 per cent are in the last week of April, and the laying dates tend to be a little later further north: for example, there is a difference of about four days in the mean dates between the south and north of England (Holyoak, 1967). In Finland there is a similar range of dates but they are a little later, from 15 April to the beginning of June (Haartman, 1969). Eggs are laid usually at one-day intervals, but occasionally there are two-day intervals. Incubation takes 17 to 19 days (Holyoak, 1967; Haartman, 1969; Eggeling and Eggeling, 1930–1) although up to 23 days has been quoted.

Soiled nest material is removed with the faeces of the young and dropped a short distance away. Unhatched eggs or newly hatched young that have died are usually removed or eaten, but after the remaining young are about 12 days' old neither eggs or dead young are removed. Lockie found that where the nest cavity was too small some young were crushed and died. Predation by grey squirrels occurs and predation by a weasel has also been recorded (Holyoak, 1967). Carrion crows are probably predators of open nests. Holyoak's investigation of a series of nest record cards showed that small clutches fail most often; the percentage of total clutch failure for different sizes of clutch was:

for clutches of 2	50%
for clutches of 3 or 4	24%
for clutches of 5	17%
for clutches of 6	12%

Holyoak (1967) divided the deaths of young birds into those occurring in each one-third of the nesting period, and found by far the highest mortality, 84 per cent, in the first one-third, with 42 per cent and 14 per cent in the remaining thirds respectively. And Lockie found that the highest percentage survival, 88 per cent, was in broods of three and the lowest in those of six at approximately 44 per cent. The nestlings leave the nest about 30 days after hatching.

During the first ten days after hatching, one or other of the parents is always at the nest; the male collects food for his mate, the young and of course for himself. When the female has been fed she may leave the nest for a short time to defecate, stretch and exercise and perhaps preen briefly. While she does so, the male remains at the nest.

A parent, as it enters the nest, gives a short 'tuk' call, which induces begging by the young. This call is repeated if the young, having been too recently fed, fail to respond.

A box with a chimney on top and lined with old chimney-bricks, but open on one side and connected to a hide, gave me the chance of watching and filming jackdaws inside the nest. The 'tuk' call was sharp and loud inside the chimney.

The eggs hatch asynchronously so that the young differ in size and in the strength with which they stretch up to beg. The head held highest at each feed gets most, so that when food is short it is the weakest that starve and die (Lockie, 1955). At the nest in the 'chimney' that I filmed the parent put down food at the side of the nest if the food needed rearranging or breaking up into smaller particles, using the same area each time. During the second ten days the young are more active and both parents feed them. Instead of stretching straight up, they beg towards the parents. Various sounds, such as that of the parent landing at the nest entrance, will induce begging, and the parent no longer calls on arriving. The parent has a standard position from which to feed the young; but the young constantly change their position and a satiated and sleepy youngster is jostled away from the feeding point, so that all tend to get their turn, if the food supply is sufficient.

By the third 10 or 12 days the young are growing feathers and are active in exercising their wings and in preening. When the nest floor and entrance are level, as in some cliff and tree nests, the young go to the nest entrance to meet their parents to be fed. In chimney nests with a vertical entrance this is not possible.

The young follow their parents after leaving the nest, sometimes until August, begging and calling and flying after them. If the young are actually begging they will not fly after their parents. If their gaping responses tire, then they will follow, so the following takes place between bouts of gaping and calling for food.

ROOSTING

Communal roosts of the jackdaw exist in all months of the year, and are used by both resident and migrant jackdaws. They are usually, but not always, combined corvine roosts, in which carrion crows, ravens, and especially rooks are present – most jackdaw roosts are also rook roosts. Of those that I know, a few small ones have jackdaws only and these are usually of a temporary nature. During the nesting season breeding birds roost at their nests, or close to them; and non-breeders, whether adult or young and perhaps those that have failed in breeding, often go to the communal roost even in May and June. After the young birds have fledged and become sufficiently strong in flight, all the birds in the area tend to go to a communal roost, the site of which may be used throughout the winter. The pattern of movements of the roosting flocks is often very complicated and varies from one area to another (Coombs, 1961; Brownsey and Peakall, 1955; Griffiths, 1955; Lint, 1971; Lundin, 1962). In the part of Cornwall with which I am most familiar jackdaws outnumber rooks in a proportion of perhaps five to one, and there are many isolated jackdaw nests as well as large and small breeding colonies. The jackdaws congregate at collecting areas and then later fly in flocks to fields where very large numbers collect near to the actual roost trees. Many of the first collecting points are at rookeries where rooks are also gathering. The two species then fly together to the collecting area near to the roost trees, and then, when the time to fly into roost comes, both species fly in at the same time. Then to some extent they separate into different parts of the tree tops, so that in some parts of the roost the trees will contain mostly, or even solely, rooks, and in others mostly, or solely, jackdaws. When the birds arrive at the roost trees there is much flying to and fro and calling but gradually the movement and the noise gets less as they settle to roost, mostly side by side in pairs. The calling may be needed to keep contact with their mates and the flying to and fro necessary for them to find their perches together. These winter roosts are not always formed in one sudden change of habit at the end of the nesting season; some birds may have used the site all through the summer, others join them as they become free of dependent young. Some smaller roosts are found in other areas which later, sometimes in November, join up with the main roost of the area. The areas from which jackdaws go to make up a main roost may overlap, so that jackdaw flight lines leading to two different main roosts may be passing each other in opposite directions, or crossing at an angle to each other.

'Black crows' have an evident attraction for each other, for one may see jackdaws on a flight line to a roost drop suddenly towards, for example, a group of carrion crows collecting together before roosting. The jackdaws may do no more than deviate from their flight path, but they may perch for a short time before resuming their normal direction.

Where jackdaws and rooks gather at a pre-roosting collecting area and then fly to the roost in one flock, the difference in breeding time becomes conspicuous: the rooks stop going to the communal roost and remain at the rookery where they have collected about five weeks before the jackdaws, so that for these few weeks the roost flocks are composed entirely of jackdaws.

Some jackdaw roosts are very large, such as that described by Lundin (1962) in the Uppsala district, where the winter roost had 40,000 birds, and in Estonia by Lint (1971), where migrants augmented the local flocks, in both cases buildings were used as well as trees. The time of going to roost and departure from it are related to sunrise and sunset, and they tend to leave earlier in the morning on bright and fine days.

FOOD

There have been three intensive studies of the jackdaw's feeding habits: those of Campbell (1936–7), Lockie (1955) and Holyoak (1968). This summary is based on their work, though there have also been a number of other interesting observations.

Holyoak gave an analysis of 222 jackdaw gizzards and expressed the results in terms of the frequency of occurrence of the materials found. The most important among vegetable foods were grain and wild-plant seeds, and of animal foods grassland insects – although many other animal foods had also been eaten. There are, of course, local variations: bread may be found in some places and animal feed stuffs on farms, while fish carrion, ticks or birds' eggs are also substances which must vary in their availability.

Campbell's analysis gave vegetable matter as 84·4 per cent and animal as 15·6 per cent by volume of the materials found, but this does not take account of the more rapid digestion of much animal matter.

Lockie found that throughout the year jackdaws spent 50 per cent of their feeding time on grassland, often in the company of rooks. In May some birds moved from grassland to oak and elm canopy to collect defoliating caterpillars and these provided the bulk of the food given to nestlings in the Oxford area. The jackdaw nestling period is five to six weeks later than that of the rook, and jackdaws are not dependent on earthworms for a food supply for their nestlings as rooks are. Indeed, of 98 gizzard analyses between October 1951 and May 1953 only six contained earthworms. The jackdaw nestling period coincides with the larval stage of various defoliating moths, especially those of the *Tortrix* group and *Operophtera wurmata*. On grassland jackdaws are surface feeders, thus they do not compete to any great extent with the rooks with whom they associate as they exploit different food resources. Many foodstuffs are used. Holyoak listed peas and beans, birds' eggs and nestlings, earthworms and woodlice, in addition to those already mentioned. They also take ticks from sheep and cattle.

In cold hard weather, when food is short, they resort to rickyards and animal feeding troughs and waste-disposal tips.

There are a number of examples of specialized feeding, by this nearly omnivorous and adaptable species. A jackdaw has been seen carrying a nestling song thrush in its foot although mobbed by missel and song thrushes (Williams, 1946), and is also recorded as killing and plucking an adult starling (Van Oss, 1950). A bantam breeder near my home complained of the depredations among his chicks of nesting jackdaws, especially when they had young and in very dry weather. Jackdaws may learn to rob puffins of the fish they bring for their young, and scavenge round herring gull and great black-backed gulls' nests for eggs and surplus food (Mylne, 1960). Jackdaws also hawk for flying ants (Cornish, 1947) or rob wasp nests, ignoring the wasps (Birkhead, 1974).

They are less inclined to hide food than other corvines and when doing so tend to use existing cavities, rather than dig out a cache for themselves (Simmons, 1968). Turcek and Kelso quote Novikov for the record of a jackdaw which had stored 1 kg of acorns in a hollow tree, and they sometimes use their own nest holes for this purpose (Fairhurst, 1974).

As a final note on the feeding habits of jackdaws (and men) King (1973) records that at Lands End jackdaws were selecting and swallowing pieces of fish-and-chip wrapping paper, but only those parts soaked in oil, discarding the dry bits.

PREDATORS, PARASITES, MORBIDITY, ABNORMALITY AND MORTALITY

In some places the peregrine falcon and goshawk are avian predators of the jackdaw. Jackdaw remains appear in the pellets of red kites and remains of adult and juvenile jackdaws were found in 14 kites' nests in Wales. Indeed jackdaws may be a useful food for young red kites (Walters Davies and Davis, 1973). I have found jackdaw remains in a tawny owl's nest, and they are recorded as prey of the long-eared owl (Glue and Hammond, 1974) and more surprisingly of the little owl (Williams, 1944; Chappel, 1950). In one instance, one of two jackdaws in flight was attacked and killed by a little owl at roosting time. Whether a raven persistently attacking a juvenile jackdaw (Dickson, 1969) did so as prey is hard to say. The jackdaw was one of about 20 mobbing a raven when first seen. It was caught and clutched by the raven, rescued twice by the mobbing of the remaining jackdaws, and finally escaped. I have seen a jackdaw in flight knocked to the ground by a raven. It escaped but there had been no obvious reason for the attack.

Jackdaws' nests are enclosed, protected from the weather and used year after year and this favours the remarkable assortment of fauna which inhabit them and which were so interestingly recorded by Rothschild and Clay (1952). Their nests may contain, among others: bugs, ticks, lice, mites, earwigs and spiders, and no less than 50 species of beetle have been identified from them.

Jackdaws, although they do suffer from gape worms, do so to a less extent than rooks, which consume great numbers of earthworms. Parasites have evolved with their host species and their distribution tends to match that of the host. Their evolved species adaptations can give some indications of the relationships of those host species. The flea *Ceratophyllus vagabunda*, found especially on Alpine choughs, has a subspecies living in these islands and has been found most frequently (5 out of 24 times recorded) on jackdaws, with herring gulls and shags next on the list. Rothschild and Clay (1952) suggest that it may have adapted itself to the jackdaw, as the nearest substitute to the now uncommon chough, and it is not known whether it parasitizes the red-billed chough or not. While parasitic infestations can cause the death of the host, it is not normally to the advantage of the parasite that this should happen and out of the total deaths of jackdaws this must be a very infrequent cause.

In March 1944 I found a very wasted female jackdaw which at post mortem was found to have a sarcoma (red-cell type) growing from the thoracic wall and mainly within the thoracic cavity (Coombs, 1945).

During the investigations into an outbreak of poultry Newcastle disease (Keymer, 1961), it had been noticed that before the virus had been confirmed among the poultry, some of the jackdaws that habitually fed there had been looking dejected, ruffled and sick, and one of them had been killed by the hens. Later, one of the jackdaws was confirmed as having the virus, although they are normally resistant to inoculation with this infection. Keymer and Blackmore (1964) mentioned sight records of several species of birds suffering from alopecia, among them a jackdaw. A number of cases were discussed by them and they also record pox in a jackdaw, another skin disease affecting especially the legs and feet.

Various degrees of pigment abnormality have been noticed, from a few white feathers (Cowin, W.S., 1932–3) to complete albinism (Sage, 1963). One of the birds that I saw at my nest-box colony showed erysthristic colouration especially noticeable in the greater and median wing coverts and tail, but some other feathers were also abnormal, having a fairly bright rusty red colour. No doubt accidents, such as being killed by a moorhen (Rolls, 1971) or trapped in sludge at a sewage farm (Webber, 1965), account for a few deaths. Food shortage, when young, and injury must account for many. Severe weather, however, such as the winter of 1963, had little effect on the jackdaw (Dobinson and Richards, 1964). Holyoak's (1971) survey of mortality of British corvines showed that adult mortality in jackdaws is low and the highest mortality was in June and July of the first year.

MOBBING AND DEFENCE

That mobbing by jackdaws can be a very successful defence is shown by the 'rescue' of a jackdaw from a raven quoted in the section on predators. Their mobbing attacks are especially elicited by a 'black crow' being held, by a mammalian or bird predator or man, or even another of their own species. The urge to mob when a 'black crow' is held is very strong and jackdaws imprinted to a human being will mob that human if he is holding a jackdaw (Lorenz, 1970). I have seen combined mobbing by rooks and jackdaws when two magpies become locked together in combat on the ground. They also join in the combined mobbing of tawny owls by birds of several species together. Seeing other birds mobbing may itself be a stimulus: Rolls (1973) described how jackdaws were attracted by the commotion of swallows mobbing a tern fishing and joined in the mobbing with them.

DAURIAN JACKDAW *(Corvus dauricus)*

This species is similar to the jackdaw (Plate III) in size and proportions. A wide band across the base of the neck and upper mantle and much of the underparts are a light creamy grey colour. The forehead and crown are very glossy black, with blue and purple sheen. The throat and central part of the upper breast are black, glossed with blue. The wings, mantle and scapulars, back-upper and under-tail coverts and the tail are all glossy black. The ear coverts and sides of the head are streaked with white. The irides are dark brown and the bill, legs and feet are black. The light-coloured areas are the sides of the upper breast, lower breast, abdomen and flanks and a broad band across the base of the neck forming a collar. These areas are a greyish-cream colour but with a suggestion of the pinkish shade of the jay.

This is an eastern Asiatic bird only recorded as a vagrant in Europe. All have been in Finland; one was shot in May 1883 at Unsikaarlepyy, and three were observed at Tammela in May 1915 (Merikallio, 1958).

Daurian jackdaws nest in trees and do not use cliffs and buildings like the jackdaw. They are more prone than the jackdaw to build open nests (Koslova, 1933).

Their feeding habits are probably very like those of the jackdaw. A complete account of the species is given by Goodwin (1976).

7
Red-billed chough
(Pyrrhocorax pyrrhocorax)

European names

Dutch – ALPENKRAAI
French – CRAVE Á BEC ROUGE
German – ALPENKRÄHE
Russian – KLUSHITSA
Spanish – GRAJA
Swedish – ALPKRÅKA

Vernacular names (all Cornish)

CORNISH DAW
CORNISH JACK
CORNISH KAE
HERMIT CROW
KÌLLIGREW
MARKET JEW CROW (from a street in Penzance)
PALORES
TSHAU-HA

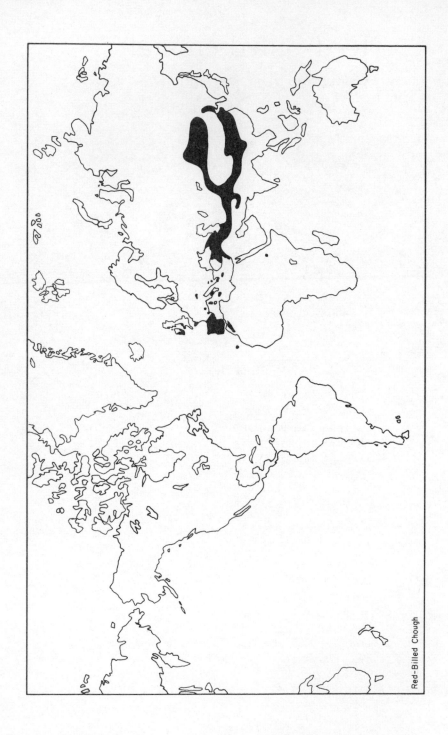

Red-Billed Chough

FIELD CHARACTERISTICS

The chough is most easily confused with jackdaws, rooks and carrion crows. On the ground it is larger than a jackdaw; its wings are much longer and the tips of the primaries extend to the end of the tail or just beyond it, noticeably longer than those of the jackdaw. Choughs walk or run like a jackdaw, but in haste they move with characteristic long bounding hops. At closer quarters the down-curved bright red bill and red legs make it unmistakable. Its wings are long and broad, and the primaries are themselves large and often well separated, even when the wings are angled back at the carpal joint, so that the flight silhouette is characteristic. The buoyant action is no less so, although choughs may go straight and direct, the beauty of their flight enhanced by great swoops and dives, sometimes from cliff top to sea level and up again. There are few more agile and graceful fliers.

In areas where both the chough species co-exist, some confusion can arise as juvenile red-billed choughs have shorter bills than adults and at first the bill is yellowish or buff and easily mistaken for the yellow of the Alpine species. But the wings of the Alpine chough only reach part way down the length of its longer tail.

DESCRIPTION

The entire plumage is black; the whole of the head and neck, mantle, scapulars, back, lesser and median coverts and underparts have a bluish gloss. The iridescence is greener on the upper and lower tail coverts, the tail, the greater and primary coverts, alula, primaries, secondaries and tertiaries. At many angles, the gloss on wing and tail feathers is sufficient to make a contrast with the head, mantle and scapulars, which appear darker. The bill, legs and feet are bright red, and the iris is dark brown.

The nestling has pinkish flesh-coloured skin with grey down except on the underparts, but the skin is blackish in the region of the down tracts. The bill is mauve with pale tip and edges and pale-yellow gape flanges. The mouth is orange pink with whitish palate spurs, and a yellowish base to the tongue. The legs and feet are flesh pink (Williamson, 1939–40; Harrison, 1975). As the nestling develops, the beak becomes yellowish white along the culmen, cutting edges and gape flanges and flesh coloured at the tip. The gape becomes pinkish with white palatal spurs, the base of the tongue is still yellowish. The tarsi darken to a purplish brown with orange pink at the interstices between the scutes and the claws are black brown (Williamson, 1939–40). The bill changes to pale red and the legs and feet to orange red while the bird is still in juvenile plumage (Ryves, 1948). There are individual variations in the rate of development of these colours.

The juvenile has browner duller back-body plumage and the wings and tail are also less glossy than in the adult. The juvenile plumage is suffused with a dull-green gloss and the irises are brown (Williamson, 1939–40). The tail, primaries and secondaries are not renewed at the first moult, which begins during the first summer, and these feathers become faded and browner than those of the adult. The body feathers and small coverts are renewed and become like those of the adult. The adult moult starts in June and takes about 92 days, all the feathers being replaced (Holyoak, 1974).

Choughs from the British part of the species range are the smallest, those from parts of the Himalayas are the largest and may be 38mm (1½in) longer.

DISTRIBUTION

The European distribution of this species, apart from the Iberian Peninsula, is confined to comparatively small scattered coastal and mountainous areas. In the west it is found in some of the Scottish islands – notably Islay – the north, west, and south coasts of Ireland, some areas of North Wales and Pembroke-shire, but is extinct in Cornwall. There are a few in Brittany and it is present in the European Alps, in the Italian Apennine mountains and also in Greece and Crete. It occurs in greater numbers and with a more even spread through-out the Iberian Peninsula and is also in the Atlas Mountains – where I have seen them sharing the cliffs with a colony of bald ibis – and in the Canary Islands. There is a very isolated colony in the Simien Mountains in Ethiopia, 1500 miles from the nearest area inhabited by them, which may date from the last ice age (Voous, 1960). In Asia the species is more widespread, with distribution continuous from eastern Turkey, the Caucasus and Iran, through the Elbruz Mountains to Afghanistan, north to about 53° in the Altai Moun-tains and eastwards to Ulan Bator and beyond in Mongolia. They are probably absent from a large central area in Sinkiang, but numerous in the Himalayas, reaching as far as the Yellow Sea coast about 122° east. The most northerly point in their range is in the Scottish islands about 57° north. The most westerly is the Blasket Islands off south-west Ireland, 10°30' west, and the most southerly the Abyssinian Mountains at about 12° north.

This species has an exceptionally wide range of distribution in terms of altitude. It is less confined to mountains than the Alpine chough, but in some ranges, such as the Himalayas it breeds at up to 2400 to 3500m (7874 to 11,483ft) (Sálim Ali and Dillon Ripley, 1972) and can be seen at much higher altitudes than this. Especially in the western part of its range, it makes much use of coastal cliffs, breeding in caves literally within a few feet of the high-tide level.

There are changes in the altitude of its habitat between summer and winter in areas of very high mountains such as the Himalayas, where it comes down to about 1600m (5250ft) in the winter (Sálim Ali and Dillon Ripley, 1972). Apart from this, it is a sedentary species and there are no true migrational movements within its European range and most of the British recoveries of choughs have been within 29 miles of the place where they were ringed (Holyoak, 1971). Most British ornithologists are aware of a general decline in numbers in the British Isles during the last 200 years or so. There is evidence (quoted by Voous, 1960) of a decrease in widely separated areas. Its breeding range in central Europe seems, for unknown reasons to have gradually diminished in the course of the last few centuries. Interspecific competition with the Alpine chough and jackdaw has been suggested as a cause: in Spain it is said that the chough is being ousted from its breeding places by the jackdaw, which is everywhere expanding its range, and there is also said to be competition for nesting holes in north-west China (Kansu) between choughs and daurian jackdaws.

Parslow, in his survey of the changes in status among breeding birds in Britain and Ireland, and Rolfe have summarized a great deal of evidence which showed that in Scotland the decrease has been continuing for about 200 years. Choughs are now entirely coastal, whereas they used to be found inland; they are now confined to Jura and Islay and certain other Western Islands. There may have been some local recovery recently in some of these areas. In England there are now no choughs, except on the Isle of Man. They were always coastal and were found in Yorkshire, Kent, Sussex – from which counties they disappeared in the first half of the nineteeenth century – and in Cumberland, Dorset and south Devon, where they remained until the latter half of the nineteenth century. By 1940 they had gone from north Devon, and there are now none left in Cornwall. In Wales they breed in Pembrokeshire, on some of the Welsh islands and in North Wales, where it is found inland and seems to maintain its numbers. In 1967, when Parslow was writing, the estimated numbers were about 700 pairs in the whole of the British Isles and of these about 600 pairs were in Ireland. Ireland is the chough's stronghold in the British Isles: they are present in all the coastal counties from Waterford to Antrim, except for Leitrim and Londonderry.

This has been a long slow decline and not a recent event in terms of human generations. Writing to Thomas Pennant Esquire on 9 November 1773 Gilbert White says: 'Cornish Choughs abound, and breed on Beachy Head and on all the cliffs of the Sussex Coast.' Yarrell wrote in 1845: 'I have seen it on the highest part of the cliffs between Freshwater Gate and the Needles Lighthouse in the Isle of Wight, Mr Thomas Bond tells me this bird inhabits Gadcliff and Tyneham in the Isle of Purbeck.' Writing in 1896, Bowdler Sharpe, describing the range of the chough in the British Isles, says: 'Now restricted to certain localities in the South Western Counties of England, parts of Wales, the Isle of Man, but still by no means rare in some localities in Ireland.' Great changes had taken place between 1773 and 1896.

As I write in Cornwall it seems appropriate to recount a little more of the history of decline here. Choughs are associated with Cornwall in many minds and this is shown by its vernacular names given at the beginning of this chapter. At one time choughs could be found in most of the suitable rocky parts of the Cornish coast but vanished from the south coast areas by about 1820 and from the Lizard/Lands End area by about 1850. There was then a gradual retreat, starting at the southern end of the north Cornish coast, so that by the turn of the century it inhabitated only the most northerly half here, from approximately Newquay to the Devon border. Choughs were seen further south than this but no nests were found (Darke, 1971) and by 1951 only four birds remained and there had been no proven breeding success for five years. From 1957 until 1968 there remained one non-breeding pair and one of these was found dead in 1968. I have a number of entries in my diary which show that I was watching choughs feeding on ant hills on cliff tops near Tintagel in August 1926. The cause or causes of this decline in numbers and distribution remain a matter for conjecture, but once the species had become locally rare, factors such as gin traps set for rabbits, shooting, egg collecting, and the taking of young for pets may well have hastened its eventual extinction. But these factors cannot account for the initial decline in so many areas. Competition with the jackdaw has been blamed, but in some areas of the Irish coast many apparently suitable sites are unoccupied by choughs. There is a possibility that the nest-site requirements of the two species are not identical (Holyoak, 1972) although they may overlap sufficiently to cause competition for a particular site from time to time. Jackdaws are ground surface feeders and choughs are probers with a narrow bill; furthermore, choughs are, at least sometimes, dominant over jackdaws (Rolfe, 1966) and – referring back for a moment to the reported competition between choughs and daurian jackdaws – Himalayan choughs are larger than British choughs and daurian jackdaws no larger than European jackdaws.

So it is far from certain that jackdaws, in spite of their great increase in numbers, have influenced the chough population. There may be some food or climatic factor, but no real evidence exists to prove that either has been important. At present the reasons for the chough's decline in the British Isles and possibly in many other areas too remain unknown. The absence of any real knowledge about what has caused the decline in Cornwall must make efforts to reintroduce the species from elsewhere of very doubtful value. One factor which must help to prevent any natural recovery by recruitment from other areas is the sedentary habit of the species.

POSTURE AND VOICE

The chough is one of the crows in which the wing-flipping movement is conspicuous (fig. 41), as with the carrion crow and in contrast to the jackdaw. This action is often associated with a self-assertive call, rendered as 'chee-ow'; the same call is used in flight, but there is then no noticeable change in wing action. When the bird is perched, this call, accompanied by wing and tail flip, is frequently used after chasing other choughs (cf the bowing and tail fanning of rooks) (Whittaker, 1947). An extreme version of this may involve a greater degree of wing opening – for example a chough might hop briskly for several feet, stop suddenly, bow and flap its wings open above its back (fig. 42) without calling and if two met during this manoeuvre they fought and became locked

41   Red-billed chough: wing and tail flip. Compare figs 20, 21, 46, 51

42   Red-billed chough: self-advertising action. Compare figs 17, 22

together in combat. Two or three others then tend to attack. Captive choughs threatened both members of their own species and Alpine choughs with a bill-forward posture, the feathers of mantle and underparts fluffed, and one regularly threatened a magpie in an adjoining aviary with an upright posture with bill down. These are obviously similar to the postures used by other corvids in similar contexts (Holyoak, 1972).

Several calls have been described. The high-pitched 'chwee-ow', familiar to those who know this species, is possibly a contact call (Holyoak, 1972) but it is also associated with self-assertive actions too. A scolding 'ker, ker, ker' was used as an alarm call when peregrine, kestrel, merlin or raven were sighted. There is also a succession of low warbling, chittering and churring sounds which may represent a song (Holyoak, 1972) but there seems as yet to be no information as to the circumstances in which song is used.

Food begging with wing fluttering is a courtship activity and is also used to signify hunger and the calls of the female are then reminiscent of both young choughs and young crows of other species.

Copulation probably takes place on the nest and is therefore seldom seen, but as recorded by Whittaker (1947) it took place outside the nest cavity (fig. 43) on one occasion and the male remained standing on the female's back for a long time afterwards. It is evident that on this occasion there was no interference by other choughs (contrast with rooks). Holyoak (1972) gives records of choughs attacking a displaying bird.

Choughs bathe frequently and this is followed by preening, oiling and head scratching which is done by the indirect method. By contrast, bill scratching is direct. The bill is also wiped on the perch, perhaps both in cleaning and as a displacement activity. Choughs sun bathe with fluffed plumage and half-spread wings. Only passive anting has been recorded.

43   Red-billed chough: female pre-copulatory posture. Compare figs 7, 25, 38, 56

TERRITORY

Holyoak (1972) saw choughs in the Calf of Man drive away individuals or pairs that approached within several hundred metres of their nest site, and concluded that the chough defends an area around its nest site as a territory. Cowdy (personal communication) found that in some territories the resident pair were not always alone, apparently a third chough was in some circumstances tolerated by the owners. More observation on the chough's territory is needed.

PAIR FORMATION

Choughs are seen in pairs at all seasons (Whittaker, 1947) and some displaying by them in early autumn and late spring was observed by Holyoak (1972) on the Calf of Man, so it is probable that the behaviour and reproduction-cycle sequence is similar to such species as the rook, with the birds having an autumn recrudescence of gonad activity when some pairs might be formed, and many choughs probably pair for life. When choughs are in a group, an individual may hop quickly towards another, stop half a metre away, bowing 'its forward end' abruptly with tail raised and wings flicked – as in the self-assertive posture but with no call. The bird giving this bow and the one that is the object of this attention are sometimes noisily attacked by others of the flock. Again this may be compared with rooks, and sometimes there is no interference at all. A bird that had 'bowed' might approach the other and nervously preen the nape and mantle. Twice, after allopreening, the 'bower' would regurgitate and present food which was quickly accepted (Holyoak, 1972). In the absence of a study of individually marked birds, it is impossible to say to what extent these activities precede the formation of a pair, or how much they may be display activities between already paired birds.

NEST-SITE SELECTION AND NEST

For the sake of easy thinking, we tend to separate activities such as the spring gathering of birds into various courtship activities such as attracting the female, overcoming the defence of individual distance, pair formation, nest-site selection and so on. Yet these activities are closely tied together and may be occurring simultaneously in different pairs, and to some extent in the same pairs of birds. Thus Whittaker records two birds out of a flock of 13 breaking away to visit the nest site for a short time and then rejoining the flock. Choughs do nest in caves, but the actual site – the ledge or opening where the nest is built – is often more open than the narrow closed holes used by jackdaws (Cowdy, 1962; Holyoak, 1972). This is a tendency, rather than a rigid distinction between types of nest site. The situation of the nest sites of ten pairs in Carmarthenshire were compared by Rolfe (1966): four were in quarries, two in mines, two in sea caves, one on a sea cliff and one on an inland cliff. In some areas of Ireland off-shore islands are also used. The altitude varied from a few feet above sea level to more than 305m (1000ft). Choughs breed at high altitudes in some parts of their range.

Building the large nest takes two to four weeks (four nests observed). Both the birds bring material for the main structure (mainly heather stems in the Isle of Man) and the female collects most of the lining and does all the work. In one case they collected wool from as far as 2km away. The male accompanied the female on these journeys but brought very little material back (Holyoak, 1972). The nest structure varies with the nature of the site; the outer structure is composed of sticks, branches and roots, and may or may not have a clay layer. Within this, the nest is built up of thin plant stalks, grass and rootlets, and then lined with wool or hair, or sometimes moss or fine grass (Kulczycki, 1973).

The eggs have a very pale ground colour, white or white tinged with pale green or cream. They are marked all over with spots of varying size, in shades of olive brown and grey. The mean size of 100 British eggs was given by Witherby as 39·4 × 27·9mm (Witherby, 1938).

The clutch may be completed in early April (Sansbury, 1959), but often towards the end of the month (Holyoak, 1972) and in the Isle of Man and Wales the mean size of 18 clutches was 4·1 eggs with two as a minimum and six as the maximum. They are probably laid at one egg per day, but there may be intervals of two to three days. Incubation takes from 17 to 18 days and, as with most corvids, is normally done by the female only. The male feeds the female on the nest and she often flies to meet him, and may sometimes be called from the nest by him. The female may use the juvenile-type wing flutter when the male is about to feed her (Williamson, 1941), which in these circumstances may depend on the degree of hunger.

The young are fed by regurgitation (Whittaker, 1947). Both parents collect food for the young after they are 2–3 weeks old (Holyoak, 1972). The frequency of feeding visits is variable, depending on brood size and availability of food – from 20 (Cowdy, 1962) to 50 minutes (Holyoak, 1972) between each. A curious habit is that both parents often go foraging and return to the nest together, one going into the nest hole first while the other remains outside.

Nest sanitation is carried out by both parents and faecal sacs are carried to a distance and sometimes dropped in the sea (Blair, 1940; Campbell, 1966); portions of egg shell after hatching are similarly disposed of but are also some-times swallowed (Nethersole-Thompson, 1941–2).

Cowdy found that when fledglings emerged from the nest there were differences in size and degree of feather development, which suggests that the eggs do not all hatch on the same day. An accurate idea of their subsequent development is given by her account of the choughs of Bardsey Island. On 7 June 1958 the first fledgling came out of the nesting cave about 4.57m (15ft) below the cliff top at about 9.30 am GMT. The same morning, three of the young were at the cave entrance and one a little below. The one out of the cave was attempting to reach the parents on the cliff top with short flights and scrambling and fluttering up the rocks. The adult made repeated and eventu-ally successful efforts to call it back to the cave. The following day all were out of the cave and fed there by the female, by first regurgitating food into her bill and then thrusting this into the young birds' throats, following this with brisk bill wiping on a rock. On the next five mornings they moved further away from the nest up to about 91m (100yd). When left alone, they hid in rock crevices, and if separated used a single contact call, repeated at intervals. On 12 June three were able to follow the adults along the cliffs and over the sea, although flying erratically; the fourth bird was smaller and with less well developed feathers. The young were still fed by regurgitation but encouraged to forage for themselves, and the adults turned over clods at which the young soon started pecking. The family continued to return to the nest five or six times a day, the young roosting there until the end of the month and the adults about 100m away.

The young collected most of their own food after three weeks, but remained with the parents for from four to five weeks (Holyoak, 1972).

When choughs are numerous these family groups form into flocks and in Spain up to 200 of the present species can be seen together in July and August (Bonham, 1970). They also nest colonially and there may be flocks throughout the year, most noticeably in displays and aerobatics, feeding and roosting. In Wales, the Isle of Man and Islay these flocks range from about 20 to 50, but in Ireland, in County Kerry a flock of 231 was counted by Flegg in 1968, and flocks of this size can be seen in Spain and Morocco. Some data are available on the breeding success of the red-billed chough, the fortunes of ten pairs nesting in Carmarthenshire in 1963 being recorded by Rolfe in 1966. Of the 39 eggs laid, one clutch of two was robbed and abandoned, and four eggs were smashed by men, leaving 33. Of these, 21 hatched and 20 young were fledged, which equals two per pair. One particular pair was followed up from 1953–63. In 1958 the female was found dead on the nest and that year was a total failure. Another female appeared and young were reared in subsequent years. The three birds using that nest reared 35 young, an average of 3·18 per year. Another pair on Bardsey Island reared 16 young in 6 years, averaging 2·66 per year. On Ramsey Island seven pairs are known to have reared ten young, or just over 1·4 young per pair per year (Cowdy, 1973). These figures are comparable with other corvids.

Part of the population is made up of non-breeders and these remain in flocks right through the summer, although within the flock they may be in pairs (Kennedy, Ruttledge and Scroope, 1951).

ROOSTING

There do not appear to be any records of large winter roosts of choughs in the British Isles. Ravens, carrion crows, rooks, jackdaws and magpies all have some degree of communal winter roosting, and it would be interesting to know whether large winter roosts of choughs are in existence from autumn to spring. Non-breeding choughs form regular roosts, and after the young have fledged, young and parents roost at or near the nest that they have used (Williamson, 1941; Cowdy, 1962 and 1973) and some birds roost in pairs on open cliffs. Breeding birds will join flocks of feeding non-breeding birds several kilometres from their nests and, like many other corvids, most birds are in pairs throughout the year – breeders and non-breeders alike.

FOOD

The rather slender decurved bill of the chough indicates that at least the method of obtaining food, if not the food itself, must be in some way different from that of other crows. The chough digs vigorously in short cropped pasture and on certain patches of moorland to which it frequently returns while other similar-looking areas are ignored (Whittaker, 1947). They dig holes about 5cm deep in the short turf which they pull back towards them (Cowdy, 1962). These are the methods used by choughs in searching for ants. Ants are found in those areas in which they have fed, and one pellet examined by Cowdy was entirely made up of ant remains. Ants are clearly a very important component of the chough's diet but, as with other crows, there is a considerable range of animal and vegetable material used by them. In addition to the close-grazed cliff-top turf they feed on ploughed land, on the beach and along the tide line, also in areas where cliffs have crumbled away, and inland on hill sides with rock outcrops, and dry moorland as well as in wet boggy areas. In Ireland, where they are so much more numerous, they forage close to the outskirts of villages. Their methods of obtaining food are often similar to that of some other crows, perhaps especially rooks, for they probe the ground, rather than feed off the surface like jackdaws, and flick over stones to obtain insects underneath. In the sand they sometimes dig massive holes, and on the shore will often drive jackdaws away. There is a record of choughs hawking for flying ants (Rolfe, 1966).

Their ability to probe and dig is a feature of their feeding and in Islay an area a metre wide was dug over in a bank when choughs were obtaining blow-fly larvae at a place where a cow had been buried some months earlier (Dawson, 1975).

Some idea of the type of food being obtained can sometimes be judged from the way the choughs are working. Deep probing in fields may be in a search for earthworms, leatherjackets and the larvae of agrotid months. On bare earth, and where the grass is short, rapid pecking, aptly described as 'sewing-machine action' is used when they are obtaining ants, and slower pecking with more searching may be for spiders and beetles (Holyoak, 1967).

The importance of ants as an item in the chough's diet has already been referred to, and a study of this was made by Cowdy in 1973 on Bardsey Island off the coast of Wales. Five species of ant were obtained, *Lasius flavus* was the most frequent, and *Lasius niger, Lasius alienus, Myrmica scabinodis* and *Tetramorium caespitum* is the order of frequency in which the choughs were taking them. The birds were probing in the galleries of ants' nests to a depth of 5cm, using the bill at all angles and, if the turf was very thin over a rock, the bird's head was so far over to the side that the bill was almost parallel to the rock's surface. Similar actions by captive Alpine choughs were also described by Goodwin (1976).

The ants move the larvae to different galleries and take them deeper in drier weather – possibly too deep for the choughs – and there is evidence of increased mortality among nestling choughs in dry weather.

The choughs watched by Cowdy fed only where the grass was short as a result of grazing by sheep and rabbits and the ant species. *L. flavus*, *M. scabrinodis*, *M. rubra* and *M. sabuleti* are inhabitants of this type of ground – *M. flavus*, for example, can be present in great numbers, up to 15,000 per sq m. If the character of the ground changes, so that scrub replaces the close-cropped turf, other ant species at much lower population densities replace these.

Like other crows, choughs are 'food hiders' for large portions of food are sometimes hidden in rock crevices and similar places, and Turner records that captive choughs buried food in earth and covered it with small stones (Turner, 1959, 1 and 2).

PREDATORS AND MORTALITY

Choughs usually show no reaction to jackdaws and nest and feed near them without there being aggression from either species (Rolfe, 1966). I can find no record of choughs being in any way dominated by jackdaws, but Rolfe records that choughs will drive jackdaws away from food on beaches. With other corvids their relationship is interesting. Cowdy says that they called in agitation if ravens appeared, rapidly fed their young and departed, and Williamson found them feeding more frequently with hooded crows than with rooks or jackdaws. But choughs will occasionally mob herring gulls and carrion crows. And hovering kestrels are attacked fiercely (Cowdy, 1962). This may be because of their falcon shape. The chough has few natural predators, but the peregrine falcon is one of them. On Bardsey Island Cowdy recorded that young choughs were dragged from their nest for 6m (20ft) along a horizontal fissure. There is no direct evidence as to what predator was involved, but this has been compared with predation on young shearwaters by little owls (Cowdy, 1962).

With the exception perhaps of the peregrine, the choughs' only serious predator is man, Rolfe (1966) quoting the case of Sir William Jardine who in 1827 shot 30 in one morning and D'Urban and Matthew in 1896 reported: 'We know of six choughs having been killed at a single shot when feeding at a manure heap at Braunton (Devon) by a sportsman wishing to discharge his gun before returning home.' Possibly we are more enlightened now, although this cannot be taken for granted, for among the ringing returns of choughs three had been shot (Holyoak, 1971) and of three choughs examined for presence of toxic chemicals two from Wales had been shot.

Choughs are still taken into captivity and 11 were removed from an Irish colony a few years ago and brought into England in concealment with the object of breeding them in captivity and reintroducing the species into Cornwall – with no success, and of these probably only two pairs remain. There is a little evidence to suggest that choughs may be more susceptible to an extremely cold winter than other corvids (Rolfe, 1966; Holyoak, 1971).

8
Alpine chough
(*Pyrrhocorax graculus*)

European names

Dutch – ALPENKAUW   Russian – AL'PIISKAYA GALKA
French – CHOUCARD DES ALPES Spanish – CHOVA PIQUIGUELDA
German – ALPENDOHLE   Swedish – ALPKAJA

FIELD CHARACTERISTICS

The Alpine chough is a bird of high mountain ranges; its black colour and musical whistling voice make it very conspicuous against the white surroundings of Alpine winter resorts, where so many sounds are silenced by the thick snow.

The tameness of the Alpine chough makes it easier to observe at very close range than the red-billed species, and the shorter, straighter pale-yellow bill and orange legs are easily seen. It has a longer tail than the red-billed chough and this can be seen when the bird is perched or on the ground, as the tail extends beyond the tips of the closed primaries. In flight it is a jackdaw-sized bird but with longer wings and tail and smaller head, and a light airy flight like that of the red-billed chough. The usual method of progress on the ground is walking, and hopping if there is need for haste.

DESCRIPTION

The entire plumage is black, with less gloss than in the red-billed chough. On most of its plumage this is a colourless sheen but on median and greater coverts, secondaries, alula, primary coverts, primaries and tail there is a slight blue–green gloss. The bill, which is pale yellow, sometimes very pale and almost ivory, is covered at its base by very short shiny black bristles. The legs are orange or coral red. The iris is dark brown.

The juvenile lacks the glossiness of the adult; it looks browner in the field and has black legs.

DISTRIBUTION AND GEOGRAPHICAL MOVEMENTS

This is a sedentary species, within Europe found in the mountainous areas of central and northern Spain, in the Alps, the Apennines and the Balkan Peninsula. It is also present in the Atlas Mountains, Lebanon, Iran, Trans-caspia, Afghanistan, Russian Turkestan and the Himalayas. Its movements are seasonal and local and are mainly changes in altitude. In the Alps in the summer they tend to feed in high pastures and come lower and feed in greater numbers round villages in winter. In the Himalayas, Alpine choughs may move to 2400m (7874ft) or even 1800m (5906ft) from their normal habitat of between 2700m (8688ft) and 5000m (16,400ft).

POSTURE AND VOICE

Perhaps the most frequently heard call is the far-carrying musical note, variously written as 'tseeou' or 'tseeop', accompanied by a crow-like dip of the head and flick of the wings and tail, probably a self-advertising call. There is a jackdaw-like, scolding, mobbing note and another note, familiar to those who know the bird in Alpine villages, is a call of varying pitch rendered by Fergusson-Lees as 'chirrish'. It may well be a contact call. When birds are at ease together, warbling, squeaking, chittering and chirring sounds are used (Holyoak, 1972). There appears to be no record of sounds which observers have felt able to describe as song. The sounds produced when a female is fed on the nest by her mate are similar to those of many other crow species.

The nests are usually hidden and inaccessible and actions normally taking place on the nest are particularly difficult to observe. Allopreening of the nape and mantle occurs between paired birds in the nesting season. Aggressive threat by a head-forward position (fig. 44) is used in encounters over larger pieces of food, and the response to this is a fluffed bill-forward posture, with the bill sometimes open or an upright bill-down position (fig. 45) (Holyoak, 1972).

Feeding of the presumed female by the male occurs in September, becomes more frequent in March, and is accompanied by wing fluttering (Rothschild,

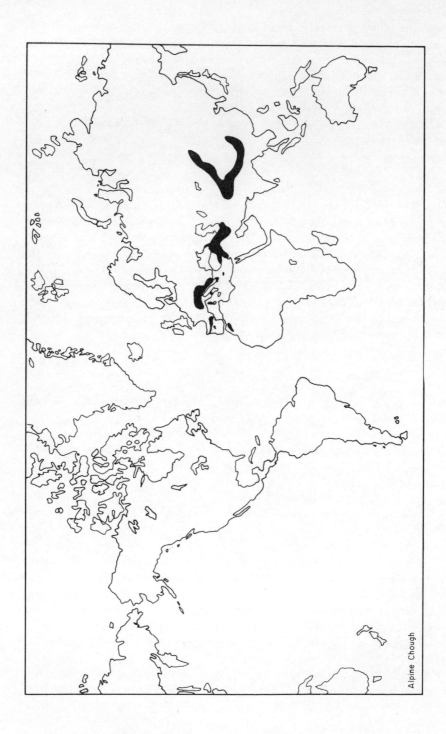

Alpine Chough

Red-billed choughs over the sea

II Jays

(a) *Garrulus glandarius*
Two male jays from the same area in W. Cornwall,
showing individual variability in colour
(b) *G. glandarius*, from Ireland (c) *G. glandarius:* juvenile (see also Keve 1967)
(d) *Perisoreus infaustus:* Siberian Jay (e) *G. glandarius*, Roumania

44   Alpine chough: head-forward posture. Compare figs 1, 16, 29, 37b, 47, 53

1956; Holyoak, 1972). There is a strutting display by the presumed male, with puffed-out feathers, not unlike that of the rook, probably a self-advertising posture. There is also a bill-up display in which the head position makes the bill, back and tail fall into line, perhaps for an intention posture for attack. Copulation probably takes place on the nest, but I can find no record that it has been observed.

Alpine choughs bathe frequently in water, following it by oil-gland preening and indirect head scratching. They also sunbathe, raising the plumage and partly spreading their wings.

NEST BUILDING

Nests are built in caves or holes in cliffs, which are usually large enough to allow the choughs to fly straight in; sometimes they are in buildings, chalets or cable-railway stations.

45   Alpine chough: bill-down posture. Compare fig 2

Although both the chough species will nest at high altitudes, the Alpine chough does not come down to lowland or sea-level cliffs. In the Alps the range of altitude for nesting is from 1280 to 2920m (4200 to 9600ft); in the high Atlas of Morocco from 2300 to 3965m (7600 to 13,000ft); and in the Himalayas from 2928 to 3268m (9600 to 15,600ft) (Voous, 1960). The lowest nesting altitude appears to be at from 600 to 900m (1968 to 2952ft) in south-eastern Europe (Reiser, 1926).

The nest is built by the female with material brought by the male, the outer layer being made of sticks and plant stems and roots and the cup formed of plant stems, dry grass and rootlets, lined with sheep wool and animal hair (Kulczycki, 1973).

EGGS TO FLEDGING OF YOUNG

Three to five eggs are laid of greenish white or buff ground colour, with mainly longitudinal grey and brown or red-brown markings. Their average measurements are $37 \cdot 5 \times 28 \cdot 0$mm. Incubation as in other crows is by the female only, although Rothschild has described an occasion when she saw what appeared to be a change-over at an inaccessible nest built inside a cable-railway shed. The bird, which from below appeared to have been incubating, left the nest and another took its place. The nest contents could not be examined and the sex and pair situation of these two birds remain unknown. Incubation takes about 21 days, the young leaving the nest 31–32 days after hatching, with only one brood reared per year.

ROOSTING

Rothschild described the pattern of roosting in the area of Wengen in the Bernese Oberland; most of her observations were made during the winter months December to March and the flight-line pattern described refers to that season. In the Wengen area the choughs roosted and nested in inaccessible cliffs above the tree line, and each roost was small, containing from 25 to 50 birds. They had some feeding grounds adjacent to their roosts, but there were regular flights to villages where they spent most of the day foraging and returned to the roosts in the late afternoon. The number of choughs going to each village might be in the region of 300 and the distance from roost to village feeding area might be from less than one mile to about five miles. Some observations made in July suggested that most choughs fed at higher altitudes then and nearer their roosting and nesting cliffs; foraging round the villages was presumably more necessary in winter weather. The larger winter flocks feeding in village areas might have a climb of as much as 1100m (nearly 3500ft) on their return journey to the roost and this might involve great changes in climatic conditions. So the weather changes may have been responsible for the great variations in the time of departure to roost; in Wengen between December and March this varied from 1 pm to 5 pm (cf rooks). Alpine choughs are gregarious and travel in groups and flocks but pairs are to be seen together as in other crow species, both feeding and in flight and in roosting flight lines.

FOOD

The food of the chough species might be similar, but in some places the two species do overlap and there may be food differences which prevent them coming into competition with each other. Alpine choughs take spiders, small snails, beetles and other insects. They take berries, such as those of juniper, rose hips and seeds, and evidence can be found in the droppings. They collect around sewage pipes from hotels where these empty down the rocks, and at garbage waste areas, and take food thrown away or thrown to them by climbers and tourists. They are often tame and will visit mountain restaurant picnic tables after the picnickers have left. Human food supplies are probably an important part of their diet in many tourist-frequented mountain areas. They are recorded as following an Everest expedition to its camp at 9500m (26,000ft) in search of food scraps. They also collect wind-blown insects from snow slopes (Holyoak, 1972). Most of their natural food is collected on the ground, on rocks and from crevices. Food is sometimes hidden in crevices and covered (Strahm, 1960; Goodwin, 1976).

Alpine choughs drink running water, which they can find round hotels, either from thaw or overflow and have been seen standing with open bill at a thin spout of water from a cracked pipe; presumably melting snow provides comparable natural sources.

9
Nutcracker
(*Nucifraga carvocatactes*)

European names

Dutch – NOTENKRAKER   Russian – OREKHOVA or KEDROVKA
French – CASSE NOIX MOUCHETÉ Swedish – NOTKRÅKA
German – TANNENHÄHER

FIELD CHARACTERISTICS

The nutcracker is jay-like in appearance, both on the ground, where it hops, and in flight but its heavier-looking head and shorter tail are noticeable. Its flight has also been likened to that of a hoopoe. Nutcrackers have a habit of perching on the extreme top of conifers, in winter dislodging the snow as they land. The dark-brown colour with white spots gives an overall greyish appearance to the body at a distance, while the head appears darker. From below, the white under-tail coverts and tail tip are very conspicuous so that only a small part of the dark colour of the tail feathers is visible.

DESCRIPTION

The nasal bristles are creamy-white with dark bases and the lores creamy white. The forehead and crown are very dark brown. The body colour is chocolate brown, most feathers having a drop-shaped white spot at the tip. At

148

the sides of the head and neck the spots are larger relative to the size of each feather, so that this area looks paler. The rump is darker with few spots. The wings are black with a blue-green sheen and the lesser coverts browner than the remaining part of the wing. The median coverts have white tips, the outer greater coverts, the primary coverts, the outer secondaries and the inner primaries very narrow white tips. The tail feathers are brownish black with a blue-green gloss; they have white tips which are small and inconspicuous on the middle feathers, getting progressively larger towards the outer ones, so that the tail looks dark from above and mostly white from below. The under-tail coverts are white. The irides are dark brown and the bill, legs and feet are black.

The slender-billed nutcracker is slightly smaller than the thick-billed race and has more white on the outer tail feathers.

The juvenile is like the adult but a paler shade of brown and with fewer white spots.

This juvenile body plumage is moulted in the first summer, the remiges, retrices and primary and greater coverts are not lost until the moult in the bird's second calendar year, and they become faded and brown with the white areas much abraded.

DISTRIBUTION

The distribution of the nutcracker depends on the distribution of the *Pinus* species on whose seeds it feeds. The various races extend from southern Scandinavia right across northern Europe and Asia to Kamchatka, Formosa and Japan, with a small separated area in the Alps and Carpathian Mountains, and also in the Himalayas. Clark's nutcracker occupies the corresponding area in North America. Of the two races that occur in Europe the nominate form is found in southern Norway, Sweden, Finland, the Baltic states, Poland and Germany down to about 55°N, and eastwards into western Russia as far as the Ural mountains. There is a separate area of distribution in the Alps, Carpathian Mountains, Switzerland, Austria, Czechoslovakia, Romania and Jugoslavia. The slender-billed race continues the distribution eastwards in Russia and across Siberia to Kamchatka and Japan, and it is this race that is involved in most of the invasions into western Europe, including that of the autumn of 1968.

GEOGRAPHICAL MOVEMENTS

In some years there is a failure of the 'nut' crop on which the bird depends, though this is infrequent. The effects of such a crop failure make themselves felt at the end of the summer, when the birds are starting their intensive food-storage activities, and when the young birds are dispersing to new areas. The most recent such failure, and the best documented, was in the summer of 1968. Accounts of the nutcracker invasion are available from Europe and beyond,

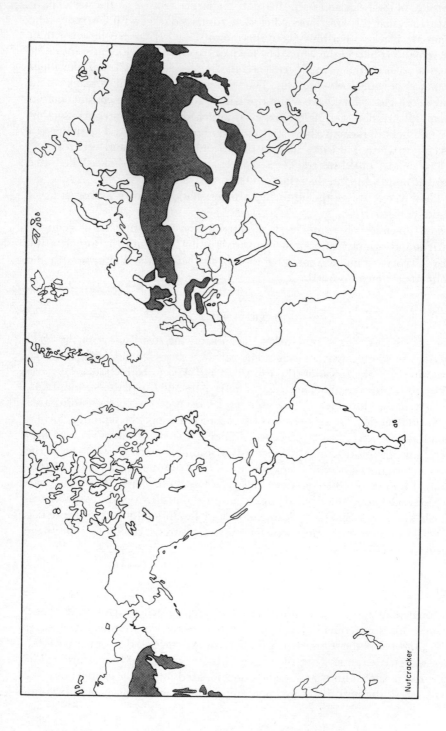

Nutcracker

and a complete summary of this material was made by Hollyer (1970 and 1971). The birds spread gradually outwards. Although one or two were seen in the Netherlands in June, the movement really became apparent in July, when they were observed in some numbers in parts of Sweden outside their normal range and also in Estonia, Lithuania, Latvia, East Germany, Poland, West Germany, Denmark, the Netherlands and Belgium. Large numbers were recorded by observers in each of these countries. In the Soviet Baltic states thousands were present by the first ten days of August and that was the peak. There were less in September and in October, small groups only. In Finland there were large flocks in mid-August. This was also the time of maximum numbers in East Germany, the highest number recorded there being 2200, decreasing to fewer than 150 by the end of October. In West Germany and Denmark the story was the same. In the Netherlands, too, August saw the peak of the invasion: 100 corpses were received by one Dutch taxidermist alone, and 6000 records were sent in. The nutcrackers tended to come in waves; in Belgium the passage was in small daily numbers from 6 to 16 August and then came a gap with none between 17 and 19. The main peaks were from 20 to 25 and on 28 August and then again on 11 September. In Sweden on 11 August 4400 were counted flying north-north-west at Holmön Island and the peak was not until the end of the month. In Poland, the maximum numbers were from mid-August until the end of September. The story is then one of wider spread and declining numbers. By December only single birds were seen in the Soviet Baltic states. In West Germany only four were recorded at the end of December; in France about 15 in widely separated areas; small numbers reached Czechoslovakia, Austria, Switzerland and north Italy, and one was recorded in North Africa and one in Portugal. Some going eastwards had reached the Gobi Desert. Almost all the records from all areas were of the slender-billed race and the majority were adults, as was the case in the United Kingdom. While most of the eastern counties had had their maximum numbers in August they spread widely, reaching as far as west Cornwall. In the United Kingdom as in the rest of Europe the numbers declined steadily until probably only about ten remained by the end of the year. The eastern counties total had reached its maximum of 138 birds in September. The 1968 exodus of Siberian nutcrackers was aided by exceptional weather conditions in the early autumn, with an unusual high-pressure area and cold, calm conditions over northern Europe in place of the westerly winds normally experienced at that time of year; this anticyclonic weather continued in August, September and October.

In many areas the birds were described as very tame and by October were in deteriorating condition, many being found dead. There were several reports that the nutcrackers fed ravenously and later they were described as being listless. In Britain, although they lived in such (for them) unusual places as gardens and by roadsides and near the sea, they had a tendency to choose conifers. Some of the nutcrackers were mobbed by other birds, three by swallows, three by missel thrushes and one was stooped at by a hobby. Such action may be due to unfamiliarity, their resemblance to a jay or may be something which occurs in their normal habitat but which has not been recorded. Such mass emigrations from the area of normal food supply must cause a great reduction in population. A few in the Netherlands remained until the following summer and one pair is known to have bred successfully there.

POSTURE AND VOICE

Little has been written about nutcracker postures. Territory is defined by harsh cries from conspicuous points near the territorial boundary and not by posturing, gestures or song. Nutcrackers do have a song which Swanberg describes as piping, whistling and whining notes uttered rhythmically and, in addition, a distinct clicking. This song is given by the males only. The bird stands in the bill-up posture with throat dilated, and Swanberg suggests the song's function is to facilitate synchronization of the sexes.

Referring to the 1968 irruption of nutcrackers, Hollyer in 1970 described a low-pitched, far-carrying 'krark' or 'kraaa', harsh but less grating than a jay, and repeated five or six times; Thorpe (1923) in the Swiss Alps mentioned that the common sound of the pine woods was a high-pitched 'gurr', probably the same harsh far-reaching cry that Swanberg described, and that another peculiar note that he heard sounded like a spring rattle.

During the nutcracker invasion of autumn 1968 nutcrackers were not often seen to drink but some, in both England and West Germany, were seen to drink like a pigeon by continuous action, and not the interrupted scooping and swallowing of the other crows. This requires further observation, especially in view of the special oesaphogeal development described by Swanberg (1956).

TERRITORY

The nutcracker's territory is very specialized. During a ten-year study in Sweden, Swanberg (1956) found that nutcrackers usually pair for life and their territory is held for life; one pair is recorded as holding the same territory for 14 years. The average area was 13·2 ha (32·7 acres). The highest density was in the Åland Archipelago where the average was 9 ha (22·2 acres) per pair. Swanberg suggested special reasons for this higher density and I shall refer to these later. The territory is not defended by fighting and not much by display and posture. Ownership is proclaimed by loud harsh cries, especially from points along the territory boundary and facing favourite call points of neighbours. Although fighting and display are not conspicuous, the territorial calls are seasonal, as with the displays that are conspicuous with other species. They are most marked just before nest building and absent when the eggs have been laid and occur again when young are with their parents and in the territory which is in use throughout the year.

The territory is the area within which the nest is built, but it is also the area within which both members of the pair have their food stores. This ensures that food is stored within a limited area known to the owners. The fact that the storage area is limited in extent obviously makes it easier for the birds to remember their own store places, and memory is vital when snow changes the whole scene in winter. The territory being a food store guarantees accessible food at nesting time, with consequently shorter foraging flights when the young are being fed. In general, food competition with other nutcrackers is avoided, although they will watch to locate a cache being made by a neighbour, and if the owners are absent will empty it. Having a storage area of this size ensures that the food caches are well scattered and this is a protection against the loss of too much stored food to rodents. As the territory is in use all the year round and for many years a place with which both birds become very familiar, it may also serve as a well-known refuge from predators.

PAIR FORMATION

Species that pair for life provide few opportunities for observation of pair formation behaviour, and such behaviour may be less conspicuous than that of a species where the difficulties inherent in pair formation have to be overcome frequently. It is not known whether pairs are formed in autumn or spring nor how juveniles enter the social structure. Like many other crow species there are social gatherings usually in the early morning and especially before and during nest building. If pair formation is the main function of these gatherings, it might be expected that they would take place earlier in the year than this, but the age composition of the groups forming such gatherings is not known. During the gatherings, pairs may leave to go to their own territories (Swanberg, 1950), about 8 to 10 birds usually taking part in these ceremonies. As with other crow species, these gatherings do not appear to excite territorial defence responses.

NEST SITE AND NEST BUILDING

Nutcrackers always choose a nest site within their territory and the nests are always built in conifer woods (Swanberg) in spruce (*Picea*), *Pinus sylvestris*, *P. cembra* and in larch (*Larix*). At an average height of 5·5m (ranging from 2 or 3m to 11 or 12m) (evidence from published accounts shows that the Siberian subspecies nests at about the same height), the nests are usually in the side shoots of branches close to the trunk so that they rest on a number of small branches (two to five) and are not well attached to them.

Nest building takes about 12 days (von Haartman, 1969). The nest is rather loosely built in appearance, like a jay's nest, but it is of three-layered construction, the outer layer forming the floor and walls of the stick 'basket', and is made of thin twigs 0·2 to 0·6cm thick and 15 to 30cm long, usually with green shoots of the bramble woven in. In some nests the bramble may be as much as 30 per cent of this external layer. All the twigs are fresh. At the base they are laid obliquely or transversely and folded if they are too long. At the sides, the twigs are laid more or less parallel to each other and short dry twigs and bits of rotten wood and dead leaves are stuffed in between them. The next layer is cup-shaped and made of clay and rotten wood, up to 2cm thick in the middle and thinner at the sides. Inside this, is the third layer of the lining, woven circularly of fresh 'bast' (mostly from the sallow) but with bits of rotten wood, dead leaves and tufts of moss and stalks of grass added.

The mean dimensions of seven nests examined were: outer diameter 26·42cm, inner diameter 14·10cm, height 14·50cm, depth 7·64cm. This description of the structure and measurements are from those examined by Kulczycki (1973) and were of the nominate race. He quotes several authors to show that the nests of the Siberian nutcracker *N.c. macrorhynchos* are very similar.

EGGS AND INCUBATION

The nutcracker's eggs are pale blue or greenish-blue, very finely marked with grey and grey-brown spots. The mean measurements are 33·9 × 24·9mm (Witherby, 1938). At the time when nutcrackers start their nesting, temperatures can be very low, − 10°C, for example while the bird is incubating. Laying in Finland begins in early to mid-April.

Dementiev (in Swanberg, 1956) gives the incubation period as 16–18 days. Swanberg found that true incubation starts with the last egg and he measured incubation periods from the date on which the last egg was laid. From the time that the first egg is laid, it is covered by one or other of the pair, for this is the only corvine genus in which the male regularly takes part in incubation and in fact plays an important part in it. This unusual feature is, like so much of the nutcracker's life cycle, linked to its food-storage requirements. The food stores, although they are within the territory of the pair, are made and remembered by the male and the female separately. The combined stores are needed for the pair and their young and it is therefore impossible for the male to feed the incubating female, as in the other crows, because he does not know where her stores are and the female must have sufficient time to collect food from her own stores. So the male takes his turn throughout the laying period. The maintenance of egg temperature by an incubating bird depends on the development of highly vascular brood patches and six male nutcrackers had brood patches as large as and macroscopically similar to those of the female.

It has been found that very little embryonic development takes place at temperatures lower than 30°C. The nutcracker's clutch is usually three or four and all four eggs may hatch on the same day. Until the last egg is laid, the bird is sitting high and not applying the brood patch. Swanberg found that the temperature of the first egg averaged 22°C, of the second 23°C, of the third (of four) 26°C and the fourth egg 30°C. When full incubation began the average temperature rose to 35°C. All these were the egg temperatures when the ambient temperature was about − 10°C. He found that from the laying of the last egg, the average incubation period of three egg clutches was 18 days and 16 hours, and of four egg clutches exactly 18 days. The sexes were found to have a time-table for their shares of incubation. The female brooded at night, and the male from before until after sunrise, and during a few shifts of from 20 minutes to 1 hour 20 minutes by day. The female took over from several hours before sunset until the following morning. The day activity period is from 30 minutes before sunrise until 20 minutes after sunset (comparable with other crows such as raven, rook, carrion crow and jackdaw). Of this the female incubates for 66 per cent of the time and the male for 34 per cent. The male Clark's nutcracker *Nucifraga columbiana* also takes a share in incubation.

Swanberg poses a final and interesting question. How does the male nut-cracker know when to change from merely protecting the eggs to actual incubation? For true incubation starts only with the last egg of the clutch and the number in the clutch is variable. Goodwin (personal communication) suggests that he might react to the temperature of the eggs, when the female has begun to incubate.

YOUNG

While they are in the nest the young are fed on the stored food provided for them by the parents. After leaving it, they stay for two or three weeks in the territory, or at least with the territory as a base. Then during the summer and before the ripening of the 'nuts' they go (in Sweden) with their parents to deciduous woods to feed, but each evening both parents and young return to the territory to roost. Nutcrackers help their young to feed for a long time. For example, young at 105 days were being fed by their parents within the territory and probably for another nine days after that (Swanberg, 1956).

As with several other corvine species, the main time for dispersal to new areas is when the young are fully grown, at the end of their first summer. This may partly coincide with the hardening of the flight feathers by keratinization, making longer flights possible; the distances they travel are usually short, and six Swedish nutcrackers ringed as nestlings were recovered at from six months to five and a half years later at distances of from 7·5 to 40km away (5 to 25 miles).

FOOD

Nutcrackers are mainly dependent on a continuous supply of pine seeds and hazel nuts, and the means of achieving this continuity is the cause of much of their specialization. The Old World nutcrackers divide into a group of sub-species, two of which come within Europe. They cover the area of pine species,

P. cembra, P. sibirica, P. pumila and *P. koraiensis* and the seeds taken from the cones of these trees are the most important item of their diet. Turcek and Kelso (1968) have gathered together a great deal of information about the relationship between the nutcracker and its food trees, from their own work and from many others whom they quote. The trees, and hence the nutcracker, have considerable economic importance. The pine seeds have a very high energy value. Stores of these seeds provide 5000 calories per gm compared with 4000 calories from the same weight of insects (Turcek, 1961). He suggests that this enables the nutcracker to be independent of insects at its early nesting time in a cold and snowy climate. The protein requirements of young birds are usually met by a change to an animal diet, and it would be interesting to know how this is accomplished by the nutcracker. In studies in Sweden and Finland Swanberg found that hazel nuts were the main food. Seed production is, of course, a late summer and autumn phenomenon; and to ensure a continuous supply for many months ahead the nutcracker has had to develop behaviour for efficient storage of these foods. There are also some associated anatomical and physiological adaptations for food transport and storage. The shape and thinness of the nutcracker's bill enables it to pick out the seeds from the cones, and they can also break open cones by hammering them against hard wood or rock, with sufficient vigour for the sound to be heard as much as 50m away. The lower mandible has a thickening and a rhamphothecal bulge (Swanberg, 1956; Richards, 1958) to strengthen the grip on the seed, cone or nut. The bill shape of each European subspecies is related to the type of cone which is its main food, the slender-billed being dependent on *Pinus sibirica* and the thick-billed on *P. cembra*. For carrying its food stores the nutcracker uses its bill, its throat pouch and, like the jay, its enlarged oesophagus. In the spring and early summer and again in late summer and fall it uses an oesophogeal diverticulum or pouch opening under the tongue, which Swanberg records as being developed at these times. Nuts and seeds are dry material and to make the business of regurgitating them into the chosen store easier, this bird has an unusually copious supply of saliva.

Swanberg says, referring to the hazel-nut crop in Sweden, that the nutcracker's life in the two or three autumn months was completely devoted to storing nuts. The hazel nuts fall in October and the nutcrackers started making their stores in August. They left the spruce forest where they lived before sunrise and went direct to the hazel coppice which was as far as 6km away. Within one hour after sunrise many had returned with a full load of nuts. They continued all day and only stopped at sunset. The maximum activity was reached towards the end of September when it began to lessen and this continued throughout October, and finally tailed off during December.

The actual stores put away consisted of three or four and up to eight or nine hazel nuts, together pushed down about one bill length and then covered with lichen. The average time taken to make each store was about three minutes – then back to the hazel bushes for a fresh supply.

The information assembled by Turcek and Kelso provides a similar picture. The choice of storage site was not in existing cavities or in dense moss or grass but where there was a soft substrate into which the pine seeds could be pushed, each such cache containing anything from 3 to 48 seeds. The number of pine seeds carried on each journey is far greater than the number of hazel nuts: of *P. sibirica* up to 167, of *P. pumila* up to 218, of hazel nuts up to 26 and of beech up to 11. These quantities were carried in some cases as much as 15km (9·3 miles).

Turcek estimated that 70 per cent of the hidden seeds are recovered by the nutcrackers. Other animals recover 20 per cent in the forest and more in tundra areas, 80 per cent of the recovery by other animals being by rodents. But it is ecologically, and in some areas economically, important that many of the seeds are not recovered but are effectively sown by the birds. The seed species that they use are not airborne like the winged seeds of ash or sycamore. The distances that the birds carry them and the large number of scattered small stores where they are hidden to ensure a food supply for the birds, also ensures a very efficient scatter of seeds for the trees. The number of seeds sown in this way is enormous, for according to Bibikov (in Turcek and Kelso, 1966) there are anything from 417 to 3334 caches per hectare, perhaps as many as 4000 to 34,000 per hectare in dry ground throughout the enormous area of Taiga. The numbers of cached pine seeds actually sprouting has been recorded as from 100 to 60,000 per hectare (Reimers, Reimers and Smirnov; and Pivnik in Turcek and Kelso, 1968). The nutcrackers are probably the main agent for continued planting of these tree species. It was also found that the nutcracker's food caches provide cluster sowing which, through competition, makes stronger trees compared with those sown separately. This seed planting by nutcrackers is of such value to the pines that it may be that the high calorie value of the seeds has evolved because it enables the nutcrackers to use them as stored food, thereby serving the survival of the pines by acting as their seed distributors. Just as many plants, by evolving coloured flowers, can make use of insects for pollination.

The stores are made by pushing the nuts (and this word includes pine seeds too) into suitable ground and covering them. At the chosen site, the bird makes nodding head movements while it regurgitates the nuts; a few pokes with its bill puts them in place and then it conceals them with reindeer moss or lichen. This done, it moves a short distance away and surveys the site. If another nutcracker comes, it makes no further caches until the other has gone. The caches may be in line in the forest floor to 25 to 100cm intervals (Bibikov, 1948; Mezhenyi, 1954, in Turcek and Kelso, 1968). None of this elaborate storage system would have any value unless they had developed an equally remarkable ability to recover their supplies by means of visual memory. Swanberg recorded that in recovery operations 86 per cent of the nuts were found by the birds, about one-third of these was in each of the months January, February and March and the success rate remained consistent throughout, indicating that the birds must know which caches have already been emptied. It must be remembered that these areas are covered by snow during much, perhaps most of this time, and the nutcrackers will dig through up to 1m of snow to reach the store, the dig being large enough to admit the bird, rather than a wide exploration (Zykov, 1953, in Turcek and Kelso, 1968). Apart from any other considerations this depth of snow would seem to exclude a sense of smell as a factor, and indeed it has been shown experimentally that the visual memory is lost if the hippocampal or archaeocortex (the relevant brain area) is removed (Kushinskaya, 1966, in Turcek and Kelso, 1968). The stores are the remembered store of each individual and not of the pair, although sited within the territory of the pair.

The 'nut' crop supplies their food for many months and enables them to start nesting at a time when they are dependent upon stores. Supplementary food may be brought into the food store territory from outside, after the snow has gone, if this proves to be necessary. Nutcrackers also use other food sources such as other fruit and seeds, as well as some insects and animal food.

The periodic invasions by the nutcracker of wide areas of Europe where they are not normally recorded has produced a great many observations from several countries which provide further information about food, although the choice of food will have been influenced by starvation.

During the 1968 nutcracker invasion Hollyer described the nutcracker as digging and probing in the ground, pecking at cracks and stripping back bark to look for insects. Grasshoppers, beetles, bees, wasps and ants were eaten, and other records include (in Norfolk) one live rodent and house sparrows. Nutcrackers are known to have fed on a variety of animal food, house mice, brown rats and voles, as well as vegetable material such as seeds and fruits, hazel nuts, walnuts, peanuts, acorns, elderberries and blackberries and various bird-table offerings.

MORBIDITY, MORTALITY AND PREDATORS

Nothing seems to be known about disease or parasites with this species nor of the normal expectation of life or the mortality of juveniles. Swanberg (1956) mentions one male which was at least 15 and probably 18 years.

The irruption emigrations of nutcrackers that happen from time to time must cause an immense mortality – 'death wanderings' as they have been called.

The most serious avian predator is probably the goshawk, as with other crows within its range. The pine marten is likely to be a nest predator but its depredations are probably much reduced by the wide spacing of the nutcracker nests ensured by the size of the territories.

10
Magpie
(Pica pica)

FIELD CHARACTERISTICS

The magpie's black and white colour is unmistakable. In flight the long tail, narrow when closed and diamond-shaped when open, and mainly white primaries are also characteristic and conspicuous. Its chattering call, likened by some to a machine gun, can be heard at a distance and is also unmistakable.

DESCRIPTION

The sexes are alike and there are no differences in appearance between summer and winter.

The whole of the head, neck, mantle, inner scapulars, back, upper- and under-tail coverts and tarsal feathers are glossy black. The rump varies in the different geographical races and in individuals within the same race from black to greyish white or brownish grey. The outer scapulars, flanks and abdomen are white. The secondaries, lesser, median and greater coverts are glossed with blue-green and bronze. The primaries are black with a green gloss on the outer webs, the base and tip of the inner webs are black and the remaining part of the inner webs is white. The tail is glossed with green and bronze, with a band of reddish purple about 75mm (3in) from the tip; the terminal part is dull greenish blue.

The bill, legs and feet are black and the iris is dark brown.

The nestling is without down and has a bright-pink mouth lining with white spurs at the base of the tongue and on the palate; the edges of the gape are pale pink.

The juvenile has the same colour pattern as the adult, but all the glossy areas are less bright, and the white is less pure. The tail is short when the nestling leaves the nest. The first primary is larger than that of the adult and has less white on it.

When the young magpie leaves the nest it still has some of the nestling's pink colour at the angles of the gape but within about ten days this has become the same creamy yellow as the bare areas of skin that still show around the eyes, especially noticeable behind the eye. A moult into adult-type plumage may start in July and some glossy feathers begin to appear among the dull black of the head mantle and breast; the dull-green greater and median coverts are replaced by much bluer and glossier ones. This moult ends about the end of September. Sometimes the tail feathers are replaced, but usually tail, primaries, primary coverts and secondaries are retained and these gradually become faded and browner. The areas of bare skin around the eye do not become covered until the new head feathers are complete, but the skin colour has gradually changed from creamy yellow to pale greyish blue; in the North African race the area behind the eye remains bare and becomes a brighter blue, noticeable in the field. The iris, blue grey in the nestling, darkens to adult colour within six to eight weeks of leaving the nest.

Various subspecies have been separated, but they show features which are present in varying degree in the magpie with which we are familiar *P. p. pica*. *P. p. melanota*, in Spain, has a black rump, and in some British specimens it is nearly black. *P. p. maritanica* of north-west Africa also has a black rump; it also has a blue patch of bare skin behind the eye, and this, as we have seen, is present to a lesser degree in the sub-adult British specimen. More noticeably different is *P. p. bactriana* of northern Asia, which is larger, has a white rump and has bigger white areas on the inner webs of the primaries so that they look

III   Jackdaw: adult males
      (a) *C. monedula spermologus*, Cornwall (b) *C. monedula ibericus*, Madrid
      (c) *C. monedula soemmeringi*, Moscow
      (d) *C. dauricus* (e) *C. monedula collaris*, Turkey

IV Azure-winged magpie

different in the field. The most northerly of the European races is *P. p. fennorum* and this is slightly larger and has more white on the wings than *P. p. pica* and more bronze and less green on the tail. *P. p. pica*, the nominate race described above, ranges from the United Kingdom across southern Scandinavia to central and south-east Europe; moving westwards *P. p. galliae* is slightly smaller and has less white on the wings and less often white on the rump. *P. p. melanotus* is similar to *galliae* but often has a wholly black rump or sometimes dark grey (Goodwin, 1976). The trend therefore is for the size to get smaller and the white areas to get less from north-east to south-west.

DISTRIBUTION

The distribution of the magpie has been very dependent on human influence. In England and Scotland the number of magpies decreased in the nineteenth century, and increased again after 1914, probably due to the decrease in game preservation. Again there was a marked increase in 1939–45. But this was followed by a decline in the eastern counties of England from about 1950. The removal of hedgerows and the widespread use of toxic chemicals and the post-war increase in gamekeeping are probably responsible for this. Afforestation may have produced an increase in some areas like central Scotland, for this is one of the species that can live in conifer plantations (Prestt, 1965; Parslow, 1967).

Ireland was first colonized within historical times, towards the end of the seventeenth century, and the magpie has increased steadily since then. It now breeds in every county in the British Isles up to a line from the Forth to the Clyde, except for some areas in south and south-east Scotland. There are also local areas of breeding in the eastern Highlands as far north as Easter Ross. It is a wanderer to the Western Isles.

In some areas of urbanization magpies have adjusted well to the new surroundings. Urban parks and larger gardens with plenty of trees are a suitable habitat for it, but the denser building which has used such gardens as sites for smaller houses involves the cutting of trees and is much less favourable.

In rural areas they prefer clumps of shrubs or trees rather than forests (Klejnotowski, 1969). They are found on the steep slopes above sea cliffs, where are suitable nesting habitats such as blackthorn scrub – a situation in which a magpie makes a spectacular, and beautiful, picture with the sea as a background. The magpie is distributed throughout Europe, with the exception of north-west Scotland; it does not occur in Iceland, nor in northern Russia, east of the White Sea.

They are sedentary in most areas, ringing returns showing the distances that they travel are usually less than 32km. In Great Britain there were only two records up to 1971 (Holyoak, 1971) of distances more than 32km. One of these had travelled 86km, and only about one-fifth had moved more than 8km.

Magpie

Continental records have also usually shown only short distance movements (Busse, 1969), although one ringed in Finland was recorded 432km from the area where it was ringed. However, there is an account of 20 magpies arriving on the Island of Thanet from the north-east on 28 September 1910 and a further 15 on 14 October (Witherby, 1912).

POSTURE AND VOICE

There does not appear to have been any specialized study of the whole of magpie behaviour, but both Goodwin in 1952 and Holyoak in 1974 have given fairly extensive accounts of some aspects of magpie displays and postures and there have been a number of short notes published on the spring gatherings of magpies, when various displays take place.

In situations of social and sexual excitement the white areas of the plumage are so arranged as to be conspicuous, the white shows little when fear prevails. In describing the postures Goodwin's terminology is used.

1   wing flirting accompanied by a 'tchuk' note (fig. 46). The head is somewhat lowered and there is a forward bow with tail raising at the same time; the folded wings, with the brightly coloured secondaries 'squared' to make them conspicuous, are lifted and sometimes slightly opened and fluttered; the lift is a 30 to 40° rotation at the shoulder joint. At low intensity this movement is only just suggested; when there is an accompanying sexual intention the head feathers are raised.

Either sex may give this display towards its mate, sometimes quite spontaneously if they are just foraging together, but more typically if they have become separated the display is given as they rejoin. This is commonly used at full intensity at the spring gatherings. For example, when there had been 14

46   Magpie: wing flirting. Compare figs 20, 21, 51

birds at one such gathering and only four remained, the male of one of the remaining pairs drove off the other pair, then first the male and afterwards both of the final pair gave a high-intensity wing-flirting display on top of a bush which may have been their nest site.

2   aggressive wing flirting is similar but is a relatively slight movement with no fluttering, and the tail is jerked up more vigorously, accompanied by an upward head and body movement and an aggressive 'tchuck' note. The crown feathers are flattened and this display too is often used at gatherings. It may have a sexual connotation but includes a threat.

3   the tilting display. This is a display which is partly a threat and may also be part of the male courtship. It may be homologous with the lateral version of the pre-copulatory display of the rook. The magpie approaches the object of its posturing with its secondaries displayed as described in the wing flirting; it tilts its body slightly, raising the further wing without unfolding it, and switches its tail towards the object, at an angle of 130° to the body, with head held high, and using low-pitched monosyllabic notes.

4   aggressive display is similar to the tilting display, but the side of the tail towards the object is spread, the feathers of the mantle are lifted and the head lowered and held forward.

47   Magpie: tilting threat. Compare figs 1, 16, 24, 37, 50
48   Magpie: begging. Compare fig 32

5   begging. The wings are lifted high at the shoulder and fluttered as the bird stands high on its perch. The white of the primaries is very conspicuous and the flutter is accompanied by a loud call 'cheeuch'. This is an appeal for food by juvenile or female. The upright attitude is unlike that of other crows when begging for food.

6   blinking. This is the action of drawing the nictitating membrane across the eye, and is common in social excitement, whether sexual or aggressive. A slow movement of the nictitating membrane, which is held closed for a short time, is also used by the female. There is a brilliant orange patch in the corner of the membrane, which is conspicuous and a similar action is used by the carrion crow, although in that species there is no orange patch. In both species this seems to have a submissive or appeasing significance.

7   bowing. An action apparent when the bird is excited, a quick bow and an upward jerk of the tail.

8   hammering. Hard hammer blows with the bill at its perch are made by the magpie as a displacement action when conflicting drives – for example of escape and attack – inhibit each other. Another displacement activity is bill wiping, which occurs in similar situations.

9   female pre-copulatory display. The female crouches with legs flexed and tail lowered and head slightly raised. The wings are half open and drooped and quivering slightly; in an example observed by Clegg in 1962, it was not quivered and the male's response to this display by the female was to approach her with his tail at an angle to the body and slightly raised, wings held stiffly out in front and vibrated so that the white of the primaries became a blur. The effect was very striking to the observer. With two or three hops in this position he then mounted the female from behind and copulation took place. There were no post-copulatory displays by the female and neither made any sound which the observer could hear.

The spring gathering of magpies, the 'great magpie marriage' of the Rev. W. Damion Fox (Stubbs, F.J., 1909) may well be concerned with pair formation. Such gatherings are usually in early spring but can be from mid-December until May (Holyoak, 1974). No observations on individually marked birds at such gatherings have yet been made, but assuming that birds arriving and remaining together are pairs it seems that at such gatherings paired birds predominate, but single birds arrive and depart and most of the birds within the area, whether paired or unpaired, are attracted to the group. The group moves across territories without interference. Display flights are conspicuous. The displaying bird rises with slow flight using a slow wing flap to an 'unnecessary height', as Holyoak puts it, circling round and back. They sweep round covering a rough circle of 50 to 100m diameter. They are also described as hanging in the air in front of their mates (Stubbs, F.J., 1909; Brown, R.H., 1924–5; Holyoak, D., 1974). Fig. 49 was drawn from a field sketch of one that I watched hovering in front of its mate.

Allopreening does occur in this species, although rarely, and when it does, only briefly.

49   Magpie: male hovering in front of female

The maintenance activities used by the magpie include frequent bathing, sometimes in shallow pools, sometimes in falling rain, and a magpie has been recorded as bathing in snow, and after bathing preening and oiling the plumage. Magpies also sun-bathe, sometimes half lying on one side with the wing nearest the sun open and raised. Head scratchings, as in other passerines, is indirect. Anting must be regarded as a feather-maintenance activity and in this species only passive anting has been recorded (Simmons, 1966).

After feeding the bill is cleaned by hammering against hard objects and by wiping against the perch.

Goodwin (1952) has recorded captive birds as making a rattling chatter of alarm, of varying loudness and pitch, sometimes with two notes preceding the chatter 'skah skah chá-cha-cha'. The call might be the product of conflict between fear and the impulse to flee, and curiosity or aggressiveness. Another sound produced by captive and wild birds is a harsh two syllabled 'shrak-ak' repeated at intervals but not as a chatter; captive birds gave this call when ill at ease, for example in a new cage. The juvenile begging call, which follows the clamour of nestlings as they grow up, is also used by the female in food begging from the male and as a greeting between paired birds, and during allopreening. It is well rendered as a two-syllable 'cheeuck' and can often be heard from wild birds (Goodwin, 1952; Holyoak, 1974).

A sudden explosive 'tchuck', together with 'aggressive wing and tail flirting' in captives, accompanies aggressive display and may precede attack. It is often heard at spring gatherings and in territorial advertisement (Goodwin, 1952; Holyoak, 1974).

Some calls are not often heard from wild birds – for example a loud hoarse screech, when a captive is handled; and there is also a protest note given by a juvenile threatened by an adult, or by a captive pushed away by its owner, and this context suggests that the rather quiet 'tsaree' note, fading away, is submissive. There is a prolonged (up to half a minute without intermission), hoarse throaty call used by captive females at the nest site. This may be used to call the mate to the nest site and stimulate him in nest building (Goodwin, 1952).

There are various low-pitched notes between paired birds at the nest and Holyoak also recorded a possible example of singing at the nest (1967[1]). Captive magpies are good mimics but no copied note has been heard from a wild magpie.

Individual distance appears to be greater in magpies than in *Corvus* species, and rather greater than in the jay. Fighting, which occurs rarely, might be due to this or over territory. It is sometimes very savage. I have seen two magpies, which started their fight about 9m up in a tree, fall to the ground locked together and continue fighting there. This incidentally provoked a mobbing reaction from jackdaws and carrion crows similar to that which occurs when a member of their own species is held by a predator.

TERRITORY

Magpie territory has not been studied intensively but the nearest nests in the Tring area were 108m apart (Holyoak, 1974), much the same distance as between two nests in my own garden.

Nests were about 82m apart in Leicestershire (Holyoak, 1974). In Leicestershire farmland, 195 ha (480 acres) held five breeding pairs and ten non-breeding in 1966; 247 ha (610 acres) of Isle of Man moorland held two breeding pairs and six non-breeding birds in 1967; 287 ha (710 acres) of farmland near Tring held seven breeding pairs and 14 non-breeding birds; while in 1968 there were nine breeding pairs and 16 non-breeders in an area of 1040 ha (2570 acres) of farm and parkland near Tring. In these instances there was an area of 10 ha per bird in pure farmland, 24 ha per bird in moorland, 30 ha per bird in mixed farm and parkland (Holyoak, 1974). This data can do no more than give an indication of the size of territory because the role of non-breeders and the area they occupy are not known. Intruders and predators are mobbed by both territory-holding breeders and by non-breeders. Among intruders, non-breeders are much more easily driven away than are neighbouring-territory holders.

Territory is advertised by the plumage, and in late winter and early spring magpies can often be seen perched on high points. In my garden they use the tops of *Pinus radiata*, and they are made very conspicuous especially in sunlight by the fluffing of the white areas and the sleeking of the black. 'Tchuck' calls, self-advertising postures, and occasional chases presumably help to indicate the territorial boundaries.

In the breeding season, between a quarter and a third of non-breeding birds were paired in the Isle of Man, some holding territories without suitable nest sites, but in Leicestershire and at Tring some non-breeding territories contained old nests and so, presumably, suitable nest sites. The failure to breed might be due to partial sexual development of one or other of the pair – perhaps a young bird hatched the previous year, as is sometimes the case with rooks, or as in crow failure to secure a territory.

Territory-holding magpies show no resentment towards spring gatherings within the territory and this may be similar to the change in the resident pair's defence when flocks of carrion crows are at pre-roost assemblies within a territory.

PAIR FORMATION

Pair formation very probably takes place at the spring gathering. There are many unpaired magpies in all months of the year and in late winter the proportion may be 40 per cent. In many cases, pairing by young birds may not take place until they are 17–22 months and, once formed, the pair bond presumably continues until one or other of the pair dies. They can be seen in pairs throughout the year but, if one dies, the remaining bird will usually obtain a new mate. Many of the replacements may be yearling birds, some birds of this age being capable of breeding.

NEST AND NEST BUILDING

Some nests are started as early as January (Goodwin, personal communication), but many not until April, with nest building taking about three weeks (Brown, 1924). The sites chosen vary with the terrain and the availability of trees. Scots fir, larch, hawthorn, oak, ash, sycamore and alder are all used and on the slopes above Cornish cliffs nests in blackthorn thickets are quite common. Occasional nests are built on the ground (Felton, 1969) and have been recorded in such unusual and unlikely places as a ledge on a quarry rock face, and 12m up a quarry crane still in use (Fairhurst, 1970).

The frequency with which various species of tree were selected in Finland was recorded by von Haartmann (1969) and is indicated by the following figures (the choice to a great extent reflects availability):

Spruce	232	Cembran pine	
Pine	123	Birch	
Bird cherry	7	Mountain ash	} 1
Willow	6	Juniper	
Alder	3	A pile of fallen branches	

Nests are often built on old nests and if this continues for a number of years an enormous structure can result. One that I knew was built in a rhododendron in Snowdonia and after several years use there was an oblique pile of sticks more than 1·8m deep.

Both sexes take a share in building this structure – a cup of sticks and earth, lined with more earth and a final lining of fibrous roots – the finest towards the centre for the eggs to lie on. The dome is generally made of thorny sticks and the small branches of the nest tree are entwined with it, one opening is usual but there are sometimes two. There are individual variations in materials and structure, with the most eccentric I have heard of being a nest built entirely of wire (Burton, 1971). Instead of the usual fine roots, the lining can be made of horsehair, binder twine, oak leaves and sometimes bits of paper may be added. The dome may occasionally be omitted altogether; it is a defence against predators, especially carrion crows.

If the nest is destroyed and the eggs taken, a second nest is often built. The replacement is soon made, and a new nest with full clutch of eggs may be found three and a half to four weeks after destruction of the first clutch (Brown, 1924). After destruction of a second nest or clutch there is no replacement, and the second nest is usually less well built than the first.

EGGS TO FLEDGING OF YOUNG

There is, as in most species, a geographical variation in the time of laying. There are records in England of full clutches from before the end of March to as late as the end of May, but most common is the third and fourth week in April. A similar range of dates appears to prevail in Finland (von Haartmann, 1969).

Although the eggs are normally laid daily, there is sometimes a two- or three-day interval. They are covered by the female at night. Full incubation starts with the fourth or fifth egg, so that with a small clutch of three or four it begins with the last (Brown, 1924). The estimation of the incubation period requires close observation and has been given as 17–18 days by Brown (1924) and as an average of 22·3 days between the extremes of 18 and 23 by Holyoak (1967[2]).

The eggs range in colour from pale blue or greenish blue to yellowish green and are densely mottled and spotted with brown and ash grey. The average size of 100 British eggs was given by Witherby (1938) as 34·1 × 24·2mm.

Magpies sometimes lay quite large clutches – up to eight – and the average of 179 samples was 5·6, and within the geographical range of England there is little difference in clutch size. Nor is there any great difference as a result of the altitude: clutches of 5·7 are the average for 0–150m and 5·4 from 150–300m. Clutches laid late in the season tend to be smaller (Holyoak, 1967[2]). Some clutches are total failures, resulting from accidents to the nest or the parent magpies, or nest robbing by predators. Excluding these total failures, the mean success rate is 83 per cent. Unhatched eggs often disappear after the rest of the clutch has been hatched for a few days but after the young are 12 days' old this rarely happens. Carrion crows, rooks, magpies and jays are said to eat their own unhatched eggs (Holyoak, 1967[2]; Goodwin, 1976). Some dead nestlings are also probably eaten, while large ones are removed. A very high proportion of failures are caused by man, especially perhaps when disturbance drives away the adults, allowing predators free access to the nest. There is a very high rate of failure in undomed nests.

The young are blind until seven or eight days and are brooded during the day until ten or eleven days, being fed by both parents. For the first ten days the male collects the food, usually within a half mile of the nest, carrying it in his throat pouch and feeding both female and young. The female also feeds the young with some of the food he has given her. When the young grow larger and are no longer brooded by day, the female joins the male in foraging.

The young are fledged and leave the nest at 21–30 days (Brown, 1924). Their tails are very short, their flight weak and for the first few days they remain inconspicuous among the foliage. Family parties remain together until the end of July or August.

Colonel Ryves recorded a case in Cornwall in which seven young magpies were with their parents on 12 November 1929 – they had evidently only just left their nest. Physiologically this is probably not a case of late breeding in 1929 but rather of premature breeding in what would in normal circumstances have been the spring of 1930. It is unusual for autumn breeding to be successful (see p. 79).

FLOCKING AND ROOSTING

Magpies become partially gregarious in the autumn and this continues during the winter, when there is a degree of communal roosting. 'Flocks' are usually parties of fewer than 20, but communal roosts may contain far more than this number. Roosts are often in the same group of trees as other 'crows' – ravens, carrion crows, rooks and jackdaws. Communal roosting continues until late March or April, breaking up when nesting starts in earnest. While small foraging flocks are in existence some birds continue as pairs and in some areas pairs may be found roosting together rather than in any communal roost. If two or three pairs in an area are robbed they may flock together until they start re-nesting.

FOOD

Magpies are mainly ground feeders, far more so than are jays. They favour places near to trees, either rides in woodlands, woodland edges or in fields close to the tree or shrub cover. In woodlands near Oxford, their foraging tended to start at the edge of the wood and work outwards towards the middle of the field (Owen, 1956). They used a wide variety of invertebrate food, but caterpillars especially, of *Tortrix* spp., were picked up from the ground under broad-leaved trees; they took large numbers of Coleoptera (*Carabidae* and *Elaetaridae*) and Diptera (*Empis tesselata* and *Sarcophaga* spp.) – both larvae and newly emerged adults. They also took woodlice (*Isopoda*) and earthworms (*Lumbricus* spp.) (Owen, 1956). They will take wasp larvae from the nests (Birkhead, 1973[1]). Grain, fruit, acorns, chestnuts, small mammals, small birds and their eggs and carrion all form part of the diet. Grain is the most important vegetable food.

The magpie's predatory activities are very varied. For example, they rob the nests of cattle egrets and purple herons in Spain (Mountfort, 1958) and are frequent predators of wood pigeons' and many other eggs of small birds in this country. At a roost of tree sparrows south of Zaragoza in Spain, 60 magpies made repeated dives into a reed-bed roost trying to capture the tree sparrows (Rolfe, 1965). There are reports of magpies killing and eating larger prey such as a song thrush (Boog, 1966), a female starling (Butlin, 1971), snakes (Mountfort, 1958; Carr, 1969) and there is circumstantial evidence of their having killed a full-grown rabbit during snowy weather (Thompson, 1925–6).

Like other crows, magpies are food storers, but they are far less dependent on their stores than jays or nutcrackers. Animal food may be hidden and stored – the female starling mentioned above was well hidden in long grass (Butlin, 1971) – but vegetable food, such as walnuts and chestnuts, are also stored (Boev, 1958; Toleshkov and his colleagues, 1960; Turcek and Kelso, 1961). Like jackdaws, magpies are surface feeders but feed in longer vegetation than the former do. They pick food off the surface, turn over the ground with the bill, occasionally scratching aside with the feet also (Holyoak, 1974). Grain is obtained by deeper probing and some insects are caught by jumping. Small food items which can be swallowed quickly are usually eaten on the spot, those carried away and hidden are the larger ones, whose possession might be disputed by another bird (Henty, 1965).

PREDATORS AND PARASITES

In a few areas in Spain magpies are preyed upon by Spanish imperial eagles and no doubt by other raptors in other countries where these still survive in any numbers. In southern Spain the magpie is the main subject of brood parasitism by the great spotted cuckoo, which I shall treat in a separate chapter.

As with other crows, abnormal skull and bill development occurs in magpies (Birkhead, 1973[2]) and abnormalities of pigmentation are not rare; they range from shades of brown, grey and cream to full albinism (Harrison, 1963).

11
Azure-winged magpie
(*Cyanopica cyana cooki*)

European names

Dutch – BLAUWVLEUGELEKATER Spanish – RABILARGO
French – PIE-BLEUE A CALLOTE NOIRE Swedish – BLASKATA
German – BLAUELSTER

FIELD CHARACTERISTICS

The azure-winged magpie is unmistakable. It is smaller and more slender than the magpie (*Pica*), its general colour is more reminiscent of a jay, but the body colour is browner, less pink and paler than a jay. In the field the whole of the wings and tail appear as a slightly greyish light blue. The black of the upper part of the head contrasts very sharply with the creamy white of the throat. Its movements are magpie-like with frequent tail flicking and its usual method of progress on the ground is hopping.

DESCRIPTION (Plate IV)

The sexes are alike and the summer and winter plumage are the same. The head is glossy black above a line running from below the bill and passing below the eye and there is a slight crest. The upper parts are greyish brown, browner than a jay but with a hint of the jay's pinkish shade. The under parts are similar but paler and the throat is creamy white, contrasting with the black of the head. The wings and tail, which often look blue grey at a distance, are a very beautiful hyacinth blue, brightest on the primaries and secondaries. The distal part of the outer webs of the outer seven primaries is partly white. The tail feathers in the European race have narrow white tips, and the white tips are much larger in the eastern Asiatic race. The bill and legs are black and the iris dark brown.

The nestling has a pale scanty down, a bright pink mouth lining and pink edges to the gape. In the juvenile the blue areas are less bright than in the adult and the remaining plumage is browner, most of the feathers having narrow buff tips.

DISTRIBUTION

The world distribution of the species is very unusual as it is found in the Iberian Peninsula in Europe and in temperate eastern Asia, including Japan. There are now no populations in the intervening space, and although it is thought that the distribution may at one time have been continuous, there is no definite evidence for this. The species has no close relatives. There seems to be no historical evidence for the theory that it was introduced into Spain or Portugal by a traveller returning from the Far East in ancient times, attractively romantic though the theory may be. In its European range in Spain and Portugal it is rather local with a possible increase in density in the southern and western two-thirds of the peninsula. It frequents woodlands and open country with trees, but not at high altitude.

POSTURE AND VOICE

Although there seems to be no account of its behaviour in the wild state, Goodwin (1976) has described some of the postures of the Asiatic race in captivity.

The birds used a tilting display, like that of the magpie, a self-assertive display in a threatening context. The tail was partly spread on both sides and not only on the side nearest to the threatened object as in *Pica*. The folded wings were slightly lifted and fluttered, with the far wing more raised than the near one. A male hopped round his mate after feeding her, with head a little lowered and the head feathers not erected, wings partly opened and fluttering, and tail only slightly tilted towards her (fig. 50). This may have been a sexual version of a tilting display.

The male may erect the conspicuous black head feathers, sometimes done when a male approached his mate, often, but not always, when feeding her.

Only a few sounds produced by wild birds of the European race have been described. The call most often heard was described by Mountfort (1958) as a

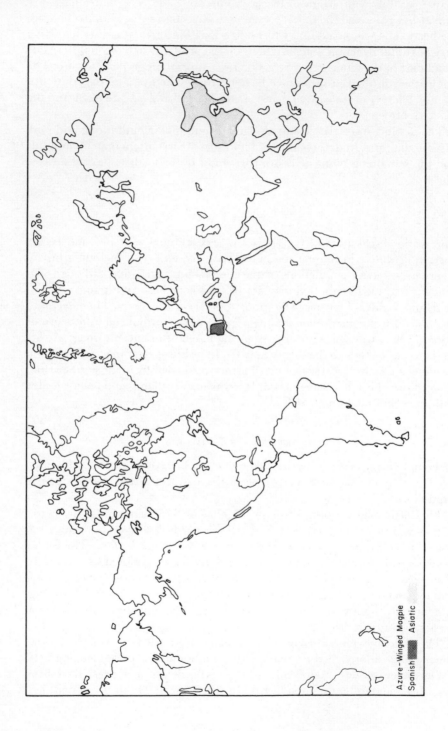

Azure-Winged Magpie

Spanish ▨

Asiatic ░

50 Azure-winged magpie: tilting display of male to female. Compare figs 1, 16, 24, 37, 47

hoarse, high-pitched 'zhree'. The bands of azure-winged magpies were noisy, calling to one another as they went, and this call may be a contact note. Three alarm notes were given by birds whose nest was approached, a lower version of the call note just described, a high-pitched urgent squeak phonetically rendered as 'guer', and a harsh 'churring' like a missel thrush.

ANTING

The captive bird of the Asiatic race observed by Goodwin applied the ants to the underside of its primaries, and then, instead of discarding each ant as it had been applied, it collected more until it had a small bundle of ants in its bill. The same wing movements as a jay were used.

NEST BUILDING, EGGS, INCUBATION AND YOUNG

Nests are built 2·74 to 4·86m (9 to 16ft) up, usually in trees with plenty of foliage: stone pine (*P. pinea*), ash (*Fraxinus*), cork (*Quercus suber*) and orange trees (*Citrus aurantium*) and more recently in eucalyptus. This is a somewhat gregarious species and colonies of as many as 150 birds have been described. In winter they remain gregarious and use communal roosts (Dos Santos, 1968).

Nesting begins towards the end of April or early May and the nest is built with an outer layer of thick plant stems, small sticks and rootlets; in some nests this outer layer is made up mainly of twigs such as those of the stone pine. The bottom contains most of the rootlets and sometimes earth or clay; the nest cup is formed of freshly picked plant stalks, lined with tightly packed hair and wool (Kulczycki, 1973).

EGGS TO FLEDGING OF YOUNG

The eggs, usually six or seven in number, but quite frequently up to ten or eleven are buff in ground colour, densely marked at the large end and less so all over, with ash grey and a few dark spots. Their average size is 27·9 by 20·6mm (dos Santos, 1968). Incubation is by the female, who is fed at the nest by the male. The duration of incubation for the Asiatic form in captivity was 15 days (Porter, 1941). The young are brooded at first and both female and young are fed by the male. Later, as the young develop feathers and become more active, they are covered less by the female, and as they come to require more food both parents take part in feeding. At a nest observed by Mountfort, small young were fed 12 times in an hour, by regurgitation.

The Iberian range of the azure-winged magpie comes within that of the great spotted cuckoo, and it is one of the species on which this cuckoo is said to be a brood parasite (p. 208), although apparently much less often than the common magpie.

FOOD

Parties of azure-winged magpies may be seen picking over the ground and around fresh animal droppings. They feed on beetles and other insects, perhaps small lizards, eggs and young of small birds and carrion, and some fruits and seeds, acorns and olives. Some food may be stored (Valverdi in Turcek, 1966).

PREDATORS

The azure-winged magpie is itself amongst the prey species of the Spanish imperial eagle *Aquila heliaca* (Mountfort), and no doubt other avian and animal predators too. Some nests, for instance, are robbed by carrion crows.

1 *Raven by nest* Keri Williams

4   *Rook*   C.J.F. Coombs

2   *Carrion crow (opposite, above)*   C.J.F. Coombs
3   *Male hooded crow feeding female on nest (opposite, below)*   Bryan L. Sage

5 *Jackdaw at nest in disused mine shaft* C.J.F. Coombs
6 *Alpine chough at Furst, nr. Grindlwald, Switzerland (opposite, above)* Richard Vaughan
7 *Red-billed chough, on Islay (opposite, below)* Rodney Dawson

8 *Jay (opposite, above)*   J.B. & S. Bottomley
9 *Siberian jay (opposite, below)*   Arne Blomgren
10 *Greater spotted cuckoo (left)*
J.B. & S. Bottomley
11 *Nutcracker (below)*   P.O. Swanberg

12 *Azure-winged magpie*
R.G. Carlson
13 *Magpie*
C.J.F. Coombs

12
Jay
(Garrulus glandarius)

FIELD CHARACTERISTICS

Jays are most often seen flying away from the observer, when the white rump, contrasting black tail and the black and white secondaries are particularly conspicuous. This species, and the Siberian jay, are the most arboreal of the European crows. The jay moves in trees by jumping from branch to branch, often only just opening its wings; on the ground it usually hops. The flight among trees is quick and agile but across open spaces it appears weak and slow, with an intermittent flapping action. The longish tail and short, round wings are noticeable. Its loud harsh screech, the reason for some of its local names, is familiar to most people, while the much quieter, buzzard-like mew – often uttered from the depths of a thicket – is much less so, although very characteristic of the bird.

DESCRIPTION

The pattern and colour of the jay's plumage is shown in Plate II and so I shall. mention here only details which are not easily seen. Faint blue-grey barring is present on most of the pinkish-brown feathers of the upper parts, and this gives the appearance of a bloom on these areas. This is very marked on the nape, where the feathers are elongated like those of the crown to form the crest. Here the pinkish brown has an almost purple shade in some birds and the 'bloom' is very marked. The blue-grey cross banding is most easily seen on the pinkish-chestnut lesser and median coverts. The black-blue white barring on some of the outer greater coverts, primary coverts and alula is repeated on covered areas at the base of some of the primaries and secondaries. All the primaries are dark grey-brown with off-white outer webs, except the first. This is black. The innermost secondary is a rich chestnut with a black tip. The inner greater coverts are black and are conspicuously placed against the white part of the secondaries during many displays. The iris is light blue with a narrow, brown outer ring and a very narrow brown inner ring where the iris meets the pupil.

Jays with a darker, redder, shade on all the pinkish-brown areas were at one time given subspecific status as the Irish jay. The lighter, greyer birds from the more easterly parts of the range, at one time termed continental jays, have all the pinkish-brown areas paler and greyer.

Nestlings, described by Goodwin – who has reared them in captivity – have no down. The mouth is pale pink inside without spots and externally the gape flanges are pinkish white. The juveniles are like the adult but the body colour is less pink and more rufous. The bill is grey, the mouth usually bright red or mauve-pink and dark grey areas form and coalesce. A young bird bred in captivity and examined at 49 and 56 days and again at 7 months showed increasing blackening of the inside of the mouth. By 7 months it was entirely greyish black, except for the upper part of the gullet and a few small areas. These were pink.

Moult

The juvenile moults its body feathers and lesser coverts in its first autumn; it retains the primaries, secondaries, primary coverts, greater coverts, and alula, and tail feathers until its second moult the following summer. The retained feathers become faded and abraded but this cannot normally be distinguished in the field. The adult jay's moult period averages 102 days, with the earliest starting birds beginning in April and the latest to finish may end the moult in early October (Holyoak, 1974).

Plumage type and distribution (Plate II)

Hartert in 1907 noticed the 'more uniform vinous' colour and minimum of greyish wash on the back of British jays, apparent when a series of skins was examined. Three years later Witherby and Hartert together drew attention to the warmer colour of Irish jays and quoted Edward Williams in 1885 as having given the first description of these differences (Hartert, 1907–8; Witherby and Hartert, 1910–11).

In the *Handbook of British Birds*, published in 1938, the introductory section to *Garrulus glandarius* contains the following on the genus *Garrulus* 'Five or six species, only one European one, *G. glandarius*, in many different sub species'. Separate sections are given to the continental jay, no. 10, the British jay, no. 11, and the Irish jay, no. 12. The description of the plumage of each of these birds is given and attention drawn to the differences. In the following year Sir Julian Huxley (1939) suggested the use of the word cline for geographical variation in which gradation is measurable. In 1954, Professor H.K. Voous presented a paper to the British Ornithologists' Club on clines and their significance in zoological studies. There he pointed out that the colour of the pinkish plumage of the upper and under parts of the jay depends on the relative as well as the absolute quantities of two pigments: eumelanin and phaeomelanin. This causes a great range of colour variation from grey to reddish brown and from dark to light; birds with the different plumage type occur in all populations. The proportions of these pigments and resulting colouration may be only a biproduct of some gene combination which had survival value for some quite different reason and which evolved under environmental influence (Voous, 1954).

DISTRIBUTION

It is a species found only in the old world, inhabiting woodlands wherever there are oak trees and its range extends from Ireland and the Atlantic coast of Spain and Morocco in the west, through North Africa to the Middle East as far as the western shores of the Caspian Sea. It is found in the whole of Europe, except for the west coast of Ireland, north of Scotland and north-west Scandinavia. Here the jay reaches to about 67°N and it extends across Siberia and central Asia, north of the central mountainous area and south of 60° latitude. In eastern Asia it reaches to Sakhalin and the Japanese islands, and south into Indo-China and Taiwan. The systematic status of the jay has gone through various degrees of 'splitting' and 'lumping' and views about jay 'migration' have also changed since the first recognition of birds from the continent in 1910 (Ticehurst, 1910–11). There have been many records of 'continental'

jays in England, mostly east and south (Riviere, 1919; Curtis Edwards, 1919; Gurney, 1918; Harrison, 1935–6). The continental jay is described as a migrant in Great Britain in the *Handbook of British Birds* (Witherby, 1938), while the nutcracker is described as a vagrant. The invasive movements of both species are probably of the same kind, arising when the food supply is inadequate for the number of birds present. In both species these invasions are perhaps more truly emigration from their own area, occurring in the autumn at a time when a food crop on which each specializes is normally collected and stored – acorns for the jay and the seeds of *Pinus siberica* and hazel nuts for the nutcracker.

Invasion movements by jays are widespread in Western Europe. Writing from Cognac, about 80 miles north of Bordeaux and 50 miles east of the Atlantic coast, Delmain (1935) described the autumn movements of jays in south-west France. The first movements of a few birds occurred on 25 September, on 8 October there was a 'rush' of jays, and on the 9th the woods were swarming with them, feeding on acorns and chestnuts. The movement decreased in the next three days and had ended by 15 October. Most flew at 50–100m and in small groups of up to a dozen or so. That was described as an exceptional year.

There was an invasion of south-east England in the autumn of 1957, with 600–1000 jays recorded in Essex on 21 September (Cramp, Pettit and Sharrock, 1960).

Normally jays probably move only short distances and even young birds, ringed as nestlings and juveniles, are usually recovered near their birth place; records of only four recoveries at more than 20 miles were found by Holyoak (1971).

When England was covered in deciduous woodland, and oak was a predominant species throughout the country, jays were probably very numerous and widespread. There had been a general decrease, most marked in the north of England and Scotland and in areas of intensive game preservation up to the 1914–18 war, when a general increase began. The reduction in gamekeeping during the war must have contributed to that increase, but I remember seeing jays hanging in bundles with crows, magpies, sparrowhawks and barn and tawny owls on a barn door near Exford on Exmoor in 1916.

The increase which started in those years has continued, possibly accelerated during the 1939–45 war. The species is still absent from the Isle of Man, the extreme west and north of Ireland, and some parts of southern Scotland, but otherwise is evenly distributed as far north as Argyll, Perth and Kincardineshire. New conifer plantations in Scotland have favoured its spread, but the normally limited range of movement of jays from their birth place probably makes this a slow process. It has increased westwards in Cornwall and Pembrokeshire and in many suburban areas (Parslow, 1967). The distribution and increase of the jay in the London area has been particularly well documented (Wallace, 1974; Simms, 1962; Cramp and Tomlin, 1966). First breeding was in the garden of Holland House in 1929, followed by a pair in Kensington Gardens in 1950. Many other London parks are now inhabited by jays, whose adaptability has led to colonization of suburban gardens in a number of towns.

The most detailed studies on the behaviour of the jay are those made by Goodwin – especially on captive jays nesting and rearing young in his aviaries – and with reference to wild jays too (Goodwin, 1952[2], 1956).

Wing and tail flick

Flight-intention movements are shown in the wing and tail flick, which jays share with many other species. The jay gives a quick down flick, the tail and wings are lifted, the tail is partly spread (fig. 51), then closed and then wings

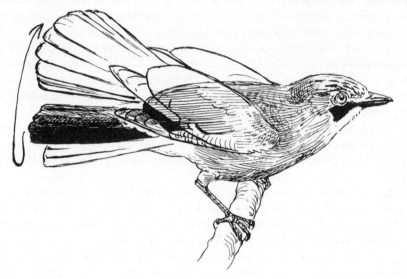

51　Jay: wing and tail flick. Compare figs 20, 21, 41, 46

and tail drop back to normal. This action is modified at times of serious alarm. In mobbing a predator, for example, the head and body swing down and sideways with a flick of the tail and flexing of the legs at the same time (fig. 52), the body feathers are compressed and the crest is erect and the alarm note may accompany this gesture. Goodwin (1956) suggested that this may be an intention movement for downward flight.

These actions occurring in agonistic and sexual situations are influenced by the fact that jays are not colonial species and individual distance, even between members of a pair, remains important always. Adults keep apart, pairs roosting about 1m apart and showing either aggressiveness or appeasement, according

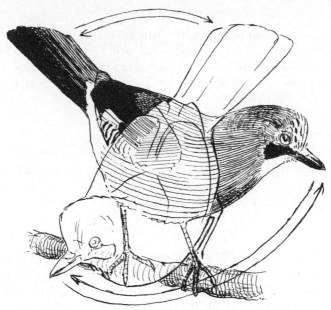

52   Jay: serious alarm

53   Jay: head forward threat with crest raised. Compare figs 16, 29, 37ᵇ, 44

to circumstances, if this distance is reduced. This is unlike the behaviour pattern of rooks and jackdaws, which roost almost in contact with each other. Young jays roost in contact, but individual distance becomes important from about the time that they become completely independent of their parents.

Bill snapping

The threat gestures used by jays include the generally effective bill snapping, with head stretched towards the threatened bird. If this is not effective, there may be an actual attack or, if this is thwarted or inhibited, a defensive element is introduced and the crest is raised (fig. 53) with perhaps partial raising or fluffing of other body plumage.

Defensive posture

In a fully defensive posture most of the contour feathers are raised and the wings are uncovered by the body feathers and may be partially spread or drooped (at very high intensity, fully spread). The tail is slightly spread and the bill open. In high-intensity threat the jay faces the enemy.

The defensive threat

Defensive threat appears to be a conflict posture when the urge to attack and to escape are both aroused, for example when a threat to another jay proves ineffectual and the 'enemy' stands his ground, or in dealing with a predator at the nest. In mobbing a predator the jay moves about all the time, taking up new positions, while in defensive threat it faces the enemy from one position.

Lateral display

54   *Jay: lateral display. Compare fig 13*

In the lateral display, the bird is broadside on to its 'enemy', although there are some similarities to the previous posture. The body feathers are raised and the tail lowered, making the shape of the lower back and rump very 'humped' and conspicuous. The fluffing of the abdominal feathers partly hides the legs and feet and the general effect is to make the jay look bigger. The crests may be raised, perhaps when there is a conflict of drive between attack and escape, as in other circumstances the crest may be flat. The posture may be accompanied in the female by clicking notes. This display occurs most commonly in late winter, spring and early autumn (the times of maximum physiological sexual activity) but can continue at any time. It is used by the male towards the female in the early stages of the breeding cycle, when the problems of individual distance have to be overcome, and it occasionally ends in copulation. This is a self-assertive display common to either sex. A female displaying may not be lateral to the bird 'displayed' to, and may switch suddenly from self-assertion to submission. Indeed, either male or female can show lateral display and submissive posture within a few moments of each other. Goodwin suggests that this may be derived from intention movements for copulation. Certainly the necessary physiological condition is present in both spring and autumn. Finally, there is also an element of conflict in approaching another jay closely: the urge to approach and also the fear of reprisal.

Chin-up display

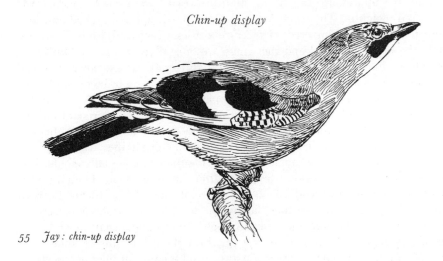

55   *Jay: chin-up display*

The chin-up display is not well developed in the jay but is much clearer in use and form in the lanceolated jay (*G. lanceolatus*), which crouches with fluffed-out belly plumage, the head held up at right angles to the body and the bill pointing almost vertically. It makes chirruping notes and faces towards the object of its display, presenting the throat, the feathers of which are flattened down, making it conspicuously white. In the jay the bill is only a little above the horizontal so that, although the throat feathers are flattened, they are much less conspicuous. The female responds to the male's lateral display with her own lateral display or, less often, the submissive display but sometimes with the chin up as also when he offers to feed her or to solicit courtship feeding. The male uses it much less often, perhaps when approaching the female or after courtship feeding.

Submissive display

56   Jay: female pre-copulatory display. Compare figs 7, 25, 38, 43

In the submissive display the bird is perched with head, body and tail horizontal, tail and rump if anything slightly raised and the tail is jerked and
quivered violently. The wings are spread, or partly spread, arched and presented frontally and quivered; at lower intensities, which are the most frequent,
only the tail is quivered and the wings are only slightly spread. This is the
female invitation to copulation, but it is also used by jays towards social
superiors and sometimes by paired birds exchanging food or inedible objects.

An action which seems to have a dependent, if not actually submissive
connotation, is juvenile-type food begging, which I think is derived from the
intention to fly towards the parent carrying food. The action is used first by
nestlings not capable of flight, but it continues for as long as they are dependent,
and again later, when the female is about to incubate or is actually incubating.
She is then dependent again, this time on her mate for food. The posture is
accompanied by hunger and food-begging calls and the bird leans forward
with bill open, fluttering wings, facing the food bearer. Courtship feeding,
which may have the function of reinforcing the pair bond, occurs in wild birds
from February onwards, and in captives throughout the entire nesting cycle
and occasionally in late summer and autumn. Of course it may also occur in
wild birds throughout this long period, but does not seem to have been
recorded. The male prepares the food by tearing it into small pieces and holds
it in his gullet or at the back of his mouth. He offers it to the female, who takes
it with her bill at right angles to his. Both birds use the appeal note: the male
if the female is at some distance, and the female to solicit feeding. When the
moment to feed her comes, he sometimes proves reluctant to part with the food
and in any case often keeps some and swallows it. The male's approach to the
female is interesting as he usually looks for her in order to offer the food and the
female may be nervous and hesitant. If the offer fails, the male then approaches
from below – a position of disadvantage and the antithesis of aggression.
Sometimes the male will approach giving snatches of song, and sometimes with
low-intensity sexual display; occasionally the female will try a wing flutter

(hunger begging) and Goodwin has proved experimentally that this form of food begging is used by a hungry jay, and I have recorded in the section on rooks how hungry female rooks used the same action.

Early in the spring, before nest building, the female sometimes approaches the male with food in her bill – not concealed in the gullet – and offers it to him with submissive display. If the male receives it, he also gives a submissive display and passes the food back; it may in fact be passed to and fro several times and sometimes an inedible object may be used instead. If the male can find no suitable perching space, he may hover in front of her to make the offer.

Displacement, or thwarted activities include bill wiping, pecking at the perch and tearing at objects with accompanying jerky body and tail movements. Goodwin saw one of his jays hammering a perch or branch with closed bill as do crows and magpies.

Jays, like magpies and some other species, have spring gatherings of three or four birds and occasionally as many as 30. Unlike the lek of black grouse or ruff there is no set time or place for these 'meetings', nor is there any regular duration, birds may come and go and eventually the gathering may come to an end when they all leave in ones and twos. There are frequent lulls in the excitement and not all the birds seem equally involved. Some of the postures described above may be seen, especially perhaps the lateral display, which is probably directed at other jays. On these occasions jays also demonstrate their version of display flight, a slow deliberate action when the wing movement appears to be of greater amplitude than normal and with the wings more widely spread than in ordinary flight. This wing action, which is clearly homologous with that of the other crows, seems to be shown whenever the bird flies while in self-assertive mood, and the plumage may actually be arranged as in the lateral display.

Goodwin (1952[2]) has described the following calls.

A   an appeal note, a cat-like mewing of variable volume. Used in differing contexts it may be used in hunger, in making contact, in offering and soliciting food at the nest site, as a juvenile appeal call (like the fledgling feeding food call), and used by the female with wing fluttering to solicit courtship feeding. It is also used in flight at the spring gatherings and in pursuit flights and by birds looking for a food hiding place and when seeking food for their young.

B   chirruping notes, which express the bird's need to be en rapport with the creature at whom these are directed (another jay or human keeper), with perhaps an appeasing function. The subordinate partner of a pair may give these notes if it is afraid that its mate will drive it from food or perch. There may be chirruping duets given with the chin-up position. They are described as soft, stammering notes interspersed with louder and longer drawn-out calls derived from the appeal note. As each monosyllable is uttered, the body and tail are jerked slightly and the longer note is preceded or followed by gaping.

C   the alarm note, the familiar rasping screech of the jay from which some of·its local names are derived. Usually given a couple of times with a pause before being repeated, this is used in mobbing, or fleeing from, a predator, perhaps when an escape drive is inhibited by aggression or curiosity. There is also another alarm call, termed by Goodwin the hawk alarm note, a low monosyllabic note given when the jay has seen a flying hawk. Between the appeal note and the alarm screech, and intergrading with either, is a grating note used at the moment of attacking or defending and also when quarrelling with other jays.

D   a call used at the spring gatherings, which may have some sexual significance, is a loud and resonant crow-like 'kraah', in captivity uttered most often by unpaired females.

E   a low warbling song, which Goodwin thinks is mostly made up of mimicked sounds. He also suggests that copied sounds may be used when conditions are similar to those present when the jay first heard the sound: for example, birds mobbing a human intruder at the nest may intersperse their own calls with the alarm notes of a blackbird or magpie.

Development of behaviour of young jays

The development of some of the behaviour patterns of young jays hatched and reared in captivity were described by Goodwin (1951). They are blind and naked when hatched and, like other passerines, very weak so that few movements are possible. By nine days, when the feathers in many areas have begun to break through the sheaths, the young jays have begun to preen and stretch and may even show signs of fear. At first, begging for food is accompanied by a faint chirruping noise but within a few days it becomes almost completely silent and remains so until the young birds have left the nest. The food is prepared by the parent and a subdued parental note is a stimulus to begging. If nestlings are really frightened – for example by a predator at the nest – they give an alarm screech not unlike that of the adult.

At 26 days one young bird swallowed a morsel of food which it had picked off another's face. No further attempts at feeding were seen until the 38th day, when the food placed on the perch was picked up. At this stage, the young birds were still inexpert at closing the bill to hold the food and not until they reached 40 days were they seen to place food under the foot to control it while breaking it up with the bill. Feeding, like flying, is an innate behaviour pattern with expertise added by skills acquired by practice. At this stage, about 40 days, the parents, 'worried' by the pestering of the young, tended to put down the food in front of them, and the female did not actually feed them after the 42nd day. They continued to beg from the male for several more days, so thus apparently recognized the male and female as separate individuals. By the 54th day all voluntary parental feeding had stopped and the parents' reaction to begging was aggression. However, the young birds continued to rob their parents for about two more weeks. They were robbed if they were carrying food, or if they put it down to free the bill for threatening the young. The male of this particular pair learned to fly up above the young, striking down at them with his feet, thus managing to hold the food still.

Parental care

The reactions of adult jays are modified before the start of incubation so that from about two weeks before she begins to incubate the male bird brings prepared food for the female. When the young hatch, the insect food provided is broken up into very small particles; harder and larger pieces are discarded. This behaviour change is induced by the sight of the newly hatched young and applies to both the parents. The male brings prepared food in his gullet, feeds it to the female and both feed the young, or he may sometimes refuse food to the female and feed the young direct. The parents use a subdued version of the appeal note to induce the young to gape, and place the bill into the nestling's gullet and eject the food with the tongue. Sometimes there may still be food in the parent's bill when it is withdrawn and this is either given to another nestling or swallowed by the parent.

The adult remains motionless after feeding the young, waiting for the faecal sac, which is taken direct into the bill; the young bird makes no attempt to defaecate over the side of the nest. If the female takes the faecal sac she swallows it, as she may have no opportunity for depositing it away from the nest – at least during the first week after hatching, when she is still brooding the young. The male, on the other hand, drops it at a distance. The nest is kept clean because the adults treat all foreign matter in the same way, whether bits of foliage, drops of water, morsels of food, faeces or dead small young, and the probing of the nest bottom that one sees when watching jays at the nest is thought to be the removal of insect parasites.

After the young have left the nest and are in the branches of nearby thickets, both the parents seek them out to feed them. The adults remember where their young are and return to the right branch to find them. The young do not start moving about and following their parents until the latter begin to tire of feeding them.

Anting

Jays indulge in active anting (Goodwin, 1947; Simmons, 1957–66), running the bill down the inner edge of the primaries and secondaries, without an ant in the bill. At the same time, the wings are spread and pushed forward so that the primaries are touching the ground, and the tail is pressed to the ground and brought forwards, sometimes so far that the bird is sitting on its tail and may actually fall over backwards. Anting takes place less than once in two or three weeks. It is followed by a vigorous water bath; water bathing is in any case frequent, perhaps several times a day, and young birds first bathe in water at 28 days.

TERRITORY

There is surprisingly little firm evidence about the territorial habits of jays. Goodwin (1976) notes that there is circumstantial evidence for acceptance within the territory of certain jays other than the territory-holding pairs who normally defend the area. Food may be obtained both inside and outside the territory, which might in some cases be about an acre in extent. Much more research is required.

NEST SITE AND NEST BUILDING

Nests are often built in the branches of a small tree, sometimes in the peripheral branches of a larger one, or in ivy on the trunk, at a height of from about 1·2m to 18m and nests more than 9m from the ground are often in dense evergreens (Holyoak, 1967). One in my garden in an ilex was about 12m up and was unusual in that it was easily visible from the ground.

Nests have been found in hollow trees (Tutt, 1953; Goodwin, 1953[1]). One was used after the normal nest of the pair in a low bush had been robbed. There have been no records of jays using a nest a second time, when a clutch of eggs has had to be replaced (Holyoak, 1967). Von Haartman's (1969) data on the nest sites of jays in Finland also puts some unusual sites on record, as well as giving the frequency of choice of a number of different species of tree. Nine nests were on buildings, one in a firewood pile, and one 17m up on a rock face. The tree sites were usually low, and 93 were in spruce, 6 in pine, 3 in juniper and 1 in birch.

The selection of a nest site by a captive pair, and the building of their nest, was described in detail by Goodwin (1952). The nest site was probably chosen by the male, who was the less nervous of the two and seemed to take more interest in the site. An exposed wire basket had no attraction for them until concealed with conifer branches. At the start of building, both birds – but especially the female – began to pull at small branches near the perch, and then a day or two later small sticks were actually broken off, held for a moment and then dropped. These actions became more purposeful and synchronized and sticks were actually carried to the nest site. But during the first week there were many visits but very little progress with nest building. Both the birds worked at the nest but the female spent more time at the site and pulled out twigs which hung down or protruded. The male worked more at the stick collecting and building than the female, the female more on the lining.

They worked independently of each other, as do wild jays. If one was working at the nest and the other arrived the first usually left and they often approached and departed with a short display glide. If they were disturbed when carrying nest material, they dropped it while their attention was on the disturbance. Nest building was interrupted in cold weather, and a cold spell on 25 April with sleet and hail and 6in of snow on the 26th delayed their work for a few days and it was not resumed until the 29th, with the first egg being laid on 2 May.

With this species, as with other corvines, the time in which a nest can be built can be very variable and Swanberg recorded a nest in Sweden built in 5–6 days (Swanberg, quoted by von Haartman, 1969).

EGGS, INCUBATION AND HATCHING

The eggs are pale olive to blue-green, finely speckled and spotted with darker olive, buff and grey-green. Their average size (British specimens) is 31·7 × 22·8mm.

Holyoak has presented data of the jay's nesting period, much of the material summarized from the British Trust for Ornithology nest record cards. The mean clutch size was 4·5 eggs and there was little variation between areas from the south coast to the north of England or westwards into Wales. The range of clutch size was from 3 to 6 in a sample of 124 nests. In Finland, a series of 35 nests showed a range of from 4 to 9, with a mean figure of 6 (von Haartman, 1969).

A captive pair of jays laid their first egg between 7 and 7.40 pm on 21 April 1948 and the next four at daily intervals; the nest and its contents were covered from dawn on 21 April, before the first egg was laid, but true incubation did not begin until the laying of the third egg (Goodwin, 1948). At another nest, in which six eggs were laid, incubation began with the sixth egg, the first having been laid on 14 May, and the sixth before 10 am on 20 May. There is a wide range of laying dates, as shown by the nest record cards, wider than for other corvids: from about 10 April to the end of the first week of June, but the majority were in the period from about 20 April until about 30 May. Clutches laid much later than this are probably replacements of earlier failures.

Incubation time must be taken as full incubation, that is to say from the laying of the last egg. It is given as 16 days (Hosking, 1942; Holyoak, 1967). Incubation is by the female only, although there is one possible record of a male incubating (Niethammer, quoted by von Haartman, 1969). The female is fed on the nest by the male, leaving it only briefly for exercise, water and defaecation, usually at the time when the male has fed her, and he is therefore at the nest. Jays sometimes sit very closely, especially towards the time of hatching, and may almost be touching before leaving. However, especially in the early days of incubation, they may desert if disturbed, and it is difficult to assess the effect of the observer on desertion, as a factor in the total failure of some broods. Unhatched eggs may be eaten by the parents and, as with other crows, small but not large dead young are removed from the nest. The success rate for hatching improves as leaf cover thickens and is therefore better later in the season (Holyoak, 1967). The improvement of cover and the effects of disturbance are, of course, interconnected factors as nests are far more vulnerable to predators when ill concealed or unprotected by the parent birds.

FOOD

Although the jay is an adaptable and a rather opportunist feeder, the part of its diet made up of acorns is specialized and very important. It is important for both the jay and the oak trees and, if oak trees are important to man, the jay is important to man also. The jay's range is the same as that of various species of oak, so it may well be the greatest natural distributor and planter of oaks. Jays have a specially enlarged oesophagus to enable them to carry acorns, beech mast or hazel nuts to their chosen point of concealment and a very liberal supply of saliva to make it easier to regurgitate dry food into the concealment site (Turcek and Kelso, 1968).

Their exploitation of the acorn harvest is of course an autumn activity. Chettleburgh (1952) recorded that in southern England this started on 8 September, when only eight birds were seen to be involved, and this number increased at the end of September, until there were 35 to 40 active by mid-October. After 20 October the number of birds decreased and the acorn collecting had ended by 16 November, when all the supplies had been exhausted. At the start, when only a few birds were engaged, they worked from about 9 until 12 GMT but at the peak this had become a ten-hour day. Then each bird's flight, collecting, bringing and returning took about ten minutes, this peak period lasting for about ten days. It is easy to see that the number of acorns planted becomes very large, for this rate of work by jays means that 35 birds will make 21,000 flights in the ten days and, if the average load is assumed to be as low as only three at a time, this means the planting of 63,000 acorns in ten days (Chettleburgh, 1952). Schuster (1950) calculated that 65 jays would plant 200,000 acorns in one month.

The number of acorns carried per flight is from 1 to 9 for as far as 1200m or, in a few cases, 4 or 5km (Turcek and Kelso, 1968; Bossema, 1968; Schuster, 1950).

When eating an acorn, the jay holds it against the perch with both feet, the two innermost toes on each foot holding the acorn and the outer toes holding the perch, with constant changes of position and angle. The jay does not hammer the acorn but breaks away bits of shell with its bill and levers them off until an opening has been made. The acorn is rotated to make this easier, and some of the pieces wrenched off are swallowed (Goodwin, 1952[2]).

In the autumn, jays, as well as wood pigeons and in some places rooks and ravens, rapidly use up the supply of acorns, so the jays must store them, and most effectively in damp ground. These may germinate by the spring and give young plants of several inches height by June. The cotyledons of these seedlings are still in good condition. They are like fresh autumn ones and remain thus until the end of the summer, when the new crop will be available. Acorns are used by jays for feeding their young in June and consumption by adults and young is at a rate comparable with that in the autumn. When retrieving acorns in the summer, jays appear to select green-stemmed seedlings to pull up. The seedlings of a previous year with brown stems are ignored, as are seedlings of other species. The acorns are given to the older young and only very rarely to small nestlings (Bossema, 1968).

The hiding of the acorns and hazel nuts and beech mast – these are also used – probably varies from place to place. In the Hainault Forest, Chettleburgh (1952) found that the most favoured place was under a thin covering of dead leaves, or pushed under roots of brambles. Occasionally a hole was dug, but natural holes were preferred. One acorn was put in each hole and the site was never far from a cover of bushes or trees.

In eastern Europe Turcek and Kelso (1968) described jays as carrying up to 9 acorns or 15 beech 'nuts', and hiding them 2 to 8 at a time in the mossy litter in light timber stands and forest edges.

When collecting the acorns, a jay sometimes shows aggression towards another jay by dropping on to its back and thus displacing it, but as a rule, when burying the store, there is little aggressiveness towards jays or other species. Occasionally they will remove an acorn to a new site almost as soon as it has been buried or when retrieving acorns for food, an occasional one will be reburied.

Apart from the ability to identify the current year's supply of stored acorns by the appearance of the seedlings growing from them, jays appear to have an accurate memory of where they have placed their treasure. These actions appear deliberate and they go straight to the spot, dig it up and fly away. Recovering acorns begins about one week after storing of them has ceased (Chettleburgh, 1952). In winter jays retrieve their acorns individually – one bird at a time, not in groups as when they are storing them, and far more will be retrieved on one day than another. Like nutcrackers, they can dig straight down through snow to a buried nut. For example, peanuts from the bird table, buried when the ground was clear, were recovered accurately ten days later when it was covered by snow (Salfeld, 1969).

The habit of burying acorns is a specialized feeding development, but jays take a wide variety of other foods both vegetable and animal. They frequently feed on the ground, hopping from place to place, and often carrying both wing tips on one side of the tail. They open up crevices and turn over soil like other crows with a swing of head and bill (Goodwin, 1952[1]). Holyoak (1968), comparing the food of *Corvidae*, divided food substances into very important foods, numerous foods and few records only. In class 1 were acorns and beech mast, birds' eggs and woodland insects, and in the rather less important group peas and beans (*Pisum vicia*), and grain (*Triticum, Avena, Hordeum*).

A note in *British Birds*, Vol. 12, 1918, described several jays making tree-to-tree flights and then out into the open, taking wheat heads and returning to the wood with them. Wild plant seeds, pear, cherry and plum, wild fruit and cultivated soft fruits are all taken, as are nestlings and terrestrial molluscs, grassland insects, spiders, woodlice, centipedes and, finally, bread. There are also a number of records of unusual and perhaps opportunistic food selection, such as plane buds in Kensington Gardens (Goodwin, 1949). With this opportunism there is sometimes a degree of learning, as with a male jay who accidentally discovered that shaking a peanut holder at a bird table made the nuts fall to the ground and then, bending down from its perch, seized the bottom of the holder to turn it upside down (Salfeld, 1963). Jays have an innate behaviour pattern for dealing with wasps, first disabling them by biting, then biting or crushing the stinging end of the abdomen several times before swallowing the insect (Goodwin, 1952; Birkhead, 1974). Certainly one of the most unexpected examples of opportunism was exhibited by a jay that stalled in mid-flight and dropped to the surface of the river Avon near Bath to catch a fish and fly with it still alive and wriggling to the bank (Sharrock, 1963).

These varied animal and vegetable foods are also presented to the young, but the proportions of animal and vegetable components change with the age of the young. Nestlings in the first few weeks (8–24 days) receive 5 per cent by volume of vegetable matter, mostly oak galls and bread, and vertebrates made up 15 per cent of total animal matter, especially defoliating caterpillars, but also coleoptera, arachnids and others collected within a short distance of the nest (Owen, 1956). The young birds of 16–24 days receive more vertebrate prey than the younger and for nestlings and fledglings eggs do not seem an important item. For fledglings in June and July acorns become more important than eggs or young birds (Bossema, 1967).

The use of high-protein animal food for young birds in the nest is comparable with many other species for which the bulk of food is also vegetable matter at other times. It is interesting to compare the reactions of some passerine birds (potential prey for jays) to stuffed jays, when compared with their reactions to certain other species. Mistle thrushes, song thrushes and blackbirds attacked the dummy jay and the latter ignored a stock dove. Woodlarks largely ignored the stock dove but reacted to the jay with intense distraction display. White-throats, chiffchaff, willow warbler, and wood warbler all attacked a stuffed cuckoo but only threatened the jay vocally. A dunnock continued to brood with a stuffed stock dove near the nest, but both parents stayed in the bushes near and remained silent when the jay was at the nest. Both male and female red-backed shrike attacked barbary dove, cuckoo and jay but, when all three of these were placed at an equal distance, the jay and the cuckoo were attacked and the dove ignored. The only small bird which really attacked and struck the stuffed jay was a chaffinch. They will attack but not strike a live jay.

The jay often takes little notice of mobbing; its response may be to start looking for the nest (Goodwin, personal communication). An attack by the nest owners may deflect it from its purpose, but if it is urgently feeding nestlings, it will continue its search. A jay that has found a nest may react to attack as it would if being robbed of its food and will attack the defending parent (Goodwin, 1953[2]).

Eggs are not instantly recognized by the jay as food and if initial testing pecks do not puncture the shell the egg may be left. If the shell is opened, the contents are nibbled away and lifted out with small pecks and not sucked. Many insects are eaten and some rejected – the burnet moth, the black and red soldier beetle, and the red soldier beetle for example. Captive jays attacked the larvae of the elephant hawk moth from behind where there are no warning 'eyes'. The privet hawk moth larva, which has no such warning 'eyes', was taken with no hesitation (Goodwin, 1952[2]).

PREDATORS AND PARASITES

Predation of eggs and young of the jay must be much more frequent than the killing of adults by predators. Nests are obviously more vulnerable when the parents are absent, perhaps as a result of disturbances. Carrion crows, magpies and perhaps grey quirrels are nest predators of jays. In my garden the carrion crows are frequently mobbed by jays. Their nest is in a thicket in an old orchard and at that time crows are often to be found on low branches nearby. Jays themselves may also be among nest predators of their own species.

Adult jays are among the prey taken by the goshawk in countries where this predator is found. In Wales, fully grown jays were found in four red kites' nests (Walters Davies and Davis, 1973), although there is no evidence as to whether the kites caught them or found them dead. The long-eared owl takes woodland and woodland fringe birds – in fact bird prey makes up about 15 per cent of its food requirements – and jays are one of the species taken (Glue and Hammond, 1974). Perrins (1959) described seeing a jay caught by a weasel near Oxford in cold weather.

Jays, like all living creatures, are host to various parasites, both internal and external. Plasmodium blood parasites with a complex life cycle have been isolated from jays among other British species. Trypanosoma also, usually blood parasites and not necessarily pathological, have also been found. They are variable in form and the trypanosome species are not certainly confined to a particular host species. Jays, like other corvines, are hosts to *Syngamus trachea* but are probably less afflicted than rooks. Like all birds, they are subject to feather mites (Rothschild and Clay, 1952).

The reaction of jays to enemies, and potential enemies, reflects the danger to which they are exposed from these various predators. Sparrowhawks, for example, cause a strong mobbing reaction, while owls are mobbed rather less and with a more variable intensity. All black corvids are treated as nest enemies and mobbing is less outside the nesting season when jackdaws cause hardly any reaction at all.

MORBIDITY AND ABNORMALITY

Albinism and melanism have both appeared in the jay (Sage, 1962). There are a number of completely white or creamy white jays in collections; absence of pigment in a few feathers also occurs. Two years ago, one which frequented our garden had white inner secondaries in both wings. This bird was only seen during the summer and may have disappeared, but stunted and distorted feathers occur when feeding is inadequate and with captive reared jays this defect improved with Vitamin B and calcium (Goodwin, 1949). Abnormal pigment can also occur in the eggs and erythristic jays' eggs have been described (Taylor, 1926–7).

13
Siberian jay

(Perisoreus infaustus, formerly Cractes infaustus)

European names

Dutch – ONGELUKSGAAI   Russian – KUSHKA or RONZHA
French – MESANGEAI IMITATEUR   Swedish – LAVSKRIKA
German – UNGLÜKSHÄHER

Other names

BOREAL JAY – NORTHERN JAY – RED-TAILED JAY

FIELD CHARACTERISTICS

In the field, the Siberian jay appears to be a grey bird intermediate in size between the missel thrush and jay; its colour is cryptic, but it may be easily seen as it is often very tame, a characteristic of the genus, which made its Canadian relative familiar to the trappers as 'Whisky Jack'. The rufous colour of the flight and especially the tail feathers can be very striking, however, and this is especially so seen against the light in flight or during some movement when the wings or tail are spread.

DESCRIPTION

The sexes are alike and there is no difference between the winter and summer plumages. The nasal bristles are soft and buff to rufous at the base, darker at their tips. The forehead is paler than the rest of the head, because the feather bases are visible. The scalp is dark chocolate brown, and on the nape this colour changes by shading into the colour of the mantle. The mantle scapulars and back are greyish brown. The rump is yellower and the upper-tail coverts rufous. The chin and throat are grey with pale buff central streaks on the feathers; these are very conspicuous on the chin so that this is noticeably paler. The breast is grey, merging to rufous buff.

The lesser and median coverts are greyish brown. The outer web of the outer greater coverts is rufous, the inner web and the whole of the inner greater coverts are greyish brown. The wings are grey-brown, and rufous on some of the outer greater coverts, primary coverts and at the base of the outer web of some of the outer secondaries. The central tail feathers are grey-brown, with increasing amounts of rufous towards the outer ones. The bill and legs are black and the iris very dark brown or black. Juveniles have the head less dark and the head and occipital feathers are shorter than those of the adult and the rufous colour is much less conspicuous, especially on the tail, primary coverts and primaries. There is one moult per year, starting about mid-June and ending about the middle of September.

The plumage in this genus is very soft and fluffy, and no doubt an excellent insulator, for these are comparatively small birds whose environment is very cold during a large part of the year. These conditions apply throughout the whole range of the genus. A further adaptation to winter living in cold climates, described by Dow (1965), is the presence in this genus of a pair of mandibular mucous-secreting glands, unique among crows, and probably unique among passerines. It is believed that the mucus from these glands coats the tongue to make it sticky, so that probing for insects in crevices and seeds in cones is more successful, and helps to make winter feeding possible. Or the value of this saliva may be in forming a sticky mass of food for easy storage in trees.

Some workers have been inclined to separate subspecies, but these appear to be geographical colour variations, with no sharp colour division at the boundaries of the supposed areas of distribution of each subspecies. For example, *P. i. ruthenus* in Norway may be rather more rufous. The closely related Canadian jay (*P. canadensis*) has similar geographical variations which have been separated subspecifically. The Canada jay is a much greyer bird, with contrasting dark-grey and white or pale-grey head, and no rufous colouring.

DISTRIBUTION

The Siberian jay is largely sedentary; local movements of 7·5 to 15km were occasionally noted among the birds studied by Lindgren (1975). Its distribution is in the coniferous forest of spruce, pine, cedar and larch in the Taiga areas. In Fenno-Scandia it reaches as far north as 61° (Blomgren, 1971) and in Russia and across Siberia up to the conifer limit to about 70°N, and occasion-

Siberian Jay

ally in birch areas adjacent to the conifers. In the Soviet Union the conifer line extends further south than in Fenno-Scandia and the Siberian jay may be found as far south as Moscow and the southern Ural Mountains. In European Russia it overlaps the jay, and it is not known if the two species are in competition, but in Fenno-Scandia the northern breeding limit of the jay has shifted northwards and, correspondingly, so has the southern limit of distribution of the Siberian jay. In Asia it extends south to the Altai, northern Mongolia and probably northern Manchuria and east to Anadyr, the Sea of Ohkotsk, Sakhalin and Ussuriland (Vaurie, 1959). The distribution tends to be uneven, so that it may be common in one area and scarce in another that is apparently equally suitable. Its occasional nomadic movements may be responsible for its accidental occurrence, in winter, in such places as Denmark, the Tatra Mountains and Hungary and, in autumn, in Chakalov (Dementiev and Gladov, 1951–4; Merikallio, 1958; Curry Lindahl, 1963).

POSTURE AND VOICE

In one of its displays the male jay swings to and fro like a weathercock in front of the fluffed-up female. His wings and tail are slightly spread, he bobs his head and hops sideways to and fro, making a 'laboured chirrupping sound'. The female makes little response or may move away with small hops. The male ends his display by diving out of the tree canopy, at a great pace and swings up into another tree top. This is a sudden flight (Blomgren, 1971; Lindgren, 1975). Both the swaying to and fro with partly spread wings and tail and the dive and upward glide may emphasize the chestnut colour of the wings and tail. This display is most frequent in March and can be seen as early as February. Lindgren says that it can take place outside the 'pairing time', for example on 5 June when there were fully fledged young in the nest. Two males have been seen performing this display in front of one female.

There is also a display performed by both sexes, but more often by the male, which Blomgren termed the spruce dance and Lindgren the spiral dance. The displaying bird moves quickly (with closed wings) down and round the trunk of a spruce or pine and up again, spiralling rapidly round the trunk from branch to branch.

Copulation is not preceded by either of these displays, but at times by mutual feeding or billing.

Two sounds made by the Siberian jay are very like those of the jay, a loud scream and the buzzard-like mew. There are quiet contact notes used between the sexes, and also mimicry of other species (Blomgren). The song contains a range of sounds, soft and harsh, whistling, creaking and trilling with additional mimicked notes. It is most used during the nesting season, but also at other times of the year, even in the extreme cold, and is subdued and can only be heard from a short distance. Both sexes can sing (Lindgren, 1975), and singing may have some function in the synchronization of the sexes for breeding (Blomgren) as it is not used in connection with territory.

TERRITORY

Territory is, according to Blomgren, a food territory within which the jays breed. It varies in size and in the area studied by Blomgren was about 150 ha (370 acres) and was slightly larger in the autumn and winter than during nesting. In places where the population is denser, as in the Arvidsjaur district described by Lindgren, the territories were between 50 ha (123 acres) and 100 ha (247 acres), and during nesting most activity was in the nest area and little towards the boundaries. In the autumn and winter, when the birds are actively food hoarding, they used the territory to its limits. The difference in population numbers and territory size may depend on the food available, and Lindgren states that in very sparsely populated districts territories are separated and do not come into contact. Typically the territorial habitat contains dry pine heath interspersed with small bogs and lakes, often with mixed spruce and pine trees growing in open or dense formation. Foraging birds go out into the open and away from the trees, perhaps into areas that have been cleared, collecting berries and insects among the cloudberry tussocks and dwarf birches.

Siberian jays are sedentary and remain paired for life in most cases; territorial ownership and boundaries are remarkably constant. One female was present in the same territory for 12 years and boundaries remain unchanged, even when both of the occupying pair are replaced within one year (Blomgren).

It is known that intrusion into a territory by birds from as much as 1·5km away may take place. Such intrusions have been noted during autumn and during the nesting season. They are met by a form of pursuit flight. A relationship not unlike the third bird described by Charles in his account of the carrion crow occurs with this species too. Lindgren described 'the odd jay' as being unattached, but not an intruder from another territory. They remain within the territory for a period lasting from a few days to a few years. One, or sometimes two, become 'fellow travellers' with the territory holders, and are tolerated by them except in the nest area or where special food supplies have been put. They are recognized by their calls and behaviour. In the presence of the territory holders they give a cheeping, probably submissive, note.

The odd jay takes over territory defence if either of the holding pair should disappear and, if of the right sex, the odd jay will often succeed to a vacancy if the disappearance is permanent.

In spite of territorial defence being greatest at the nest site, promiscuous attacks by other males can occur. A male came with 'purposeful approach from afar off' and landed 20cm above a nest where the female was brooding. The female went to chase away the intruder and copulation took place. The female then returned to brooding. Lindgren also recorded a case of joint brooding. In 1961 an 'odd jay' joined a territory-holding pair and remained until 1968. On 10 April 1963, egg-laying had started and on the 15th two jays were sitting on the nest, one of them on the edge. There was difficulty in both females finding room to brood but no actual quarrelling. Five days later both were brooding; they changed upper and under positions, the longest spell without change being two hours 55 minutes. Sometimes the heads faced the same way and sometimes in opposite directions. There were six eggs, some of which hatched. Both females brooded the young, and both fed them, but a week after hatching the nest was robbed. In 1964 the same male and both females were present, but the nest was high and inaccessible and information could not be obtained. By 1965 the female of the territory pair had gone, but the 'odd female' remained and continued until 1968. For the last two of these years she was with a new male that had been an 'odd jay' in 1965.

NEST SITE AND NEST BUILDING

The nest is built in pine or spruce. Blomgren found 8 in pine and 47 in spruce, and Lindgren 74 in pine and 17 in spruce. The average height in the tree is 4–6m, the lowest only 2m above the snow surface, and the highest 17m. In Lindgren's study, many more nests were built on the south side of the tree than the north. The figures were:

North – 2	North west – 1	North east – 1	Total 4
West – 4	East – 9		Total 13
South – 28	South east – 9		Total 37

The nest is usually close to the trunk, often built against it and once between two trunks of a divided spruce. Two were a metre from the trunk, both in larger pines.

When selecting the nest site, the male jay first creeps in close to the trunk 'testing the site' but both sexes take part in this. There may be several false starts at building, as many as six by one pair were recorded and both sexes take part in these abortive efforts. If there is a breeding failure, a whole new nest is built.

Both sexes build the nest, with the base and side being made from dry twigs broken off the trees. Its outside diameter is about 20cm but with some twigs projecting beyond this. Interstices between the twigs are packed with pieces of birch and sometimes pine bark. The nest is lined with beard lichen, moss, down and feathers, sometimes wads of cobwebs, fragments of wasp nests, and fur of reindeer, fox and squirrel. The cup is deep and the thick lining has to provide very good insulation against external temperatures of $-20°$ to $-30°$. A remarkable adaptation against the difficulties of nest building in March in the far north is the hoarding of the nest-lining material long before nest building (Lindgren, 1975). This starts in late March and takes about three weeks (Blomgren, 1971).

EGGS TO FLEDGING OF YOUNG

The eggs are pale blue-green or blue-grey, spotted and blotched with grey-brown and grey, and more heavily marked at the large end. They are similar in colour to magpie's eggs but less heavily marked and smaller. The average size is 31·6 × 22·9mm (Harrison, 1975). They are laid between 31 March and 22 April, the mean being about 13 April. The average clutch is four, and clutches of three to five have been recorded.

The female covers the eggs when the first is laid, but incubation proper starts with the third. The female sits very close and can sometimes be touched or even lifted off the nest and replaced. The intensity of incubation and reluctance to leave are also presumably adaptations to early nesting in a very cold climate.

The incubation period is 19 days and heavy snow may fall during this period. The newly hatched young are almost naked and are closely covered by the female, who remains at the nest. All food is collected by the male for the first week or so. His foraging may take an hour, and the food, mainly insect larvae, is stored in the throat pouch and perhaps the oesophagus until he returns to the nest.

The young birds leave the nest 21–24 days after hatching; they remain in the parents' territory through the remaining part of the summer, autumn and winter. Some move away in the late winter, while some stay on into the following nesting season, when they are tolerated within the territory by their parents but not near the nest site. It is not known how far away young birds move at this stage.

Nest predation takes place at all stages after the eggs have been laid. Potential predators are squirrels (although no snow tracks have been found), ravens, crows and magpies. In Lindgren's study the success rate was surprisingly low, 80 per cent being unsuccessful. There is some evidence that other Siberian jays, possibly non-breeders or neighbouring territory holders, may be predators.

FOOD

Siberian jays are omnivorous. In autumn and early winter berries (especially bilberries) are collected and stored behind loose bark or in hanging beard lichen and between forked twigs. The stores are hidden throughout the territory, and this enables the birds to remain within their territories throughout the winter and provides a food source during early nesting. Conifer seeds that have fallen on the snow are also gathered. More protein food is brought to the young, especially insects and pupae, but small rodents are quite often caught; and one bird was seen to transfer heavy prey from bill to claws in flight. They will also take carrion, offal from slaughterhouses, eggs of small birds, and I have seen one pursue a small bird with an almost sparrowhawk-like dash, but without success.

ADVERSE FACTORS

Timber forest is an exploited commercial asset. The disturbance caused might be an adverse factor for this species. If timber felling leaves part of the jay's territory still with standing trees they will sometimes continue to nest in them, foraging out into the open clearings. Felling may cause them to move, but they are persistent, although many breeding failures are caused.

14

Great spotted cuckoo
(*Clamator glandarius*)

European names

Dutch – KUIFKOEKOCK   German – HAHERKUCKKUCK
French – COUCOU-GEAI   Spanish – CRIALO
                         Swedish – STUTSGOK

FIELD CHARACTERISTICS

The great spotted cuckoo is parasitic on various species of corvids in Europe, especially on the magpie, although carrion/hooded crows, ravens, jackdaws and jays have all been mentioned by authors and the azure-winged magpie also – but perhaps with some reservations. In the field, this cuckoo is a short-legged, long-tailed bird, smaller than a magpie and often very noisy. When perched in a tree, its pale-cream underparts are conspicuous, and there is a sharp contrasting line below the eye where the grey of the head in the adult, black in the juvenile meets the cream. On the ground its stance with very short legs is noticeable and the light underparts are not so easily seen. The dark-brown mottled back renders the bird inconspicuous, the white spots on the feathers appear at first glance rather as a general mottling than as discrete spots. Its flight is very similar to that of a common cuckoo, with short rather quick flaps, and the juvenile has a very noticeable rufous base to the primaries. The long tail is very obvious, whether perched on the ground or in flight.

DISTRIBUTION

In Europe it is found in all but the extreme north of the Iberian Peninsula. It is present along the south coast of France from Spain to Italy, and along the Greek coast bordering on the northern side of the Aegean Sea. Its world distribution is limited and broken up into relatively small areas in Asia Minor, Egypt and scattered parts of west, central, east and south Africa (Voous, 1960). It is not a breeding species in all of these places. For example, although it breeds in the Iberian Peninsula, there is no record from Morocco (Heim de Balsac and Mayaud, 1962). Great spotted cuckoos breed in South Africa and the possibility that some may breed in both summer and winter quarters needs investigation.

REPRODUCTION

The mating of the great spotted cuckoo was described by Channer (1976). The presentation of food (a caterpillar) was an important part of the action. The male prepared the food and presented it to the female, who then began 'a regular jerking action of its whole body, keeping the wings closed'. The male mounted the female and both continued to hold the caterpillar; when the female began to swallow the caterpillar the action ceased and the male re-leased the caterpillar. The male found two or three more caterpillars and each time coition, which lasted about two minutes, was repeated.

The eggs, which are a little smaller and less elongated than those of the magpie, average $32 \cdot 1 \times 24 \cdot 0$mm (Harrison, 1975). They are pale greenish blue, like those of the magpie and marked with light brown and grey.

The female cuckoo does not as a rule deposit more than two eggs in each host's nest, although she may lay 15–16 in a season (Harrison, 1975). In the south of France most clutches are laid in the second fortnight in April and there is a synchronization between the completion of nest building by the host and the laying of eggs by the cuckoo. It has been suggested that the sight of the host building may be a stimulus to the oviduct (presumably via the pituitary) of the parasite. Once a certain stage of physiological development has been reached by the cuckoo, the process is irreversible and there is pressure on the bird to find a suitable nest in which to deposit its eggs (Gramet, 1970). This may account for the larger number of cuckoo eggs sometimes found in the host's nest. In one nest in Spain containing six magpies eggs and five cuckoo eggs, three hen cuckoos had apparently laid in the same nest.

At some nests, the magpie eggs were found to have been dented. It was also found that as the cuckoo egg was laid a magpie egg disappeared, although no cuckoo was actually seen removing them. Cuckoo eggs, on the other hand, were neither removed nor dented, so the hen cuckoo seems able to recognize other cuckoos' eggs in the nest, in spite of the very close similarity in the eggs (Mountfort, 1952).

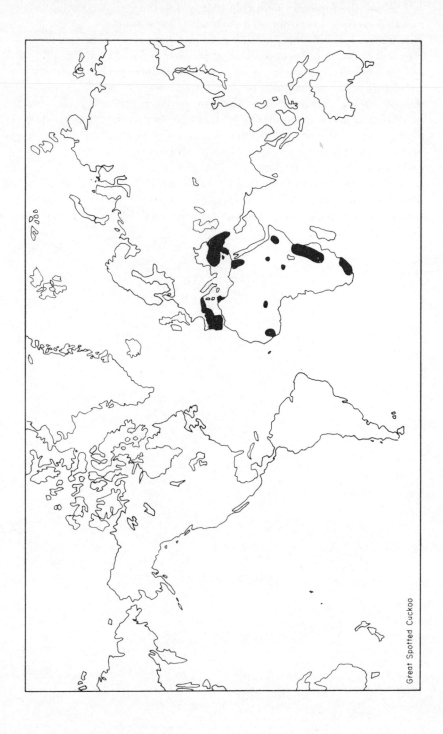

Great Spotted Cuckoo

The nestling is pinkish flesh-coloured and without down, the inside of the mouth is conspicuous, bright red with white gape flanges.

It has no reflex for ejecting the eggs or young of its foster parents as the common cuckoo has. Perhaps the most important adaptation that this cuckoo has for successful parasitism is the short incubation period of its eggs, only $13\frac{1}{2}$–14 days, compared with 18 days for the magpie, which usually ensures that the cuckoo's hatch out first. The later-hatching young magpies then have no chance of successful competition and may be smothered or crushed. The young cuckoos also have a brighter orange-red gape than the young magpies and this may provide a stronger feeding stimulus.

Accounts of the species parasitized by this cuckoo often mention the azure-winged magpie somewhat tentatively. This species is said to have an incubation period of 15 days. If this is correct, it may afford protection against great spotted cuckoo parasitism, with the parasite and the host eggs hatching at almost the same time.

15
Some comparisons

There are great differences in the form of territory that has evolved with these eleven corvid species. The size varies from a few square feet to several square miles, functions differ from species to species and there are interrelated adaptations of structure, physiology and behaviour.

Territory is a defended area and is topographically localized, unlike individual distance, which is also defended, but moves with the bird (Hinde, 1956).

For all these species the nest and its immediate surroundings are the most vigorously defended area; for colonial-nesting rooks and jackdaws this small area is the whole territory. It is defended by gestures (posture and threat) and by voice and, if necessary, by actual combat. In species with larger territories, various devices are used to advertise the boundaries. For example, magpies fluff out the conspicuous white area of their plumage perch in prominent positions where they can be seen; carrion crows also perch conspicuously in their upright posture, reinforcing this with boundary patrolling and various self-advertising and aggressive actions; and nutcrackers have their loud calls.

Lack (1954), referring to the dispersion effect of territory said: 'in both territorial and colonial species, dispersion is primarily due to the avoidance of occupied and crowded ground by potential settlers, not to the aggressiveness of those in occupation.' Perhaps the earliest view on this subject was expressed in a letter to the Hon. Daines Barrington from Gilbert White on 8 February 1772, 'Most of the singing and elation of spirit of that time (the amorous season) seems to me to be the effect of rivalry and emulation, and it is to this spirit of jealousy that I chiefly attribute the equal dispersion of birds over the face of the country.' This aptly describes the functioning of the nutcracker's calls, but the nutcracker, like other passerines, including crows, has a song but uses it without any territorial connection. Swanberg (1951, 1956) suggested that it has a sexual significance. Rooks use their song away from their territories and, as Richards (1976) has shown, captive male rooks use their song in attracting hen birds. Perhaps this is usual among crows and song once used for the double purpose, by advertising ownership of a territory, of repelling would-be settlers and attracting unpaired females, now retains only the latter function.

Postures (or gestures) and calls are important in maintaining territory, for Charles (1972) found by experiment that with carrion crows the presence of the territory holder alone was not enough, he had to use the self-advertising and border patrolling actions to keep his territory free from intrusions.

Houston's hooded crows maintained moorland territories of up to more than 240 ha (600 acres), much larger than those of Charles's birds in agricultural land, but the raven's territory is many times larger (Ratcliffe, 1962). Some of the postures of the raven and the carrion crow are obviously homologous, for example, the ear-tuft display of the raven and the pot-bellied posture of the crow and the thick-head of the raven and the bristle-head of the crow. We cannot be sure that the two species use their homologous postures in exactly similar circumstances because, thanks to Gwinner, we know more of the individual behaviour of the raven and its adaptability than we do of the crow, and we know more of the crow in the wild state, thanks to Charles, Houston, Tenovuo, Wittenberg and Yom Tov, than we do of the raven. There does appear to be a difference in acceptance of the 'third bird'. Ryves (1948) and Ratcliffe (1962) record 'nest visiting' by an extra raven so that 'twice at other eyries with eggs three ravens were present together in complete harmony'. Charles on the other hand found that carrion crows ejected the third bird from the territory before nesting began. This might indicate that the territory-holding raven does not have to contend with flock-bird intrusion and cannibalism. Some form of toleration of 'extra birds' within the territory is widespread among corvids; among the European group there is Ratcliffe's evidence of its probable occurrence among ravens, while Wittenberg and Charles have given details for the carrion crow to the effect that the third bird is always a male. Lindgren described both male and female 'odd jays' in the case of *Perisoreus infaustus* and Goodwin mentioned the possibility of 'odd jays' also occurring with jays of the *Garrulus* genus. Cowdy (personal communication) has seen a third individual with pairs of nesting red-billed choughs. The most extreme development of this kind of behaviour has been described by Woolfenden (quoted by Goodwin, 1976) in the Florida scrub jay (*Aphelcoma coerulescens*): up to three additional birds may assist in nest building, feeding the female and feeding the young. These are usually, if not always, offspring of the pair concerned. There is also Charles's record of young carrion crows of the two or three preceding seasons feeding with the adults in their territory on 13 September, at a time when seasonal territorial aggressiveness has recovered from the gonad refractory period of the summer. So that, even in this intensely territorial species, there are some elements of tolerance of 'family' birds. This, in turn, poses certain questions about recognition, because many young corvids wander away from their natal area after becoming independent of their parents. Some return later and by this time will have completed their first moult and exchanged their drab juvenile body feathers for glossy adult ones.

Territorial defence is also modified when social or pre-roost gatherings take place within a territory. Such gatherings occur among ravens, carrion/hooded crows, choughs, magpies and jays. Even territory-holding crows do not attack pre-roost gatherings within their territory (outside the nesting season): but they do attack group intrusions by flock birds and groups as large as 25 birds may be evicted (Charles, 1972). Does this imply recognition of the purpose of the birds' invasion?

There is also the situation called 'swamping' by Rowley (1973), in which defence of the territory is abandoned if the intruding birds are too numerous. Rowley was describing the territorial behaviour of the Australian raven (*C. coronoides*): a flush of food [within a territory] is soon located by the local non-breeding flock birds, and ultimately by near-by territorial neighbours. The intrusion is at first attacked and up to five or six birds can be driven off. Above this number the defence becomes ineffectual, and eventually the resident birds retire to their nest or look-out tree.' This reluctant toleration is shown both to conspecifics and to crows of other closely related and very similar-looking species coming into the territory. The tolerance shown by carrion crows to pre-roost assemblies does not seem to involve an initial resistance to intrusion, later given up, and the carrion crows continue to repel far more numerous intruders than the Australian ravens do, perhaps the difference lies in the cannibalism of the intruding carrion crows.

Territory ownership enables such reproductive activities as nest building, copulation, incubation and rearing the young to be carried out without excessive interference from birds of the same species. It may also provide an area well known to the birds within which they can find a ready refuge from predators, as was suggested by Swanberg for the nutcracker, which holds the same territory throughout the year and for many years. The territory may also be an essential part of the food-supply system of the species. In this there are contrasts within the genus *Corvus*: the rook has a very small territory that has nothing to do with food supply; on the other hand, the carrion crow defends an area which must not only supply most of its food, but where there is a measurable advantage in breeding success if the food is in sufficient quantity and close enough to the nest to enable the owners to feed in its vicinity and so be able to defend it at all times; for the nutcracker, jay and Siberian jay, territory is important in the annual cycle of food supply. These three species all have specialized adaptations of structure and physiology which may well be related to their food-storing behaviour. The Canadian grey jays of the genus *Perisoreus* have specially developed mandibular salivary glands and it is probable that the Siberian jay has them also. With these, they produce sufficient saliva to coat and impregnate collections of food items for storage; they hide each sticky bolus in trees behind loose bark, in crevices and in the hanging beard lichen; and Lindgren (1975) has also recorded that they store nest material before winter conditions make it impossible, for they are early nesters. The jay and the nutcrackers have evolved special means for transporting seeds, nuts and acorns in an enlarged oesophagus or in a sublingual pouch. The nutcracker has also a development of the horny covering of the bill to enable it to grip these hard foods. For the nutcracker, its stored food is so important that it brings it from a distance to conceal within the well-known area of its territory. Because each member of the occupying pair has its own stores, the nutcracker has evolved behaviour unusual among crows – the male takes its turn at incubation, thus freeing the female to visit her own food caches.

The nutcracker is not a migrant species. The only geographical movements that they make, apart from the dispersion of juveniles, are emigrations when their specialized food crop fails. In countries where they are not resident these movements are recorded as invasions, and the same may be said of the geographical movements of the jay, which may occur when the acorn crop is inadequate, but we do not know to what extent jays are dependent on food stored within their own territories. Regular seasonal food shortages, due to winter conditions, affect carrion/hooded crows, rooks and jackdaws, and ravens also in some of their far northern habitats; some members of all these species are migrants from these climate-affected areas. Food-dependent movements are made by members of both the chough species, especially to higher or lower altitudes in summer and winter in mountainous areas.

Nutcrackers and jays are able to recover their stored food with a high degree of success, even months later and when the ground is snow covered. The food-storing habit is common to many of the crows, perhaps to all. It is probably an ancestral behaviour pattern which has attained greater importance in the ecology of the nutcracker, and perhaps the jay, than in the other species. Simmons (1970) described the hiding of surplus food by raven, carrion crow, rook and jackdaw. They hide mainly large food items of which they might be robbed by a competitor, using single caches not connected with their territory. Gwinner described the hiding of food by his captive ravens. Before they began to feed and while they were still hungry, they hid food when it was scarce. Food for hiding is carried in the throat pouch, sublingual pouch, gullet or bill, regurgitated and then pushed into the hiding place with the bill. The hiding place may be among grass or moss, in a crevice or under stones. After pushing the food into position, soil, sand or vegetation is scraped over it with the bill, using movements like those used in raking the ground for food. Most corvids do not dig special holes in which to hide food, they use existing cavities. Rooks often do dig such holes, using the digging and probing methods by which they, more than other crows, obtain their food.

16
Lewis Harding and the rooks at Trelawne

To ornithologists who, like me, have tried to make a study of a single species or group of species, it may come as a surprise to learn that the first intensive study of the rook, and perhaps the first intensive study of any single species of bird, was made in Cornwall in 1847–8. As well as being the first of its kind, it was also remarkable, for its time, in that it was continuous for a whole year. The circumstances in which it was made were exceptional too.

The record is contained in a volume of notes bound together and belonging to Miss Foy Quiller Couch. At the beginning of the volume is this note.

The history (fig. 57)

of this volume is: – That a Gentleman had returned from a distant climate to Trelawny, in a very imperfect state of health; in which it became necessary to prescribe for him a sort and degree of occupation which should lay him under the necessity of constant attention, without inconvenience or anxiety. He was required to observe the actions and habits of the Rooks through the varying months of the year, and the Volume which follows is the result.

JONATHAN COUCH.

*F.Z.S. and member of several other learned
societies for the study of nature. 1850.*

Jonathan Couch (1789–1870) was then doctor at Polperro, and it is known that he was especially interested in what are now called psychosomatic and psychological disorders. What he ordered for Lewis Harding was occupational therapy.

On the leaf opposite Jonathan Couch's statement has been written:

The Gentleman thus set to work by my Father to chronicle the life of a rookery was Mr Lewis Harding a nephew of Sir Harry Trelawny, Bart. of Trelawny, in Pelynt[1]. He was a great invalid and resided at Trelawny for many years, from whence he moved to Polperro.
Bodmin
May 1. 1870   T.Q. COUCH[2]

In spite of being a great invalid, Harding died in 1893 at the age of 87. He had returned from Australia in 1846 after being abroad for 11 years and while there he had probably sent back a collection of Australian butterflies to Dr Couch. So he was almost certainly a man with natural-history interests and with much travel experience behind him when he was given this advice by his doctor.

He was an early photographer and left many contemporary pictures taken in and around Polperro. This side of his life has been documented by Lanyon (1976), who points out that to be a photographer at that time required some knowledge of chemistry and a scientific turn of mind.

No doubt he received guidance and criticism from Dr Couch, who is believed to have seen him at very frequent intervals. Dr Couch was himself a notable naturalist, a friend of William Yarrell and later the author of an important four-volume work *The History of Fishes of the British Isles* (1860–5). He was an artist and at Polperro had the opportunity of dissecting and painting specimens brought in by the local fishing boats. He seems to have been a realist in his view of natural history, to judge from his remark: 'The whole duty of the existence of creatures appears to be to draw nutrition, propagate and rot'. All his sons became doctors and his grandson was Sir Arthur Quiller Couch.

Harding was able to watch the rooks at quite close range from his own room at Trelawne, an old country house two miles from Polperro where some of the plantations in which the rookery was situated surrounded the house. He also walked through the plantations and rode round the grounds. But he did not have the advantages of binoculars or even a telescope – on 18 March 1848 he

---

[1] The Trelawny family originally lived at Trelawny in Altarnun. The house of Trelawne in Pelynt was purchased by the family in the nineteenth century, possibly because of the similarity of the name. The Trelawny family may have been calling it Trelawny, as this is the name clearly written by both Jonathan and Thomas Couch in their statements at the beginning of Harding's diary.

[2] T.Q. Couch is Thomas Quiller Couch who was Jonathan's son. He was in medical practice at Bodmin.

of this Volume is :— that a Gentleman
had returned from a distant Climate
to Trelawny in a very imperfect state of
health, in which it became necessary to
prescribe for him a certain degree of
recreation which should lay him under
the necessity, if constant attention, without
inconvenience or anxiety. He was requested
to observe the actions and habits or the Parts
through the varying months of the Year, and
the Volume which follows is the result—

J. Couch

Jonathan Couch (Vicch.
F.L.S. (a member of several
... the learned Societies &c &c &c.
1650

The gentleman thus set to work by my Father to
chronicle the life of a working man Mordaunt
Harding, a nephew of Sir Henry Trelawny Bart,
of Trelawny, in Cornwall. He was a portraitist,
and resided at Trelawny for many years from
whence he moved to Polperro.
J Couch
Bodmin.
May 1. 1870.

57   *Pages from Lewis Harding's MS*

says: 'It would require a telescope to be certain.' Nor was it possible for him to follow the flight lines of the rook and jackdaw flocks in the way that a modern ornithologist would take for granted.

Harding's notes occupy both sides of more than 300 sheets of paper. At the beginning of each month he gives the time of sunrise and sunset on the first and last days of the month. On nearly every day he describes the weather conditions and concludes the month with a summary of his observations. Often his notes for the day occupy many pages and his summaries usually do so. Dr Couch's original request was that Harding should 'observe the actions and habits of the rooks through the varying months of the year'. I have tried to quote especially from some of his monthly summaries with a few of the daily entries that seem to me to illustrate Harding's success in meeting this request. I have also omitted a good many of his anthropomorphic interpretations of what he had seen, although I hope I have retained enough of these to show how different was the approach then from what it is now. Yet it is striking how accurate were Harding's actual observations, in spite of the differences of interpretation from those of the present day. I have put in a few of my own comments (these are in italics). I have kept to the original spelling, punctuation and use of capitals.

The rookery at Trelawne was evidently a central roost for other rookeries in the area, a fact that gradually became apparent to Harding. The maximum number actually breeding there was about 500 pairs.

2 September . . . at 5 p.m. They all came in
 . . . at 6 p.m. they had left the rookery and were

seen in a stubble field the majority by far in a ploughed field here they were alighted blacking the surface as they stood in rank and file and crowding in silent groups – I went to observe them they were on a field close by that had been ploughed some time in a sheltered situation the wind blowing high and cold – they occupied a great extent – say a couple of acres which gradually narrowed into a parallelogram 200 yds long and 20 yards wide (about). The greater part stood still, a good number now and then left the higher ground, and invariably came flying a foot or two from the surface over the rest, towards the lower ground.

This describes well the leap-frogging effect as a feeding flock of rooks moves across a field.

Harding was anthropomorphic in his approach, especially at the beginning of his year's study. He uses words such as 'confabulation' and thinks that the rooks would talk over 'their plans for the day'. He was interested in rooks as weather prophets, and watched and recorded some flight forms with this idea in his mind.

He made many records of the movements of the rook flocks at the rookery at Trelawne, many pages of his record being taken up with this. But he had obvious difficulty because it was hard, or even impossible, to follow the flocks and he does not even mention the possibility of doing so. So there is a tendency for him to conjecture about this, and for the conjectures to become subsequent fact.

9 September . . . They came in in a body from the N.E. an immense number settled on the South Easternmost group of the rookery there they chattered and bustled and fought for places with all the clatter of a bevy of parrots and cockatoos in the bush.

On 27 September and other dates he describes the rooks as flying about in sport – probably pursuit flights.

16 October . . . I said last month that I would direct my attention to ascertain if the birds flew generally against the wind when they started in the morning – I now believe the wind has little to do with the direction of their flights then. They start off in all directions whichever way the wind is from.

19 October . . . they follow and pursue each other in threes and fours fight for a footing on the same bough – use commonly their short notes 'cuup cuup'. *He had likened this to a female voice calling in the hens.* They pursue one another in the air as well as on the boughs . . . more frequently four in number seem to fly after each other and keep together, sometimes two will join in the air and seem to fight, and call with a sharp note . . .

22 October . . . A Rook is seen fetching up a branch from the lawn into a tree, a good sized branch or stick it was . . .

23 October *Going from B to A with gale from C.* They will fly sideways all the way keeping their head to point C.

3 November . . . 4 rooks seen chasing each other for some time – then 4 or 5 more – many other rooks seem two and two perched together – one is pecking at the head of his companion who seems to sit quietly to be thus pecked at, as if his companion was rendering him a service – this lasts about a minute . . .

Five and fours and sixes together frequently yet on the wing chasing each other – often as if two males after a female then the two pursuers stop and fight – then resume pursuit.

They joined on arrival their companions in various quarters and remained on the trees making less and less noise as they got settled.

He thought more were paired by November and that there were less concerted movements than in September.

6 November *Rooks* . . . Two seem to agree together very well but a 3rd coming in is driven off from the party and pursued.

. . . Two stand for a considerable time with their bills in contact – one appears to be the master, to feed the other to peck at the grass and prepare food for it as a hen for its young – he then drives off one or more birds that may be near, then rejoins his mate. *The effect of individual and pair distance was referred to in Chapter 5.*

8 November . . . Two rooks together – a third comes near them – he is pecked at and driven away by one of them who follows him step by step pecking at him.

   . . . Generally among the pairs it is easy to distinguish one smaller than the other, the larger probably the male. *Male and female size and weights confirm this, see Appendix 1.*

18 November *He is describing rooks on the grass near the house.* . . . a pair of them after joining bills and seemingly saluting for a while desist when one of them flapping its wings and turning about, covers the other. Shortly after the rooks on the grass hearing or noticing the unusual cawing going on arose and followed.

25–30 November *He expresses the general belief that their flight and choice of trees in the rookery in the evening foretold a storm.*

Summary

The summary of observations consists of the characteristic features that mark the transactions of the rooks in November – particularly their pairing – and their behaviour in the storms and squalls.

   Frequently also has their flight indicated a change of weather and the coming storm, as when returning from an expedition flying high, and descending with a darting motion and a whirling and a vibratory sort of gyration, or rotating motion – or again appearing like a swarm of bees ascending and descending.

December

Summary

. . . Generally during this month of December the birds were absent from the rookery from sunrise till sunset and by far the greater part after their evening sport retired to roost far from the rookery probably in the more sheltered vallies [*sic*] that [*are*] a mile or two to the northward. The flock that did remain a small one comparatively instead of roosting scattered over the rookery, all congregated together in one part of the rookery that part to the Eastwards, that happens to be most sheltered and in the dark stormy nights they were most silent – the number of those who remained to roost in the rookery at nights varied however pretty considerably . . . *There follow four more pages mainly describing roosting flocks movements.*

17 January . . . wind NW. Snow falls – the 1st snow this year. 9 p.m. snowing still rooks silent but now and then one is heard – moon bright – cloudy – wind N.W. Trees and fields all white, nearly as light as day . . .

28 January/48 . . . many this evening descended on the grass which was slightly covered with snow the ground being frosty and ice everywhere in the lanes these many days back – This evening probably from hunger numbers sought for food on the grass they tore up the ground with their bills and they spared not each other, the stronger party pouncing on the weaker to rob him of the worm or the beech nut.

Summary

The most obvious traits in the manners of the rooks during this month were the forsaking their usual roosting trees and their half-abandoned rookery for other abodes and places of rest during the night. The rookery shorn of one half or two thirds of its usual inmates afforded a retreat for the remainder in its most sheltered part only that happened to be the Eastern portion of it . . .

1 February/48   Hard frosty morning – sun shining in the day – evening frosty – pairing is likewise more visible – perched on the trees in twos, they join their bills and the tremulous motions of their wings indicate their association in pairs as it did 2 months ago when the pairing began.

8 February . . . all roost with their heads to the wind lest the wind should ruffle their feathers and the cold penetrate to their bodies . . .

30 February . . . saw a rook carrying a stick and flying with it into an old nest, which he had selected and was no doubt making his permanent residence – this is the first appearance of the kind this season . . . *There does not seem to be any explanation of 30 February – nor during March was any allowance made for this error.*

Summary of the month of February 1848

The principal characteristics of this month have therefore been only 1st in their whole complement of numbers having been made up by the return of those who during the two preceding winter months seemed to have abandoned the rookery to go and roost elsewhere by night – these jackdaws also it was said would abandon the rooks to go and attend their own nests in the cliffs, have still kept with them all this month . . .

2 March/48   This morning for the first time the weather being mild and still – the rooks prevented this last fortnight by the storms, began in earnest to build, and pick up sticks in all directions carrying them in their bills up the trees where they lay the foundations of new nests, and refit and strengthen the remains of the old ones . . .

11 March (fig. 58)   . . . 63 nests in various stages of progress – the old nests are reduced to few in number . . .

Pages from Lewis Harding's MS

... one nest began a week ago, and not more than half finished – robbed by neighbouring birds and carried to their own nests – 2 or 3 neighbours arrived and took stick after stick, and tufts of grass within, – one in particular from the south end came frequently and seemed particularly ferocious driving even the other robbers off – the unlucky nest was at last reduced to the mere foundation ... *Similar behaviour by a rook 100 years later was described in Chapter 5.*

18 March   ... again counted the nests counting each side of the square separately as on 11th inst. and find.

On side A or North – 49 nests
On side B or West – 53 nests
On side C or South – 63 nests
On side D or East – 61 nests
        Total nests – 199
showing an increase of 136 in 7 days.

19 March/48   ... it would go far with other instances mentioned – such as that of the bird with the white feathers at the E. end – the bird of peculiar voice at the W. end over the green gate – to show that the birds keep their places and their quarters and return to the same, not only every night, but year after year – the only two birds that can be indentified are the two above spoken of – that one with the white feather frequented the same haunt exactly where he has now his nest – all last summer [i.e. *from 28 August*].

23 March/48   ... this conduct of the Rooks so different from heretofore when they used to take little or no notice of the Jackdaws, I attribute to the state of forwardness of their nests ... and that the rooks probably don't wish to be any more distracted by these strangers or have them about their nests.

25 March   ... egg shells have been seen at the foot of some trees – therefore already are many birds no doubt hatched – that is about 3 weeks after the first nests were completed. It may be said that the rooks began to build the first of this month.

29 March   ... again counted the nests and find them as follows

On North side   86
On West side   107
On East side   128
On South side   60
Total nests   381

Summary

This month has been the month of building nests, during which they have built 381 nests and are yet building more.

They continued their evening sports [*pursuit flights*] at the beginning of the month but gradually ceased them, as the work of building became more general . . . The number of rooks have decreased – for at first their seemed to be at least 7 or 8 birds to a nest, afterwards about 800 only seemed engaged with nest building and these have completed 381 nests . . . where the remainder of the rooks have gone is a question, there were if I mistake not more than three times that number before and since the nest building began – have they gone to build at some other quarter or part of the country . . . it appears that the eggs are hatched in less than 3 weeks after being laid . . . while building and as one fetches sticks the other stands by the nest to guard.

7 April   . . . it appears as well as can be distinguished that the male birds [*rooks*] bring food to their mates sitting on the nests, these raise their heads to receive what is brought, gently flapping at the same time their half expanded wings . . .

15 April   . . . counted the rooks nests – because in a few days the leaves will have covered the trees and it will be impossible then to count them over.

North end   101
East end   175
West end   128
South end (or clump at the back of the House)
                        74
Total nests   478

27 April   . . . birds feeding their young – one old one arrives at the nest, his mate rises immediately and allows the little ones to be fed first – then perhaps takes a bit herself – and then leaves the nest herself and goes to take a flight for exercise or for food, the other remains either in or near the nest waiting patiently . . . rooks are beginning to moult – feathers strewn about.

Summary

During this month the birds continued building nests even to the last day – but it may be said that the building properly ceased about the middle of the month . . .

15 May 1848   . . . rooks disturbed all day by the shooting . . .

16 May   . . . last night there were some boys evidently robbing some nests for the rooks that were thus disturbed set up a cry as if they were throttled and no doubt they were – this in two or three places – the disturbance however did not extend beyond these localities – the disturbance did not become general – it lasted for about ½ an hour between midnight and

one o'clock, some boys must have got up the trees, and I am informed this happens almost every year at this time and that young rooks are thus stolen from the nest and the boughs.

19 May   Birds still moulting – their feathers strewed about the lawn and rookery – collected a bundle of a few hundred of such feathers – hence many of the old birds as they fly in the air appear still, and have appeared this last month or 5 weeks to have many of their wing feathers wanting.

25 May   In the day time, and during the heat the young accompanied by the old exercise themselves on the neighbouring trees – flying from one to the other – one or two I observed, afraid to venture far in the open fields would fly a little way and turn round again screeching all the while – like children learning to swim, and afraid of getting out of their depth.

Summary

This month the rook's main occupation has been to feed their young in and out of the nests, to accompany them when sufficiently grown out to the fields and then train them to seek their own food and to feed them even there. They likewise provided food for their mates while sitting on the eggs and while sitting on the young their manner of feeding them is described . . . *referring to the young rooks* . . . they were also made careful and watchful by the experience they learned of their natural enemy man as their alarm and their movements on the occasion of the shooting show, as described on the 13th and 15th . . .

The Jackdaws scarcely ever appeared during the day time in this month, but returned regularly every evening in large numbers and in several flocks . . . but built no nests themselves nor reared any brood of their own here.

10 June 1848 *Late young are still fed*   . . . day after day they are seen yet bringing them food as much as their craw will hold, of worms some of them hanging out of their bills, and so loaded that they cannot emit a full sound, but make their approach known by a low hoarse croaking . . .

22 June 1848   . . . moulting not quite over, picked up a few feathers, and many birds with wings ragged yet . . .

Summary

During this month the old birds have been feeding the young as well in the fields as in the rookery. There were however towards the end of the month [*some*] that were unable to fly off and accompany the old in their excursions – They were regularly fed on the trees by the old ones calling every half hour . . . as the young grew up and became capable of accompanying the old ones they were seen flying sometimes at great heights as if practising and the old birds gradually returning to their old habits of going and returning in flocks . . .

9 July   From the above it is now an ascertained fact that no Jackdaws laid eggs and reared young in this rookery, this year past. *Harding had been told that some Jackdaws took over some of the rooks' nests after the rooks had left and laid their eggs there.*

14 July   During the day which was fine there was not a rook about. A great many feathers strewed about and of the larger sort, indicate that the moulting is not over which had begun long before the hay was let to grow . . .

July summary

Young rooks continued to be fed by the old at home this month until the 10th after which there were no young left at home but all were able to accompany the old out a forraging – the birds generally started very early in the morning i.e. from dawn till sunrise . . . also towards the 19th they began to hold their silent meetings . . . frequently they returned home, not flying directly for the rookery but approaching gradually and making some stay in the fields on the way – sometimes they appeared to be in such vast numbers as to warrant a belief that they had been joined by some neighbouring rookeries . . .

Summary

The autumnal cry of the birds begins to be heard in the month of August a cry different and easily distinguishable by the observer from that of other times. In this month they begin to live more at home being in and about the rookery in the course of the day. Going out later in the morning and returning earlier in the evening . . . they assemble again in flocks sport together in the mornings and evenings instead of each being occupied with his own family affairs . . . during the lightening [*sic*] and thunder, they fly off as if they had been fired at and don't return until their fright is allayed.

Harding was born in 1806, only thirteen years after Gilbert White had died. His one-year study was remarkably detailed and accurate, and using modern interpretations, a long list of data can be extracted from it, including the following; that rooks often pair in the autumn; that they remain paired throughout the year; that nest material is carried in the autumn; that pursuit flights (sporting) are resumed in August; mutual preening and bill wiping were described; males are dominant over females, and some males are dominant over others in stealing nest material, and rooks are dominant over jackdaws; that in hard weather there are specialized feeding conditions with more fighting; that rooks mob a predator (man) holding a young bird that has fallen to the ground; that worms, grain, beech mast, turnips and potatoes are among the food items; that both females and young flutter their wings when they are fed; that the incubation period is a little less than three weeks. There are many observations on flight in relation to wind and he supposed that, in modern terms, heat loss would occur if a bird sat tail on to the wind allowing ruffling of its feathers. He had satisfied himself that jackdaws do not use rooks' nests after the latter had left, and that the tumbling flight of rooks does not foretell a change of weather.

I spent much time myself during the years from 1945 to 1960 – and especially in 1947–9 – trying to learn something about the 'actions and habits of the rooks through the varying months of the year'.

'My' rookery was about 30 miles from Trelawne where Harding had made his observations exactly 100 years earlier. My admiration for his success, without benefit of modern equipment, transport, or literature, is tinged with regret that there seem to be no further natural-history records by him. He did not even put his name to the diary and it was Thomas Couch who wrote the note identifying the author. I wonder how great was Dr Jonathan Couch's influence on this remarkable record.

References

CHAPTER 1

Feare, C.J., *The Ecology of Damage by Rooks*, in press
Fisher, J., *The Shell Bird Book*, London, 1966
Harding, L., unpublished diary, 1848
Hare, C.E., *Bird Lore*, London, 1952
Jefferies, R., *Wild Life in a Southern County*, London, 1879
Murton, R.K., *Man and Birds*, London, 1971
Thomas, C., *The Taboo*, Camborne, 1951
Turcek, F.J. and Kelso, L., 'Ecological aspects of food transportation and storage in the Corvidae, *Comm. Behav. Biol.* Pr. A, 1: 277–297, 1968

CHAPTER 2

Amadon, D., 'The Genera of Corvidae and their Relationships', *Amer. Mus. Novit.*, 1251, 1944
American Ornithologists' Union, *Auk* 93: 378, 1977
Fisher, J. and Peterson, R.T., *The World of Birds*, London, 1964
Goodwin, D., *Crows of the World*, London, 1976
Kulczycki, A., 'Nesting of the Members of Corvidae in Poland', *Acta Zoologica Cracoviensia* 18: 584–666, 1973

CHAPTER 3

Allin, E.K., 'Breeding Notes on Ravens in North Wales', *British Birds* 61: 541–5, 1968
Aspden, W., 'Further Notes on Puffin Island 1928', *British Birds* 22: 103–6, 1928–9
Bolam, G., *Wildlife in Wales*, London, 1913

Bolt, A.W., 'Ravens Nesting in a Heronry', *British Birds* 41: 115, 1948
Bryson, D.K., 'Large Gathering of Ravens during the Breeding Season', *British Birds*, 40: 209, 1947
Cadman, W.A., 'A Welsh Raven Roost', *British Birds* 40: 209, 1947
Campbell, B., 'Raven Nesting in a Rookery', *British Birds* 39: 340, 1946
Coombes, R.A.H., 'The Flocking of the Raven', *British Birds* 41: 290–4, 1948
Coombes, R.A.H., 'A Supplementary Note on the Flocking of Ravens', *British Birds* 41: 386, 1948
Coombs, C.J.F., 'Roosting of Ravens', *16th Annual Report of the Cornwall Bird Watching and Preservation Society*, 49–50, 1946
Cowin, W.S. and Rogers, H.M. Jnr, 'Ravens Nesting in a Rookery, *British Birds* 38: 53, 1944–5
Cox, A.H.M., 'Raven Nesting in a Heronry', *British Birds* 19: 149–50, 1925–6
Dementiev, G.P. and Gladkov, N.A., *The Birds of the Soviet Union*, Moscow, 1951–4
Dobinson, H.M. and Richards, A.J., 'The Effects of the Severe Winter of 1962–3 on birds in Britain', *British Birds* 57: 373–434, 1964
Elkins, N., 'Raven Catching Rock Dove in the Air', *British Birds* 57: 302, 1964
Fielden, W.H., 'Ravens as Scavengers', *British Birds* 3: 57–8, 1909
Forrest, H.E., 'Raven Nesting again in Shropshire', *British Birds* 12: 19, 1918
Gilbert, H.A., 'Gatherings of Ravens in Breconshire', *British Birds* 39: 52, 1946
Gwinner, Von E., Untersuchungen über das Ausdrucks und Sozialverhalten des Kolkraben [Corvus corax corax L] z. Tierpsychol 21: 657–748, 1964
Gwinner, Von E., 'Beobachtungen über Nestbau und Brutpflege des Kolkraben [Corvus corax] in Gefangenschaft', *J. Orn.*, 106: 146–77, 1965
Gwinner, Von E., Uber den Einfluss des Hunger und anderer Faktoren auf die Versteck – Activität des Kolkraben [Corvus corax], *Vögelwarte* 23: 1–4, 1965[2]
Gwinner, Von E., 'Uber einige Bewegungsspiele des Kolkraben' [Corvus corax L], *Z. Tierpsychol* 23: 28–36, 1966
Harthan, A.J., 'Ravens Nesting in a Rookery', *British Birds* 38: 120, 1944–5
Holyoak, D., 'Breeding Biology of the *Corvidae*', *Bird Study* 14: 153–68, 1967
Holyoak, D., 'A comparative Study of the Food of some British *Corvidae*', *Bird Study* 15: 147–53, 1968
Holyoak, D., 'Movements and Mortality of *Corvidae*', *Bird Study* 18: 97–106, 1971
Holyoak, D. and Ratcliffe, D.A., 'The Distribution of the Raven in Britain and Ireland', *Bird Study* 15: 191–7, 1968
Hume, R.A., 'Successful Breeding of Ravens on City Building', *British Birds* 68: 55–6, 1975
Hunt, O.D., 'Ravens Nesting in a Heronry', *British Birds* 39: 340, 1946
Hurrell, H.G., 'A Raven Roost in Devon', *British Birds* 49: 28–31, 1956
Hutson, H.P.W., 'Roosting Procedure of *Corvus corax Lawrencei Hume*', *Ibis* 87: 456–9, 1945
Kulczycki, D., 'Nesting of the Members of the *Corvidae* in Poland', *Acta Zool Craco* 18: 583–666, 1973
Lewis, S., 'Notes on Somersetshire Ravens', *British Birds* 14: 26–33, 1920–1
Moon, H.J., 'Nest Occupied by Raven, Buzzard, and Peregrine in Successive Years', *British Birds* 17: 59, 1923
Onslow, G.H., 'Raven Nesting in a Heronry', *British Birds* 39: 212, 1946
Ratcliffe, D.A., 'Breeding Density in the Peregrine falcon, *Falco peregrinus*, and the raven, *Corvus corax*', *Ibis* 104: 13–39, 1962
Ryves, B.H., *Bird Life in Cornwall*, London, 1948
Sage, B.L., 'Albinism and Melanism in Birds', *British Birds* 55: 201–20, 1962
Simmons, K.E.L., 'Further Observations on Food-Hiding in the *Corvidae*', *British Birds* 63: 175–7, 1970

Tinbergen, N., 'Carrion Crow striking Lapwing in the Air', *British Birds* 46: 377, 1953
Ticehurst, N.F., 'On the Former Abundance of the Kite, Buzzard and Raven in Kent', *British Birds* 14: 34–7, 1920–1
Venables, L.S.V. and Venables, U.M., *Birds and Mammals of Shetland*, London, 1955
Voous, K.H., *Atlas of European Birds*, London, 1960
Walters-Davies, P. and Davis, P.E., 'The Ecology and Conservation of the Red Kites in Wales', *British Birds* 66: 184–270, 1973
Warren, E.F., 'The Fledging of a Brood of Ravens', *British Birds* 48: 172–5, 1955
Witherby, H.F., 'Raven with only one Eye', *British Birds* 11: 117, 1918
Witherby, H.F., *et al*, *The Handbook of British Birds*, London, 1938

CHAPTER 4

Abshagen, K., 'Über die Nester der Nebelkrähen [*Corvus corone cornix*]', Beitre 2 Vogelk. 8(5): 325–38, 1963
Arnold, M.A., 'Bat as the Prey of a Carrion Crow', *British Birds* 48: 91, 1955
Aspden, W., 'Herons and Carrion Crow', *British Birds* 22: 64–5, 1928–9
Axell, H.E., 'Predation and Protection at Dungeness Bird Reserve', *British Birds* 49: 193–212, 1956
Blackett, A., 'Coot Killing Carrion Crow', *British Birds* 63: 384, 1970
Broad, R.A., 'Contamination of Birds with Fulmar Oil', *British Birds* 67: 297–301, 1974
Brock, S.E., 'Carrion Crow Roost', *British Birds* 7: 203, 1913–14
Bromley, F.C., 'Carrion Crow Killing Wood Pigeon', *British Birds* 40: 114, 1947
Brown, R.H., 'Field Notes from Lakeland', *British Birds* 21: 106–16, 1926
Busse, P., 'Results of Ringing European *Corvidae*', *Acta Orn Warsz XI* 8: 263–328, 1969
Cawkell, E.M., 'Carrion Crow Attacking Magpie', *British Birds* 41: 83, 1948
Charles, J.K., 'Territorial Behaviour and the Limitation of Population Size in the Crow, *Corvus corone* and *Corvus cornix*', unpublished Ph.D. thesis, Aberdeen University, 1972
Cook, A., 'Changes in the Carrion/Hooded Hybrid Zone and the Possible Importance of Climate', *Bird Study* 22: 165–8, 1975
Coombs, C.J.F., 'Behaviour of Young Hooded Crow with Ants', *British Birds* 40: 245, 1947
Coombs, C.J.F., 'Observations on the Rook in Southwest Cornwall', *Ibis* 102: 394–419, 1960
Cornwallis, 'The Pattern of Migration in 1953 at the East Coast Bird Observatories', *British Birds* 47: 423–31, 1954
——, 'The Pattern of Migration in 1954 at the East Coast Bird Observatories', *British Birds* 48: 429–46, 1955
Cross, A., 'Carrion Crows Attacking a Jay', *British Birds* 40: 273, 1947
Croze, H., 'Searching image in Carrion Crows', *Z. Tierpsychol* 5: 1–86, 1970
Denny, J., 'Hooded Crow Dropping and Catching Object in Bill', *British Birds* 43: 333, 1950
Dickson, R.C., 'Daylight Hunting by Barn Owls', *British Birds* 65: 221–2, 1972
Dobinson, H.M. and Richards, A.J., 'The Effects of the Severe Winter of 1962–63 on Birds in Britain', *British Birds* 57: 373–434, 1964
England, M.D., 'Fight to the Death and Communal Nesting by Carrion Crows', *British Birds* 63: 385–6, 1970
Ferrier, J.M., 'Carrion Crow Attacking Squirrel', *British Birds* 25: 129–30, 1931–2
Geogehan, D.P. and Fileman, M.H., 'Carrion Crow Attacking Wood Pigeon', *British Birds* 43: 368, 1950
Goodwin, D., 'Further Observation on the Behaviour of the Jay, *Garrulus glandarius*', *Ibis* 98: 186–219, 1956

Gwinner, Von E., 'Über einige Bewegungssfiele des Kolkraben [*Corvus corax* L], 2 *Tierpsychol.* 23: 28–36, 1966

Hanford, D.M., 'Carrion Crow Persistently Stooping at Swallows', *British Birds* 62: 158, 1969

Harrison, C.J.O., 'Grey and Fawn Variant Plumages', *Bird Study* 10: 212–33, 1963

Hayman, R.W., 'Carrion Crow and Blackheaded and Common Gulls "Playing" with objects in Flight', *British Birds* 46: 378, 1953

Holyoak, D., 'Sex Differences in Feeding Behaviour and Size in the Carrion Crow', *Ibis* 112: 397–400, 1970

Holyoak, D., 'Breeding Biology of the *Corvidae*', *Bird Study* 14: 153–68, 1967

Holyoak, D., 'Movements and Mortality of *Corvidae*', *Bird Study* 18: 97–106, 1971

Holyoak, D., 'A Comparative Study of the Food of some British *Corvidae*', *Bird Study* 15: 147–53, 1968

Houston, D.C., *Report on Hooded Crows and Hill Sheep Farming in Argyll*, Department of Forestry and Natural Resources, Edinburgh University, 1974

Husband, C.I., 'Carrion Crow Carrying off Nesting Wood Pigeon', *British Birds* 59: 499–500, 1966

Kulczycki, A., 'Nesting of the Members of the *Corvidae* in Poland', *Acta Zoologica Cracoviensia* 18: 583–666, 1973

Lack, 'Radar Evidence on Migratory Orientation', *British Birds* 55: 139–58, 1962

Leach, E.P., 'British Recoveries of Birds Wings Abroad', *British Birds* 49: 438–52, 1956

Lohrl, H., 'Zum verhalten der Rabenkrähe gegenüber dem Habicht', *Z. Tierpsychol* 7: 130–3, 1950

McIntyre, N., 'Curious Behaviour of Carrion Crow', *British Birds* 46: 377–8, 1953

McKendry, W.G., 'Carrion Crow Persistently "Playing" with Object', *British Birds* 66: 400, 1973

Medlicott, W.S., 'Bird notes from the Western Front [Pas de Calais]', *British Birds*, 1918–19

Newton, I., 'Studies of Sparrowhawks', *British Birds* 66: 271–8, 1973

Nethersole-Thompson, C. and Nethersole-Thompson, D., 'Display of the Hooded Crow', *British Birds* 34: 135, 1940–1

Owen, D.F., '*Neottiophilum praestum* in Birds' Nests', *British Birds* 50: 160–3, 1957

Parslow, J.L.F., 'Changes in Status among Breeding Birds in Britain and Ireland', *British Birds* 60: 261–85, 1967

Pettit, R.G. and Butt, D.V., 'Unusual Behaviour of Carrion Crow', *British Birds* 42: 327, 1949

Picozzi, N., 'A Study of the Carrion/Hooded Crow in North-East Scotland', *British Birds* 68: 409–19, 1975

Pomeroy, D.E., 'Birds with Abnormal Bills', *British Birds* 55: 49–72, 1962

Pring, C.J., 'Time Period for Nest and Egg Replacement', *British Birds* 18: 266, 1924–5

Radford, A.P., 'Carrion Crow Stooping at Swallows', *British Birds* 63: 428–9, 1970

Ratcliffe, D.A., 'Organo-chlorine Residues in some Raptor and Corvid Eggs from Northern Britain', *British Birds* 58: 65–81, 1965

Rowberry, E.C., 'Carrion Crow Attacking Squirrel', *British Birds* 25: 129, 1931–2

Rothschild, M. and Clay, T., 'Fleas, Flukes and Cuckoos', London, 1952

Sage, B.L., 'Albinism and Melanism in Birds', *British Birds* 55: 201–25, 1962

Sage, B.L., 'Carrion Crow Killing a Kestrel', *British Birds* 55: 482, 1962

Seel, D.C., 'Moult in Five Species of *Corvidae* in Britain', *Ibis* 118: 491–536, 1976

Simmons, K.E.L., 'A Review of the Anting Behaviour of Passerine Birds', *British Birds* 50: 401–24, 1957

Symes, J.H., 'Time Period for Nest and Egg Replacement', *British Birds* 18: 244, 1924–5

Tebbut, C.F., 'Notes on Carrion Crow Displaying to Hooded Crow', *British Birds* 42: 242, 1949

Tenovuo, R., 'Zur Brutzeitlichen Biologi der Nebelkrähe [*C.c. cornix*] im Äusseren Schärenhof Südwestfinnlands. Suomal eläin-ja kasvit', *Seur van Eläin. Julk.* 25: 1–147, 1963

Tinbergen, N., *The Herring Gull's World*, London, 1953

Tinbergen, N., 'Carrion Crow Striking Lapwing in the Air', *British Birds* 46: 377, 1953

Voous, K.H., *Atlas of European Birds*, London, 1960

Walford, N.T., 'Carrion Crow Building with Wire', *British Birds* 24: 51, 1930–1

Walters-Davies, P. and Davis, P.E., 'The Ecology and Conservation of the Red Kite in Wales', *British Birds* 66: 257, 1973

Ward, P. and Zahavi, A., 'The Importance of Certain Assemblages of Birds as Information Centres for Food Finding', *Ibis* 115: 517–34, 1973

Warren, R.B., 'Carrion Crow Taking Starling in the Air', *British Birds* 62: 237–8, 1969

Wittenberg, J., 'Freilanduntersuchungen zu Brutbiologie und Verhalten der Rabenkrähe (*Corvus c. corone*)', *Zool. Jb. Syst. Bd.* 95: 16–146, 1968

Wolfe-Murray, D.K., 'Birds Observed in the North Sea, 1927', *British Birds* 21: 252–5, 1927–8

Yapp, W.B., 'Carrion Crow Taking House Martin', *British Birds* 68: 342, 1975

Yom-Tov, Y., 'The Effect of Food and Predation on Breeding Density and Success, Clutch Size and Laying Date of the Crow [*Corvus corone* L.]', *Journal of Animal Ecology* 43: 479–98, 1974

Yom-Tov, Y., 'Synchronisation of Breeding and Intraspecific Interference in the Carrion Crow', *AUK* 92: 778–85, 1975

Yom-Tov, Y. and Ollason, J.G., 'Sexual Dimorphism and Sex Ratio in Wild Birds', *Oikos* 27: 81–5, 1976

CHAPTER 5

Ash, J.S., 'Observations in Hampshire and Dorset during the 1963 Cold Spell', *British Birds* 57: 221–41, 1964

Barus, S.V., Rysavy, B., Groschaft, J. and Folk, C., 'The Helminth Fauna of *Corvus frugilegus* in Czechoslovakia and its Ecological Analysis', *Acta. Sci. Nat.* Brno 6: 1–53, 1972

Bull, P.C., 'Distribution and Abundance of the Rook in New Zealand', *Notornis* 7(5): 137–61, 1957

Burkitt, J.P., 'Notes on the Rook', *British Birds* 28: 322–6, 1934–5

Burns, P.S., 'Rook and Jackdaw Roosts around Bishops Stortford', *Bird Study* 4: 62–71, 1957

Caldwell, J.A., 'Cannibalism in the Rook', *British Birds* 42: 288, 1949

Coleman, J.D., 'The Rook in Canterbury New Zealand', *N.Z. Journal of Science* 14: 494–506, 1971

Coombs, C.J.F., 'Ectoparasites and Nest Fauna of Rooks and Jackdaws in Cornwall', *Ibis* 102: 326–8, 1960

——, 'Observations on the Rook [*Corvus frugilegus*] in South-West Cornwall', *Ibis* 102: 394–419, 1960

——, 'Rookeries and Roosts of the Rook and Jackdaw in South-West Cornwall', *Bird Study* 8(1): 32–7, (2): 55–70, 1961

Conder, P.J., 'Individual Distance', *Ibis* 91: 649–55, 1949

Dementiev, G.P. and Gladov, N.A., *Birds of the Soviet Union*, Moscow, 1951–4

Deramond, M., 'Sur la répartition actuelle du Freux en France', *Alauda* 20: 243–9, 1952

Dobinson, H.M. and Richards, A.J., 'The Effects of the Severe Winter of 1962/63 on Birds in Britain', *British Birds* 57: 373–434, 1964

Dunnet, G.M. and Patterson, I.J., *The Rook Problem in North-East Scotland. The Problem of Birds as Pests* (Ed. R.K. Murton and E.N. Wright), 119–39, London, 1968

Dunnet, G.M., Fordham, R.A. and Patterson, I.J., 'Ecological Studies of the Rook [Corvus frugilegus] in North-East Scotland. Proportion and distribution of young in the population', *J. Appl. Ecol.* 6: 459–73, 1969

Feare, C.J., 'Ecological Studies of the Rook [Corvus frugilegus L.] in North-East Scotland. Damage and Control', *Journal of Applied Ecology* 11: 897–914, 1974

——, 'The Ecology of Damage by Rooks [Corvus frugilegus], in press

Feare, C.J., Dunnet, G.M. and Patterson, I.J., 'Ecological Studies of the Rook [C. frugilegus] in North-East Scotland. Food intake and feeding behaviour', *Journal of Applied Ecology* 11: 867–96, 1974

Feijen, H.R., 'Over hat voedsal, het voorkomen en de Achteruitgang van de Roek C. Frugilegus in Nederland', *Limosa* 49: 28–66, 1976

Fog, M., 'Distribution and food of Danish Rooks', *Dan. Rev. Game Biol.* 4: 63–110, 1963

Friderich, C.G., *Naturgeschichte der Vogel Europas*, Stuttgart

Goodwin, D., 'Some Observations on the Reproductive Behaviour of Rooks', *British Birds* 48: 97–105, 1955

——, 'Further Observations on the Behaviour of the Jay [Garrulus glandarius]', *Ibis* 98: 186–219, 1956

Grace, E., 'Recruitment Behaviour of Rook', unpublished

Gwinner, E., 'Beobachtungten über Nestbau und Brutpflege des Kolkraben [C. corax] in Gefangenschaft,' *J.-f. Orn.* 106: 146–77, 1965

Harding, L., 'Diary of the Rooks at Trelawne,' unpublished

Harrison, C.J.O., 'Mottled Plumage in the Genus *Corvus*, its Causation and Relationship to Fundamental Barring', *Bulletin of the British Ornithological Club* 83: 41–50, 1963

Harthan, A.J., 'Grey Squirrels Taking Young Rooks', *British Birds* 34: 94, 1940–1

Hinde, R.A., 'The Behaviour of the Great Tit [Parus major] and Some Other Related Species', *Behaviour Supplement* 2: 1–201, 1952

Holyoak, D., 'Breeding Biology of the *Corvidae*', *Bird Study* 14: 153–68, 1967

——, 'A Comparative Study of the Food of Some British *Corvidae*', *Bird Study* 115: 147–53, 1968

Keymer, I.F. and Blackmore, D.K., 'Diseases of the Soft Parts of Wild Birds', *British Birds* 57: 175–9, 1964

King, B. and Rolls, J.C., 'Feeding methods of Rook with Malformed Bill', *British Birds* 61: 417–18, 1968

Kirkman, F.B., *Bird Behaviour*, London, 1937

Kulczycki, A., 'Nesting of the Members of the *Corvidae* in Poland', *Acta. Zoologica Cracoviensia* 18: 584–662, 1973

Lack, D., *The Life of the Robin*, London, 1943

Lockie, J.D., 'Winter Fighting in Feeding Flocks of Rooks, Jackdaws and Carrion Crows', *Bird Study* 3: 180–90, 1956

——, 'The Food of Nestling Rooks near Oxford', *British Birds* 52: 332–4, 1959

Marler, P., 'Studies of Fighting in Chaffinches. 1: Behaviour in Relation to Social Hierarchy', *Brit. J. Anim. Behav.* 3: 111–17, 1955

Marples, B.J., 'The Rookeries of the Wirral Peninsula', *Journal of Animal Ecology* 1: 3–11, 1932

Marples, G. and Marples, A., *Sea Terns and Sea Swallows*, London, 1934

Marshall, A.J. and Coombs, C.J.F., 'The Interaction of Environmental Internal and Behavioural Factors in the Rook', *Proc. Zool. Soc. Lond.* 128: 545–89, 1957

McKendry, W.G., 'Rook with Recurrent Bill Malformation', *British Birds* 66: 228–9, 1973

Mountfort, G., *Portrait of a Wilderness*, London, 1958

Nethersole-Thompson, D. and Musselwhite, D.W., 'Male Rook Incubating', *British Birds* 34: 44, 1940–1

Newton, I., *Finches*, London, 1972

Nicholson, E.M. and Nicholson, B.D., 'The Rookeries of the Oxford District', *Journal of Ecology* 18: 15–66, 1930

Niethammer, G., *Handbuch der Deutschen Vögelkunde* 1, Leipzig, 1937

Nijhoft, P., 'Herfsttrekwaarnemingen bij Cap Gris Nez', *Ardea* 46: 62–7, 1958

Owen, D.F., 'The Breeding Seasons and Clutch Size of the Rook', *Ibis* 101: 235–9, 1959

Patterson, I.J., Dunnet, G.M. and Fordham, R.A., 'Ecological Studies of the Rook [*C. frugilegus*] in North-East Scotland. Dispersion', *J. Appl. Ecol.* 8: 815–33, 1971

Pinowski, J., 'Factors Influencing the Number of Feeding Rooks in Various Field Environments', *Ecol. Pol.* 7: 435–82, 1959

Prazak, J.P., 'Materialen zu einer ornis ost-gabziens, *J. Orn.* 45: 233, 1897

Ratcliffe, D.A., 'Organo-chlorine Residues in Some Raptor and Corvid Eggs from Northern Britain', *British Birds* 58: 65–81, 1965

Report on Somerset Birds, 1953

Richards, P.R., 'Pair Formation and Pair Bond in Captive Rooks', *Bird Study* 23: 207–11, 1976

Roberts, B.B., 'Notes on the Birds of Central and South-East Iceland with Special Reference to Food Habits', *Ibis* 13: 236–64, 1934

Rothschild, M. and Clay, T., *Fleas, Flukes and Cuckoos*, London, 1952

Royama, T., 'A Re-interpretation of Courtship Feeding', *Bird Study* 13: 116–29, 1966

Sage, B.L., 'Albinism and Melanism in British Birds', *British Birds* 55: 201–25, 1962

——, 'The Incidence of Albinism and Melanism in British Birds', *British Birds* 56: 409–16, 1963

Seel, D.C., 'Moult in Five Species of *Corvidae* in Britain', *Ibis* 118: 491–536, 1976

Sevingland, J.R., 'The Influence of Light Intensity on the Roosting Times of the Rook [*Corvus frugilegus*]', *Anim. Behav.* 24: 154–8, 1976

Simmons, K.E.L., 'Anting and the Problem of Self-Stimulation', *J. Zool.* 149: 145–62, 1966

Simmons, K.E.L., 'Direct Head-Scratching by Rook in Flight', *British Birds* 67: 243, 1974

Tayler, A.G., 'Rooks' Nests Lined with Feathers', *British Birds* 33: 311, 1939–40

Thorpe, W.H., 'A type of Insight Learning in Birds', *British Birds* 37: 29–31, 1943

Tinbergen, N., 'Specialists in Nest Building', *Country Life* 113: 270–1, 1953

Tinbergen, N., 'The Activation, Extinction and Interaction of Instinctive Origins – Royal Institute of Great Britain. 24 February 1956

Tischler, F., *Die Vogel Ostfreussens*, Vol. 1, Konigsberg, 1941

Tucker, B.W., 'The Rookeries of Somerset', *Proc. Somerset Arch. Nat. Hist. Soc.* 81: 149–240, 1935

Verhayan, R., *Les Passereaux de Belgique*, Vol. 1, Brussels, 1946

Voous, K.H., *Atlas of European Birds*, London, 1960.

Walters Davies, P. and Davis, P.E., 'Ecology and Conservation of the Red Kite in Wales', *British Birds* 66: 243–70, 1973

Walton, C.L., 'Rooks and Agriculture in Mid- and North Wales', *Welsh Journal of Agriculture* 4: 353–6, 1928

Ward, P., 'Feeding Ecology of the Black-Faced Dioch [*Quelea quelea*] in Nigeria', *Ibis* 107: 173–214, 1965

Waterhouse, M.J., 'Rooks and Jackdaw Migrations Observed in Germany 1942–45', *Ibis* 91: 1–16, 1949

West Midland Bird Report, The, 1953

White, Gilbert, Letter to Thomas Pennant Esquire, 30 March 1768

——, Letter to the Hon. Daines Barrington, 9 September 1778

——, *The Natural History and Antiquities of Selborne*, 1789

Wolfe-Murray, D.K., 'Birds Observed in the North Sea', *British Birds* 21: 252–5, 1927–8

Wynne, J.F., 'The Rookeries of the Isle of Wight', *J. Anim. Ecol.* 1: 168–74, 1932

Wynne-Edwards, V.C., *Animal Dispersion in Relation to Social Behaviour*, London, 1962
Yapp. W.B., 'The Rook Population of West Gloucestershire', *J. Anim. Ecol.* 3: 77–80, 1934
Yarrell, W., *A History of British Birds*, London, 1845
Yeates, G.K., *The Life of the Rook*, London, 1934
Zahavi, A., 'The Function of Pre-Roost Gatherings and Communal Roosts', *Ibis* 113: 106–9, 1971

CHAPTER 6

Birkhead, T.R., 'Predation by Birds on Social Wasps', *British Birds* 67: 221–9, 1974
Brownsey, B.W. and Peakall, D.B., 'Jackdaw Roost Continuing Throughout the Breeding Season', *British Birds* 48: 371, 1955
Busse, P., 'Results of Ringing European *Corvidae*', *Acta. Orn. Wars. XI* 8: 263–328, 1969
Campbell, J.W., 'Food of some British Birds', *British Birds* 30: 209–18, 1936–7
Chappel, B.M.A., 'Little Owl Attacking Jackdaw', *British Birds* 43: 123, 1950
Coombs, C.J.F., 'Rookeries and Roosts of the Rook and Jackdaw in South-West Cornwall', *Bird Study* 8: 32–7, 55–70, 1961
——, 'Sarcoma in a Jackdaw', *Ibis* 87: 104, 1945
Cornish, A.V., 'Jackdaw Hawking Flying Ants', *British Birds* 40: 115, 1947
Cornwallis, R.K., 'The Pattern of Migration in 1954 at the East Coast Bird Observatories', *British Birds* 48: 429–46, 1955
Cowin, W.S., 'White-Winged Jackdaws in the Isle of Man', *British Birds* 26: 364, 1932–3
Dickson, R.C., 'Raven Clutching Jackdaw in the Air', *British Birds* 62: 497, 1969
Dobinson, H.M. and Richards, A.J., 'The Effects of the Severe Winter of 1962–63 on Birds in Britain', *British Birds* 57: 373–434, 1964
Eggeling, W.J. and Eggeling, A.H., 'Incubation and Fledgling Periods of Some British Birds', *British Birds* 24: 124, 1930–1
Fairhurst, A.R., 'Note on Food-Burying and Recovery by Rook', *British Birds* 67: 215, 1974
Glue, D.E. and Hammond, G.J., 'Feeding Ecology of the Long-Eared Owl in Britain and Ireland', *British Birds* 67: 361–9, 1974
Griffiths, J., 'Jackdaws Roost Continuing throughout the Breeding Season', *British Birds* 48: 139, 1955
Haartmann, L. von, 'The Nesting Habitat of Finnish Birds', *Comm. Biol.*, 1–187, 1969
Hinde, R.A., 'Autumn Pairing of Jackdaws', *British Birds* 40: 246, 1947
Hoffmann, L., 'An Ecological Sketch of the Carmargue', *British Birds* 51: 321–50, 1958
Holyoak, D., 'Breeding Biology of the *Corvidae*', *Bird Study* 14: 153–68, 1967
——, 'A Comparative Study of the Food of Some British *Corvidae*', *Bird Study* 15: 147–53, 1968
——, 'Movements and Mortality of *Corvidae*', *Bird Study* 18: 91–106, 1971
Hudson, R., 'Recoveries in Great Britain and Ireland of Birds Ringed abroad', *British Birds* 58: 87–97, 1965
Hudson, 'Recoveries in Great Britain and Ireland of Birds Ringed Abroad', *British Birds*, 62: 13–21, 1969
Keymer, I.F., 'Newcastle Disease in the Jackdaw', *Vet. Rec.* 73: 119–22, 1961
Keymer, I.F. and Blackmore, D.K., 'Diseases of the Skin and Soft Parts of Wild Birds', *British Birds* 57: 176, 1964
King, B., 'Jackdaws Eating Oily Fish Paper', *British Birds* 66: 496, 1973
Kulczycki, A., 'Nesting of the Members of the *Corvidae* in Poland', *Acta Zool. Cracov.* 18: 583–666, 1973
Larsson, E., 'Account of Jackdaws Overwintering in Boden, North Sweden', *Fauna och Flora* 2: 88, 1944

Lea, D. and Bourne, W.R.P., 'The Birds of Orkney', *British Birds* 68: 261, 281, 1975

Lint, A., 'Roosting of Jackdaws in Tarto Estonia', *Ornit. Kogumik* 5: 132–63, 1971

Lockie, J.D., 'The Breeding and Feeding of Jackdaws and Rooks with Notes on Carrion Crows and other *Corvidae*', *Ibis* 97: 341–69, 1955

——, 'Winter Fighting in Feeding Flocks of Rooks, Jackdaw and Carrion Crow', *Bird Study* 3: 180–90, 1956

Lorenz, K., *Studies in Animal and Human Behaviour*, Vol. 1, London, 1970

——, *King Solomon's Ring*, London, 1970

Lundin, A., 'Observations on the Habits of Jackdaws at Roosting and Wintering Grounds', *Vår Fårgel*. 21: 81–95, 1962

Mead, C.J. and Peplar, G.R.M., 'Birds and Other Animals at Sand Martin Colonies', *British Birds* 68: 89–99, 1975

Morley, A., 'Sexual Behaviour in British Birds from October to January', *Ibis* 85: 132–58, 1943

Mylne, C.K., 'Techniques of Jackdaws and Herring Gulls Preying on Puffins', *British Birds* 53: 86–8, 1960

Nicholson, E.M., Ferguson-Lees, I.J. and Hollom, P.A.D., 'The Carmargue and the Coto Donana', *British Birds* 50: 497–520, 1957

Rolls, J.C., 'Moorhen Killing a Jackdaw', *British Birds* 64: 458, 1971

——, 'Prolonged Mobbing of Common Tern by Swallows and Jackdaws', *British Birds* 66: 169, 1973

Rothschild, M. and Clay, T., *Fleas, Flukes and Cuckoos*, London, 1952

Sage, B.L., 'The Incidence of Alibinism and Melanism in British Birds', *British Birds* 56: 412, 1963

Seel, D.C., 'Moult in Five Species of *Corvidae* in Britain', *Ibis* 118: 491–536, 1976

Simmons, K.E.L., 'Food Hiding by Rooks and Other Crows, *British Birds* 61: 228–9, 1968

Spencer, R., 1961, 'Report on Bird Ringing in 1960', *British Birds* 54: 477, 1961

——, 'Report on Bird Ringing in 1961', *British Birds* 55: 523, 1962

Spring Immigration of Jackdaws on the Hampshire Coast (Ed. note), *British Birds* 13: 50,

Turcek, F.J. and Kelso, I., *Comm. Behav. Biol.* A 1: 277–97, 1960

Van Oss, R.M., 'Jackdaw Attacking Starling', *British Birds* 43: 292, 1950

Venables, L.S.U. and U.M., 'Jackdaws Breeding in the Shetland Isles', *British Birds* 40: 140–2, 1947

Voous, K.H., 'The Post-Glacial Distribution of *Corvus monedula* in Europe', *Limosa* 23: 281–92, 1950

Walters Davies, P. and Davis, P.E., 'The Ecology and Conservation of the Red Kite in Wales', *British Birds* 66: 250–1, 1973

Webber, G.L., 'Birds Trapped by Sludge on a Sewage Farm', *British Birds* 58: 296, 1965

Williams, R., 'Little Owl Attacking and Carrying off Jackdaw', *British Birds* 38: 194–5, 1944

Williams, T.S., 'Jackdaw Carrying Young Thrush in Claw', *British Birds* 39: 149–50, 1946

Wolfe Murray, D.K., 'North Sea Migrants 1930', *British Birds* 25: 6–11, 1931

Witherby, H.F., *The Handbook of British Birds*, London, 1938

Koslova, E.V., 'The Birds of South-West Transbaikalia, Northern Mongolia and Central Gobi', *Ibis* 13: 60–1, 1933

Goodwin, D., *Crows of the World*, London, 1976

Merikallio, E., *Finnish Birds*, Helsinki, 1958

CHAPTER 7

Blair, R.H., 'Nest Sanitation', *British Birds* 34: 226–35, 250–5, 1940

Bonham, P.F., 'Studies of Less Familiar Birds 157. Chough and Alpine Chough', *British Birds* 63: 28–32, 1970

Bowdler Sharpe, R., *A Handbook to the Birds of Great Britain*, London, 1896

Campbell, B., 'Nest Sanitation and Egg-Shell Disposal of Chough', *British Birds* 39: 340–1, 1946

Cowdy, S., 'Post-Fledging Behaviour of Chough on Bardsey Island', *British Birds* 55: 229–33, 1962

——, 'Ants as a Major Food Source of the Chough', *Bird Study* 29: 117–20, 1973

Darke, T.O., *The Cornish Chough*, Truro, 1971

Dawson, R., 'Choughs Feeding on Blow-Fly Larvae at Cow Carcass', *British Birds* 68: 159–60, 1975

Goodwin, D., *Crows of the World*, London, 1976

Harrison, C., *A Field Guide to the Nests, Eggs and Nestlings of British and European Birds*, London, 1975

Holyoak, D., 'Breeding Biology of the *Corvidae*', *Bird Study* 14: 61–2, 153–68, 1967

——, 'Movements and Mortality of *Corvidae*', *Bird Study* 18: 97–106, 1971

——, 'Behaviour and Ecology of the Chough and Alpine Chough', *Bird Study* 19: 215–27, 1972

——, 'Moult Seasons of the British *Corvidae*', *Bird Study* 21: 15–20, 1974

Kennedy, P.G., Ruttledge, R.F. and Scroope, C.F., *Birds of Ireland*, Edinburgh, 1954

Kulczycki, A., 'Nesting of the Members of the *Corvidae* in Poland', *Acta. Zool. Cracov.* 18: 583–666, 1973

Nethersole Thompson, C. and D., 'Egg-Shell Disposal by Birds', *British Birds* 35, 195, 1941–2

Parslow, J.L.F., 'Changes in Status among Breeding Birds in Britain and Ireland', *British Birds* 60: 261–85, 1967

Rolfe, R., 'The Status of the Chough in the British Isles', *Bird Study* 13: 221–36, 1966

Ryves, B.H., *Bird Life in Cornwall*, London, 1948

Sansbury, D.G., 'Early Breeding of Chough', *British Birds* 43: 293, 1950

Sálim Ali and Dillon-Ripley, S., *Handbook of the Birds of India and Pakistan*, Vol. 5, Bombay, 1972

Turner, B.C.,[1] 'Feeding Behaviour of Ravens and Choughs', *British Birds* 52: 129–31, 1959

——,[2] 'Feeding Behaviour of Choughs', *British Birds* 52: 388–90, 1959

Voous, K.H., *Atlas of European Birds*, London, 1960

White, Gilbert, Letter to Thomas Pennant Esquire, 9 November 1773

Whittaker, I., 'Notes on Welsh Choughs', *British Birds* 40: 265–6, 1947

Williamson, K., 'Down Plumage of Nestling and Soft Parts of Juvenile Chough', *British Birds* 33: 78, 1939–40

Witherby, H.F., *et al.*, *The Handbook of British Birds*, London, 1938

CHAPTER 8

Fergusson-Lees, I.J., 'Chough and Alpine Chough', *British Birds* 51: 99–103, 1958

Goodwin, D., *Crows of the World*, London, 1976

Holyoak, D., 'Behaviour and Ecology of the Chough and Alpine Chough', *Bird Study* 19: 215–27, 1972

Kulczycki, A., 'Nesting of the Members of the *Corvidae* in Poland', *Acta. Zool. Cracov.* 18: 583–666, 1973

Reiser, O., 'Fortpflanzungsbiologie der Alpendöhle. Beitr', *Fort Pfl. Biol.* 2: 81–2, 1926

Rothschild, M., 'Diurnal Movements of the Mountain Chough in the Wengen and Kleine Scheidegg (Bernese Oberland) Areas during the months of January, February and March,' *International Ornithological Congress* 11: 1954 (1955), 611–17, 1956

·Strahm, L., 'Observations hivernales de Chocards. *Pyrroocorax graculus* dans le haute vallée de la Sarine', *Nos Oiseaux* 25: 265–71, 1960

Voous, K.H., *Atlas of European Birds*, London, 1960

CHAPTER 9

Haartman, L. von, 'The Nesting Habits of Finnish Birds', *Coomentatione Biologicae*, 1–187, 1969

Hollyer, J.N., 'The Invasion of Nutcrackers in Autumn 1968', *British Birds* 63: 353–73, 1970

——, 'Further Notes on Nutcrackers in 1968–69', *British Birds* 64: 196–7, 1971

Kulczycki, A., 'Nesting of the Members of the *Corvidae* in Poland', *Acta. Zool. Cracov.* 18: 583–666, 1973

Richards, T.J., 'Concealment and Recovery of Food by Birds, with some Relevant Observations on Squirrels', *British Birds* 51: 497–508, 1958

Swanberg, P.O., 'Food Storage, Territory and Song in the Thick-Billed Nutcrackers', *Proc. 10 Int. Orn. Cong* (1950–51), 497–501, 1951

——, 'Territory in the Thick-Billed Nutcracker', *Ibis* 98; 412–19, 1956

——, 'Incubation in the Thick-Billed Nutcracker, *Nucifraga c. caryocatactus L.*', *Bertil Hanström Zoological Papers in Honour of his 65th Birthday*, Lund, Sweden, 1956

Thorpe, W.H., 'Notes on Some Birds of the Swiss National Park', *British Birds* 17: 160–4, 1923

Turcek, F.J. and Kelso, L., 'Ecological Aspects of Food Transportation and Storage in the *Corvidae*', *Comm. Behav. Biol. PF.* A 1: 277–97, *British Birds* 57: 314–43, 1968

Witherby, H.F., *et al.*, *The Handbook of British Birds*, London, 1938

CHAPTER 10

Birkhead, T.R.,[1] 'Magpie Feeding on Wasp Larvae and Pupae', *British Birds* 66: 119, 1973

——,[2] 'Frequency of Deformed Skulls in Corvids', *Bird Study* 20: 144–5, 1973

Boog, E.J., 'Magpie Killing and Eating a Song Thrush', *British Birds* 69: 309, 1966

Brown, R.H., 'Field Notes on the Magpie as Observed in Cumberland', *British Birds* 18: 122–8, 1924–5

Busse, P., 'Results of Ringing European Crows', *Acta Orn. Wars. XI* 8; 263–328, 1969

Burton, M., Quoted in editorial comment on correspondence about pigeons, crows and other species building nests of wire. *British Birds* 64: 77–80, 1971

Butlin, S.M., 'Food Hiding by Magpie', *British Birds* 64: 422, 1971

Carr, D., 'Magpie Preying on Snake', *British Birds* 62: 238, 1969

Clegg, T.M., 'Pre-coital Display of Magpies', *British Birds* 55: 88–9, 1962

Fairhurst, A.R., 'Magpies Nesting on Ledges and on a Crane', *British Birds* 63: 387, 1970

Felton, C., 'Magpies Nesting on Ground', *British Birds* 62: 445–6, 1969

Goodwin, D., 'Notes and Display of the Magpie', *British Birds* 45: 113–22, 1952

Goodwin, D., 'Crows of the World', London, 1976

Haartman von, L.I., 'The Nesting Habits of Finnish Birds', *Comm. Biol.* 1–187, 1969

Harrison, C.J.O., 'Grey and Fawn Variant Plumages', *Bird Study* 10: 219–33, 1963

Henty, C.J., 'Feeding and Food-Hiding Responses of Jackdaws and Magpies', *British Birds* 68: 463–6, 1975

Holyoak, D.,[1] 'Magpie Singing at Nest', *British Birds* 60: 52, 1969

——,[2] 'Breeding Biology of the *Corvidae*', *Bird Study* 14: 153–68, 1967

——, 'A Comparative Study of the Food of Some British *Corvidae*', *Bird Study* 15: 147–53, 1968

——, 'Movements and Mortality of *Corvidae*', *Bird Study* 18: 97–106, 1971

——, 'Territorial and Feeding Behaviour of the Magpie', *Bird Study* 21: 117–28, 1974

Klejnetowski, Z., 'The Biology of the Magpie', *Roczniki Wyzszej Szkoty Rolniczej W. Poznani* 56: 69–98, 1969

Mountfort, G., *Portrait of a Wilderness*, London, 1958

Owen, D.F., 'The Food of Nestling Jays and Magpies', *Bird Study* 3: 257–65, 1956

Parslow, J.L.F., 'Changes in Status among Breeding Birds in Britain and Ireland', *British Birds* 60: 261–85, 1967

Prestt, I., 'An Enquiry into the Recent Breeding Status of some of the Smaller Birds of Prey and Crows in Britain', *Bird Study* 12: 196–221, 1965

Rolfe, R.L., 'Magpie Preying on a Roost of Tree Sparrows', *British Birds* 58: 150–1, 1965

Ryves, B.H., 'Late Breeding of Magpies', *British Birds* 23: 248, 1929–30

Seel, D.C., 'Moult in Five Species of *Corvidae* in Britain', *Ibis* 118: 491–536, 1976

Simmons, K.E.L., 'Anting and the Problem of Self-Stimulation', *J. Zool.* 149: 145–62, 1966

Stubbs, F.J., 'Ceremonial Gatherings of the Magpie', *British Birds* 3: 334–6, 1909

Suffern, C.L., 'A Brown-and-White Magpie in Hampshire', *British Birds* 58: 220, 1965

Thompson, G.W., 'Magpies Killing Full-Grown Rabbit', *British Birds* 19: 252, 1925–6

Turcek, F.J. and Kelso, L., 'Ecological Aspects of Food Transportation and Storage in the *Corvidae*, *Comm. Behav. Biol.* A 1: 277–97, 1961

Witherby, H.F., 'Report on the Immigration of Summer Residents in the Spring of 1911; also Notes on the Migratory Movements Received from Lighthouses and Light-Vessel during the Autumn of 1910', *Committee appointed by the British Ornithologists Club*, Vol. XXX, *Bull. BOC*, *British Birds* 6: 323–4, 1912

CHAPTER 11

Dos Santos, J.R., 'The Colony of Azure-winged Magpies in the Barco d' Alva Region', *Cyanopica* 1: 1–28, 1968

Goodwin, D., *Crows of the World*, London, 1976

Kulczycki, A., 'Nesting of the Members of the *Corvidae* in Poland', *Acta Zoologica Cracovicensia* 18: 583–666, 1973

Mountfort, G., *Portrait of a Wilderness*, London, 1958

Porter, S., 'Breeding of the Chinese Azure-Winged Magpie', *Avicult. Mag.* 6: 3–8, 1941

CHAPTER 12

Alexander, C.J. and Alexander, H.G., 'Further Observations on the Song-Periods of Birds, *British Birds*, 1910–11

Birkhead, 'Predation by Birds on Social Wasps', *British Birds* 67; 221–9, 1974

Bossema, L., 'European Jay as a Predator, *Levende Nat.* 70: 86–92, 1967

Bossema, L., 'Recovery of Acorns in the European Jay [*Garrulus glandarius*]', *Proc. Koninkl. Nederl. Akad Wettenschaffen Zool.*, Series 71, No. 1, 1968

Chettleburgh, M.R., 'Observations on the Collection and Burial of Acorns by Jays in Hainault Forest', *British Birds* 45: 359–64, 1952

Chettleburgh, M.R., 'Further Notes on the Recovery of Acorns by Jays', *British Birds* 48: 183–4, 1955

Cramp, S. and Tomlins, A.D., 'The Birds of Inner London 1951–65', *British Birds* 59: 209–33, 1966

Cramp, S., Petit, A. and Sharrock, J.T.R., 'The Irruption of Tits in Autumn of 1957', *British Birds* 53: 109–11, 1960

Curtis Edwards, L.A., 'Continental Jays in Oxfordshire and Sussex', *British Birds* 13: 107, 1919–20

Delmqain, J., 'Movement of Jays in France', *British Birds* 29: 297–8, 1935

Editorial Note. 1918. Jays feeding in wheat. *British Birds* 12: 164

Glue, D.E. and Hammond, G.J., 'Feeding Ecology of the Long-Eared Owl in Britain and Ireland', *British Birds* 67: 361–9, 1974

Goodwin, D., 'Anting of Tame Jay', *British Birds* 40: 274–5, 1947

——, 'Incubation of the Tame Jay', *British Birds* 42: 53, 1948

——, 'Notes on Two Jays', *Avicult. Mag.* 55: 1949

——, 'Jays Eating Plane Buds', *British Birds* 42: 242, 1949

——, 'Some Aspects of the Behaviour of the Jay', *Ibis* 93: 414–42, 602–25, 1951

——, 'Jays and Magpies Eating Wasps', *British Birds* 45: 364, 1952

——,[2] 'A Comparative Study of the Voice and Some Aspects of Behaviour of Two Old-World Jays', *Behaviour* 4: 293–316, 1952

——,[1] 'Jays Nesting in Hollows in Trees', *British Birds* 46: 113, 1953

——,[2] 'The Reactions of Some Nesting Passerines towards Live and Stuffed Jays', *British Birds* 46: 193–200, 1953

——, 'Further Observations on the Behaviour of the Jay [*Garrulus glandarius*]', *Ibis* 98: 186–219, 1956

——, *Crows of the World*, London, 1976

Gurney, J.H., 'Ornithological Notes for Norfolk', *British Birds* 12: 242–57, 1918

Haartman, L. von, 'The Nesting Habits of Finnish Birds', *Comm. Biol.* 1–187, 1969

Harrison, J.M., 'Continental Jays in Kent', *British Birds* 29: 27, 1935–6

Hartert, E., 'On Birds Represented in the British Isles by Peculiar Forms', *British Birds* 1: 208–22, 1907–8

Holyoak, D., 'Breeding Biology of the *Corvidae*', *Bird Study* 14: 153–68, 1967

——, 'A Comparative Study of the Food of Some British *Corvidae*', *Bird Study* 15: 147–53, 1968

——, 'Movements and Mortality of *Corvidae*', *Bird Study* 18: 97–106, 1971

——, 'Moult Seasons of the British *Corvidae*', *Bird Study* 21: 15–20, 1974

Hosking, E.J., 'Incubation of the Jay', *British Birds* 36: 112, 1942

Huxley, J.S., 'Clines; an Auxiliary Method in Taxonomy', *Bijdr. Dierk* 27: 491, 1939

Keve, A., 'The Juvenile Plumage of the Jay [*Garrulus glandarius*]', *Ibis* 109: 120–2, 1967

Owen, D.F., 'The Food of Nestling Jays and Magpies', *Bird Study* 3: 257–64, 1956

Parslow, J.L.F., 'Changes in Status among Breeding Birds in Britain and Ireland', *British Birds* 60: 261–85, 1967

Perrins, C.M., 'Jay Killed by Weasel', *British Birds* 52: 60–1, 1959

Riviere, B.B., 'Continental Jays in Norfolk', *British Birds* 13: 25, 1919–20

Rothschild, M. and Clay, T., *Fleas, Flukes and Cuckoos*, London, 1952

Sage, B.L., 'Albinism and Melanism in Birds', *British Birds* 55: 201–25, 1962

Salfeld, D., 'Jay Learning to Feed from Nutholder', *British Birds* 56: 221, 1963

——, 'Jays Recovering Buried Food from under Snow', *British Birds* 62: 238, 1969

Schuster, L'., 'Über den Sammeltrieb des Eichelhähers [*Garrulus glandarius*] Vogelwelt', 71: 9–17, 1950

Sharrock, J.T.R., 'Jay Taking Fish from River', *British Birds* 56: 221, 1963

Simmons, K.E.L., 'Anting and the Problem of Self-Stimulation', *Journal of Zoology* 149: 145–62, 1966

——, 'A Review of the Anting Behaviour of Passerine Birds', *British Birds* 50: 401–24, 1957

Simms, E., 'A Study of Suburban Bird Life at Dollis Hill', *British Birds* 55: 1–35, 1962

Taylor, F., 'Erythristic eggs of Sky Lark, Bullfinch and Jay', *British Birds* 20: 148, 1926–7

Ticehurst, N.F., 'Continental Jay in Kent and Essex', *British Birds* 4: 213, 1910–11

Turcek, F.J. and Kelso, L., 'Ecological Aspects of Food Transportation and Storage in the *Corvidae*', *Comm. Behav. Biol.*, A 1: 277–97, 1968

Tutt, H.R., 'Notes on the Nesting of a Pair of Jays inside a Hollow Tree', *British Birds* 46: 98–9, 1953

Voous, H.K., 'Clines and their Significance in Zoogeographical Studies', *Bull. B.O.C.* 74: 25–30, 1954

Wallace, D.I.M., 'The Birds of Regents Park London, 1959–68', *British Birds* 67: 449–68, 1974

Walters-Davies, P. and Davis, P.E., 1973, 'The Ecology and Conservation of the Red Kite in Wales', *British Birds* 66: 241–70, 1973

Witherby, H.F. and Hartert, E., 'The Irish Jay', *British Birds* 4: 234–55, 1910–11

Witherby, H.F., *et al.*, *The Handbook of British Birds*, London, 1938

CHAPTER 13

Blomgren, A., *Lavskrikan*, Stockholm, 1964

——, 'Studies of less Familiar Birds', *British Birds* 64: 25–8, 1971

Curry-Lindahl, K., *Vara Faglar i Nordern*, Stockholm, 1963

Dementiev, G.P. and Gladov, N.A., 'Ptitsy Sovetskogo Soyuza [Birds of the Soviet Union]', Vol. 5, Moscow, 75–81, 1951–4

Dow, D.D., 'The Role of Saliva in Food Storage by the Gray Jay', *AUK* 82: 139–54, 1965

Harrison, C., *A Field Guide to the Nests, Eggs and Nestlings of British and European Birds*, London, 1975

Lindgren, F., 'Iakttagelser rörande Lavskrikan [*Perisoreus infaustus*] – huvudsakligen dess häcknings *biologie*', *Fauna och Flora* 70: 198–210, 1975

Merikallio, E., 'Finnish Birds: Their Distribution and Numbers', *Soc. pro Fauna et Flora Fennica: Fauna Fennica V*, 1958

Vaurie, C., 'The Birds of the Palearctic Fauna: Passeriformes', London, 1959

CHAPTER 14

Channer, A.G., 'Mating of Great Spotted Cuckoo', *British Birds* 69: 309, 1976

Gramet, P., 'Le Parasitism des Corvides par le Croucou-Geai, *Rev. Comp. Animal.* 4: 17–26, 1970

Harrison, C., *A Field Guide to the Nests, Eggs and Nestlings of British and European Birds*, London, 1975

Heim de Balzac, H. and Maryaud, N., *Les Oiseaux du Nord-Ouest de l'Afrique*, Paris, 1962

Mountfort, G., *Portrait of a Wilderness*, London, 1952

Voous, K.H., *Atlas of European Birds*, London, 1960

CHAPTER 15

Charles, J.K., 'Territorial Behaviour and the Limitation of Population Size in the Crow *Corvus corone* and *Corvus cornix*, unpublished Ph.D. thesis, Aberdeen University, 1972

Gwinner, E. von, 'Untersuchungen über das Ausdrucks und Sozialverhalten des Kolkraben [*Corvus corax L.*], *Z. Tierpsychol.* 21: 657–748, 1964

——, 'Beobachtungen über Nestbau und Brutflege des Kolkraben [*Corvus corax*] in Gefangenschaft', *J. Orn.* 106: 146–77, 1965

——, 'Über den Einfluss des Hunger und anderer Faktoren auf die Versteck – Activität des Kolkraben [*Corvus corax*]', *Vogelwarte* 23: 1–4, 1965

——, 'Uber einige Bewegungss des Kolkraben [*Corvus corax L.*], *Z. Tierpsycholiele.* 23: 28–36, 1966

Goodwin, D., *Crows of the World*, London, 1976

Hinde, R.A., 'The Biological Significance of the Territories of Birds', *Ibis* 98: 340–69, 1956

Houston, D.C., 'Report on Hooded Crows and Hill Sheep Farming in Argyll', *Department of Forestry and Natural Resources*, Edinburgh University, 1974

Lack, D., *The Natural Regulation of Animal Numbers*, Oxford, 1954

Lindgren, F., 'Iakttagelser rörande lavskrikan [*Perisoreus infaustus*] – huvudsakligen dess häcknings biologie', *Fauna och Flora* 70: 198–210, 1975

Ratcliffe, D.A., 'Breeding Density in the Peregrine *Falco peregrinus* and Raven *Corvus corax*', *Ibis* 104: 13–39, 1962

Richards, P.R., 'Pair Formation and Pair Bond in Captive Rooks', *Bird Study* 23: 207–11, 1976

Rowley, I., 'The Comparative Ecology of Australian Corvids', *Csiro Wildlife Research*, Vol. 18, No. 1, Part II, 25–63, 1973

Ryves, B.H., *Bird Life in Cornwall*, London, 1948

Swanberg, P.O., 'Food Storage, Territory and Song in the Thick-Billed Nutcracker', Proceedings of the 10th International Ornithological Congress: 497–501, 1951

——, 'The Nutcracker', *British Birds* 45: 60–1, 1952

——, 'Territory in the Thick-Billed Nutcracker', *Ibis* 98: 412–19, 1956

——, 'Incubation in the Thick-Billed Nutcracker [*Nucigraga c. caryocatactes L.*], *Bertil Hanström Zoological Papers in Honour of his Sixty-Fifth Birthday*', Lund, Sweden, 1956

Tenovuo, R., 'Zur Brutzeitlichen Biologie der Nebelkrähe [*C. c. cornix*] im äusseren Schärenhof Südwestfinnlands,' *Ann. Zool. Soc., Vanamo* 25: 1–147, 1963

White, G., 'Letter to the Hon. Daines Barrington, 8 February 1772

Wittenberg, J., 1968, 'Freilanduntersuchungen zu Brutbiologie und Verhalten der Rabenkrähe [*Corvus c. corone*]', *Zool. Jb. syst.* 95: 16–46, 1968

Yom-Tov, Y., 'The Effect of Food and Predation on Breeding Density and Success, Clutch Size and Laying Date of the Crow [*Corvus corone Linn.*]', *Journal of Animal Ecology* 43: 479–98, 1974

——, 'Synchronization of Breeding and Intraspecific Interference in the Carrion Crow', *AUK* 92: 778–85, 1975

——, 'Food of Nestling Crows in North-East Scotland', *Bird Study* 22: 47–51, 1975

CHAPTER 16

Lanyon, A., *The Rooks of Trelawne*, London, 1976

Appendix 1

The weights given here can be used for approximate comparison; seasonal and geographical variations in weight are not available in every case.

Length and wing span are also included at the bottom of this table; they are too difficult to standardize for accurate comparison, but they are useful in providing an estimate of size.

	Raven	Eurasian crow	Rook	Jackdaw	Red-billed chough
Wing ♂	390–436mm	318–345mm	305–330mm	228–246mm	257–281mm
♀	380–420mm$_w$	303–325mm$_w$	290–311mm$_w$	225–243mm$_w$	245–271mm
				Himalayan races {	290–336 ♂ and ♀$_A$
Bill from ♂ skull		Mean 57·16mm$_c$	Mean 55·75mm$_c$	Mean 34·25mm$_c$	55–59mm
♀	69·5mm$_c$		55·5mm	33·8mm$_c$	45–52mm
				Himalayan races	50–103mm
Weight ♂ {	1100–1560gm (Mean 1386gm)$_D$	740gm max. (Mean 584gm)$_D$	Aug. 1– Feb. 28 531gm mean Mar. 1–Jul. 31 486gm mean	139–225gm (194gm mean)$_D$	Feb.–June 340–375gm
♀ {	798–1315gm (Mean 1085gm)$_D$	670gm max. (Mean 520gm)$_D$	Aug. 1– Feb. 28 435gm mean Mar.–July 31 407gm mean$_c$	163–205gm (193gm mean)$_D$	
Length (bill tip to tail tip measured on flat surface)	609–660mm (24–26in)$_w$	469–563mm (18·5–19·8in) Ad.♂♂$_c$	482mm♂ (19in)$_c$ 457mm♀ (18in)$_c$	330–346mm (13–14in)$_c$	381–406mm (15–16in)$_w$ 450mm (17·5in)$_s$ Himalayan
Wing span	1219–1320mm (48–52in)$_c$	958–1021mm (37·5–40·2in)$_c$	940mm♂ (37in)$_c$ 914mm♀ (36in)$_c$	660–737mm (26–29in)$_c$	

The measurements given here were obtained from the following sources:

A   Salim Ali and Dillon Ripley, S., *Handbook of the Birds of India and Pakistan.*

C   Author's records.

D   Dementiev, G.P. and Gladov, N.A., *Birds of the Soviet Union.*

W   Witherby, H.F., Jourdain, F.C.R., Ticehurst, N.F. and Tucker, B.W., *The Handbook of British Birds.*

Alpine chough	Nutcracker	Magpie	Azure-winged magpie	Jay	Siberian jay
	173–194mm 175–190mm	187–200mm 173–188mm_w	141mm (mean) 136mm (mean)	173–189mm 170–188mm	139mm (mean) 134mm (mean)
274–298 ♂ mm 262–273 ♀ mm_A					
34–38mm 32–36mm	Thick-billed: 30–40mm Slender-billed: 38·5–46mm	39·5mm_c		31·0mm_c	
223–244gm_A 203–213gm_A	153–190gm (Mean 176·4gm)_D 124–184gm (Mean 169·4gm)_D	203–261gm (Mean 229·4gm)_D Jan.–July 239gm 165–172gm_D Jan.–July 207gm	73·0gm 69·0gm	145–197gm (Mean 165·3gm)_D 149–168gm (158·8gm)_D	81–97gm (Mean 87·6gm)_D 73–89gm (Mean 81·8gm)_D
380mm (15in)	317mm (12·5in)_w	457mm (18in)_c	♂ 335–340mm (13–13·3in) ♀ 325mm (12·7in)	330–368mm (13·5–14·5in)_c	
		584mm (23in)_c		559 mm (22in)_c	

Appendix 2

	Carrion crow	Rook
Length	483mm (19in)	489mm (19·25in)
Wingspan	1016mm (40in)	940mm (37in)
Chord of wing (leading edge to trailing edge)		
At body	184mm (7·25in)	165mm (6·5in)
At carpal joint	190mm (7·5in)	173mm (6·8in)
Tip of first to tip of seventh primary		
Length of tail	177mm (7·0in)	146mm (5·75in)
Outer	163mm (6·4in)	146mm (5·75in)
Central	190mm (7·5in)	177mm (7·0in)
Weight	695gm	509gm

The carrion crow is a larger, heavier bird with a greater wingspan and area, but with a relatively shorter tail.

INDEX